The Taiwan Tinderbox

For Ketty, my muse, for my parents, and my Taiwanese in-laws.

The Taiwan Tinderbox

The Island-Nation at the Center of the New Cold War

J. MICHAEL COLE

polity

Contents

Acknowledgments

A book is like a tree, with roots that find nourishment in a rich, sedimented soil. When it comes to this particular endeavor, the sources of that nourishment are too numerous to name them all. I will perforce list only those who more immediately informed the analysis and conclusions offered in this work.

Hsu Szuchien at Taiwan's National Security Council for his friendship, wisdom, and support for my work over the years. Colleagues Mark Chen, Lai I-chung and Norah Huang at the Prospect Foundation. Daniel Twining, Patrick Quirk, Caitlin Dearing Scott, and the CFAI team at the International Republican Institute. Russell Hsiao at the Global Taiwan Institute. Brian Crowley, Jonathan Berkshire-Miller, and Charles Burton at the Macdonald-Laurier Institute in Ottawa. Dafydd Fell and Steve Tseng at SOAS University of London. Lee Chun-yi at the University of Nottingham. Ian Chong at National University of Singapore. Martin Hala at Sinopsis. Puma Shen (now legislator) and Wu Min-hsuan at Doublethink Lab. Yu Chih-hao at the Information Operations Research Group (IORG). Lin Cheng-yi, Lin Chen-wei, and Chen Ming-chi at the Institute for National Defense and Security Research (INDSR). Alvin Yao, Lu Yeh-chung, Arthur

Ding, Simon Sung, Winston Chen, François Wu, Remus Chen, Vincent Yao, Wang Chung-yi, Antonio Chiang, Sylvia Feng, Cheryl Lai, Chris Wang, Olivia Yang, Alison Hsiao, Stacy Hsu, Natalie Liu, Thompson Chau, Eric Cheung, William Yang, Hideshi Tokuchi, Ogata Makoto, Stéphane Corcuff, Greg Bruno, Damon Wilson, and Christopher Walker at the National Endowment for Democracy (NED), Larry Diamond and Glenn Tiffert at Stanford University, Aaron Friedberg, Nadège Rolland, Richard Bush, Bonnie Glaser, Bonnie Lin, Zack Cooper, Ian Easton, Mark Stokes, Michael Mazza, Shelley Rigger, Rupert Hammond-Chambers, Scott Harold, Michael Chase, Andrew Erickson, Martin Laflamme, Grégoire Legault, Michael Hennessy, my professors Michael Roi and David Last at the Royal Military College of Canada. Ning Tung and Nicholas Maran at Elliott Advisors, Nick Greenstock at Gatehouse Advisory, and Sean McDermott at Northland Power. The list of intellectuals and academics from various institutions from whom I have learned over the years could fill several pages; you know who you are.

To the many officials in the Taiwanese and other governments who have sought my counsel, opened many doors, and empowered me over the past two decades, allowing me to do what I believe is a crucial element of my work: to bridge academia and policymaking.

Former president Tsai Ing-wen, whose offer one could not refuse, in early 2014 overturned a plan to move back to North America and led to a series of opportunities one could only dream of.

Special thanks to Jude Blanchette at the Rand Corporation for introducing me to my editor, Louise Knight, at Polity Press. Louise, and then Ian Malcolm, as well as Olivia Jackson, expertly saw this project through and were everything that a writer can hope for in a publisher.

My eternal gratitude to my parents, Réjane and Craig, who have seen their only child's stay in Taiwan expand from a planned three years to now nearly twenty. Both cultivated in me the important traits of curiosity, tolerance, and a love for the written word. May this latest endeavor, as with those that came before it, reduce the pain caused by the tyranny of distance and my far-too-infrequent visits back to Canada. Their encouragement as I do my part in trying to make our troubled world a better place has been a steady source of sustainment. To my Taiwanese in-laws, Rachel, Sidney, and Louise, like many of their people spanning the world between Taiwan and the United States, for making me a full part of their family and for their endless support, encouragement, and knowledge.

Lastly, albeit first and foremost, to my extraordinary wife and best friend, Ketty W. Chen, whose love and support, in times bonny and not, are the foundations of the person I have become. Besides being my muse, she is an endless supply of knowledge and unflagging passion for justice – a passion, no doubt, which finds its roots both in the very injustice done to her own people over the decades, and to the challenges she faced as an immigrant to the U.S. I can only hope to repay her with infinite love and support for her own important endeavors, and by trying, each day, to be the best husband that I can. And to Hanji, our beautiful Formosan Mountain Dog (at long last a recognized breed), who sadly left us as this book was being written.

Abbreviations

A2/AD	Anti-Access/Area Denial
ADIZ	Air Defense Identification Zone
ARATS	Association for Relations Across the Taiwan Straits
ASW	Anti-submarine warfare
BRI	Belt and Road Initiative
CASI	China Aerospace Studies Institute
CCG	China Coast Guard
CCP	Chinese Communist Party
CCPPNR	China Council for the Promotion of Peaceful National Reunification
CMC	Central Military Commission
CPA	Concentric Patriotism Association
CPPCC	Chinese People's Political Consultative Conference
CPTPP	Comprehensive and Progressive Agreement for Trans-Pacific Partnership
CSIS	Center for Strategic and International Studies
CSSTA	Cross-Strait Services Trade Agreement
CUPP	China Unification Promotion Party
DIB	Defense industrial base

DTL	Doublethink Lab
DPP	Democratic Progressive Party
ECFA	Economic Cooperation Framework Agreement
EEZ	Exclusive Economic Zone
FDI	Foreign direct investment
FONOP	Freedom of navigation operation
GCTF	Global Cooperation and Training Framework
GLCM	Ground-launched cruise missile
ICAO	International Civil Aviation Organization
ICBM	Intercontinental-range ballistic missile
IDS	Indigenous Defense Submarine
ILD	International Liaison Department
INDSR	Institute for National Defense and Security Research
IRBM	Intermediate-range ballistic missile
IRI	International Republican Institute
ISR	Intelligence, surveillance, and reconnaissance
JGSDF	Japan Ground Self-Defense Force
JSDF	Japan Self-Defense Forces
KMT	Chinese Nationalist Party (Kuomintang)
KSO	Special Operations Command
LACM	Land-attack cruise missile
LPD	Landing platform, dock
LSG	Leading Small Group
MAC	Mainland Affairs Council
MND	Ministry of National Defense
MODA	Ministry of Digital Affairs
MOE	Ministry of Education
MOFA	Ministry of Foreign Affairs
MOI	Ministry of the Interior
MPC	Municipal Party Committee
MRBM	Medium-range ballistic missile
NCC	National Communications Commission
NCSIST	National Chung Shan Institute of Science and Technology

NDI	National Democratic Institute
NED	National Endowment for Democracy
NFU	No First Use (nuclear policy)
NPC	National People's Congress
NPP	New Power Party
NPSU	Non-Partisan Solidarity Union
NRC	NATO–Russia Council
NRFA	NATO–Russia Founding Act
NRPJC	NATO–Russia Permanent Joint Council
OPEC	Organization of the Petroleum Exporting Countries
ORBAT	Order of Battle
PAP	People's Armed Police
PfP	Partnership for Peace
PIPIR	Partnership for Indo-Pacific Industrial Resilience
PLA	People's Liberation Army
PLAAF	People's Liberation Army Air Force
PLAN	People's Liberation Army Navy
PLARF	People's Liberation Army Rocket Force
PPC	Provincial Party Committee
PRC	People's Republic of China
ROC	Republic of China
ROCN	Republic of China Navy
RSF	Reporters Without Borders
SAR	Special Administrative Region
SEF	Straits Exchange Foundation
SLOC	Sea lines of communication
SOE	State-owned enterprise
SRBM	Short-range ballistic missile
TAEF	Taiwan-Asia Exchange Foundation
TAO	State Council Taiwan Affairs Office
TFD	Taiwan Foundation for Democracy
TPP	Taiwan People's Party
TRA	Taiwan Relations Act

TSMC	Taiwan Semiconductor Manufacturing Corporation
UAV	Unmanned aerial vehicle
UCAV	Unmanned combat aerial vehicle
UFWD	United Front Work Department
WHO	World Health Organization
WMD	World Movement for Democracy
WTO	World Trade Organization

Preface

Writing about conflict, about a war that could be, often feels like tackling an abstract concept. Many academic volumes, op-eds, editorials, and threat assessments have been written over the years about the possibility of armed conflict in the Taiwan Strait. In most cases, the worst-case scenarios are described as if this were a work of fiction or a mere intellectual exercise.

For me, the reality of such nightmare scenarios, the fact that we are facing an existential threat, was underscored in early August 2022, when China's People's Liberation Army (PLA) initiated major live-fire exercises around Taiwan in response to the "provocative" visit by then-U.S. House Speaker Nancy Pelosi. Even then, as I walked the streets of Taipei and observed the pragmatic residents go about their ordinary lives, TV screens showing coverage of the maneuvers in sea areas around Taiwan, the whole thing seemed a bit unreal. For personal reasons, what made the threat concrete was the fact that, just as the PLA was firing ballistic missiles around and over Taiwan, my spouse was on a return flight from Japan, and her flight route happened to intersect one of the "boxes" the Chinese military had drawn at sea to conduct its exercises.

With that, the abstract of military exercises became incarnate: throughout the day, I was haunted by What Ifs – *what if something happens, a collision, or a missile hits the commercial aircraft with my wife on board as it completes its ballistic arc on its way to its designated target at sea?* Eventually, with some delays, the flight made it safely home and nothing terrible happened. But as such exercises and maneuvers become more frequent, the likelihood of an accident or unintentional collision continues to increase, and this could conceivably lead to serious escalation.

As this book was being written, the PLA was once again launching major military exercises around Taiwan, this time as a "warning" against "Taiwan independence" and in response to the inauguration, three days earlier, of President William Lai Ching-te of the Taiwan-centric Democratic Progressive Party (DPP). This time, some of the exclusion zones established by the Chinese military, especially those to the east of Taiwan, were closer to Taiwan's 24 nautical mile contiguous zone than during the drills in August 2022.[1] This is Taiwan's new reality, a fact of life in a new Cold War – or cold wars – that includes another fault line in Europe, and another one in the Middle East.

In recent years, revanchist authoritarian powers led or inspired by China and Russia have sought to destabilize the international world order that has existed since the end of World War II. They are doing so by using various tools in their arsenals, from cognitive warfare and "grey zone" operations to conventional warfare on a scale not seen since World War II. And while the decision by Vladimir Putin to invade Ukraine on February 24, 2022, is no guarantee that his ideological partner Xi Jinping will use similar instruments to achieve his goals vis-à-vis Taiwan, the nature of the threat facing the democratic island-nation of 23.5 million people is becoming more pressing and multifaceted. The Taiwanese people are caught between the pincer of China's external threat and attempts to destroy their country's democratic firewall from within by proxies of the Chinese Communist Party (CCP) that benefit from an increasingly polarized political environment.

With the disruptions to global supply chains caused by the double hit of the Covid-19 pandemic and Russia's invasion of Ukraine, the essentiality of Taiwan, the world's largest designer of advanced semiconductors, to the global economy has gained primacy. This, in turn, has resulted in greater interest about Taiwan and, not incidentally, to the realization that a military crisis in the Taiwan Strait would have a catastrophic impact on the world economy.

Beyond this, Taiwan's success as a nation that transited from rigid authoritarianism for nearly half a century to one of the most vibrant liberal democracies has also positioned it as a key player in the promotion of the values that buttress the U.S.-led democratic order, with all its imperfections. By embracing democracy and successfully absorbing outside influences, the Taiwanese have built a society that, given ongoing developments in the People's Republic of China, is increasingly incompatible and resistant to Beijing's attempts to annex it.

Unrecognized officially by most of the international community yet meeting every requirement for statehood, Taiwan therefore finds itself on the front lines of a new clash of ideologies that pits the democratic order against an array of authoritarian states which, in increasingly coordinated efforts, is seeking to destroy or replace it with a system that is more suitable for their aspirations.

We do not know whether Xi will decide to do the unthinkable and, like Putin, defy expectations of "rational" decision-making by launching an invasion of Taiwan. What is certain, however, is that the Chinese party-state apparatus is actively endeavoring to change the "status quo" in the Taiwan Strait. Short of an amphibious assault and attempted occupation of Taiwan,

Beijing's toolkit involves various instruments it can use simultaneously to try to win over or co-opt the Taiwanese and undermine their democratic institutions and belief in democracy itself.

What is also certain is that Beijing wants Taiwan to capitulate and to sit at the negotiating table, where it would inevitably be the weaker party and therefore would be forced to make concessions. Such concessions, it goes without saying, would come at a cost: as the experience of Hong Kong since Great Britain returned it to Chinese control in 1997, and more recently after the crackdown on pro-democracy protests, has made perfectly clear, incorporation into the PRC entails a loss of freedoms and liberties. The central government in Beijing cannot countenance the spaces where critics operate independently, let alone have the ability to criticize the Party.

This is therefore a story of resilience in the face of extraordinary odds, the tale of a real people making their own choices amid uncertainty and an external environment that is becoming increasingly complex, in which the possibility that we are sleepwalking into a major conflagration, a return to great power conflict, is no longer unimaginable.

This book strives to tell this complex story from the perspective of Taiwan and to dispel the notion that the Taiwanese people have no agency in the Taiwan Strait, that Taiwan is a mere pawn of the United States as it faces off against an emergent revisionist power. It argues that Taiwan's fate, just as that of Ukraine, the Baltic states, Moldova, and other embattled democracies, will have a direct incidence on the ability of authoritarian regimes to rewrite the rules of the international system, and therefore determine the world that we, and future generations, will live in. It also aims to remind the reader that real people's lives are at stake, that inadequate crisis management, insufficient deterrence, and miscommunication could spark the tinderbox and have a highly destabilizing impact on the region and the world, at a tremendous human cost – including to the Chinese people. And yes, that includes you, the reader.

Taipei, Taiwan
January 2025

Introduction

The current crisis in the Taiwan Strait, a tinderbox that many fear could spark a hugely destabilizing great power confrontation between China and the United States, does not find its roots in recent history, although developments over the past decade and half or so – the main focus of this book – have unquestionably taken us ever closer to the precipice.[1] Rather, the conflict, which pits democratic Taiwan, the world's twenty-first largest economy, with a population about the size of Australia's, at 23.5 million people, and its principal security guarantor, the United States, against authoritarian China arguably originated in the late nineteenth century. More specifically, at the conclusion of the First Sino-Japanese War, when China's Qing dynasty, on the losing side of that war, was forced to "cede" Taiwan to the Japanese victors as part of the Treaty of Shimonoseki.[2] The treaty launched what Beijing would later refer to as the "century of humiliation" at the hands of foreign powers. Chief among them was Japan, which over the first half of the next century engaged in predatory practices – and a war of annihilation – on a scale similar to the worst depredations of Western colonial powers, which in many ways it sought to emulate.

From Shimonoseki in 1895 until Japan's defeat in World War II, Taiwan was therefore part of the Japanese empire. Thus, during World War II, Taiwan was part of the Axis. My wife's maternal grandmother, growing up in Chiayi County in southern Taiwan, would always remember the terror she experienced as American B-29 and B-32 heavy bombers groaned in the skies above her on their way to bombing runs in southern Taiwan – the same American military that, today, plays a key role in ensuring Taiwan's defense against the People's Liberation Army (PLA). Her wedding photos are striking for the fact that, in the background, flags of the rising sun and swastika are displayed on a wall. Before she died, whenever we visited her at home, she would have the Japanese TV channel NHK on, and for her entire life, she, like many people of her generation, was always more comfortable speaking Japanese than Mandarin, despite rigid attempts by the Chinese Nationalist Party (KMT) to impose the language (and ban others).

All this is not ancient history. All within a lifetime. During World War II, a 3-year-old boy who would have been my spouse's oldest uncle on her mother's side died of an infection due to lack of medication caused by shortages resulting from the war. A friend of the family recalls losing a sister in the U.S. nuclear bombings in Japan – both he and his sister jumped into a river to avoid being burned by the blast, but she didn't make it. Another friend of the family remembers, as a curious boy growing up in Pingtung, in southern Taiwan, defying warnings from his parents to stay away from an altercation and, drawn to it, looking between the legs of a circle of KMT soldiers gathered in the city as they shot a number of locals to death as Taiwan's period of "White Terror" began. After relocating to Taipei, my spouse's maternal grandparents lived across the street from the family of Chen Wen-chen, whom Garrison Command is accused of murdering in 1981 after a period of detention and interrogation.

During the period between 1895 and 1945, the people of Taiwan were treated as colonial subjects, subject to the vagaries of a regime that never made them full citizens of the empire. And yet, Taiwan benefited from the colonial power's modernizing instincts to turn it into a model colony. It was early during that half century of colonial subjugation that the first inklings of a Taiwan independence movement emerged, a consciousness that would carry into the twenty-first century as Taiwan continued to exist in a limbo of sorts, even after it achieved the full requirements for statehood.

Throughout its existence, and well before Japan incorporated Formosa into its empire, its people were confronted with external designs upon their land, including European powers and Chinese dynasties (the term Formosa was first used by Portuguese sailors, who upon seeing Taiwan called it the "beautiful island," or "Ilha Formosa," which Dutch colonists subsequently appropriated). Besides the Aboriginal people who first occupied the land, waves of settlers came from what is now known as China; some did so temporarily, while others, tired of the constant warring in their homeland, made Taiwan a more permanent home.

Thus were sown the first seeds of a contest of identity that continues to characterize, and in some ways to haunt, politics in Taiwan today. After World War II, this would be compounded by a second wave of Chinese settlers, this time in the form of Chiang Kai-shek's fleeing Nationalists (KMT) after their defeat by Mao Zedong's Chinese Communist Party (CCP) in the Chinese civil war.

At the 1951–2 San Francisco Peace Treaty, defeated Japan was forced to "cede" sovereignty of Taiwan. However, *to whom* it was ceded was never clearly established. Nevertheless, the Republic of China (ROC), which had been founded in 1912 when Taiwan was a possession of the Japanese empire, assumed de facto control of the island and its people. After losing control of the mainland in 1949, Chiang's Nationalists relocated to Taiwan, where they hoped to rebuild their forces and, one day, reconquer their homeland. The arrival of more than a million demoralized Nationalist forces in Taiwan was at first cautiously embraced by the people on the island, though the relationship between the local population and, as it would soon become clear, their new colonial masters, quickly soured as KMT rule proved more repressive, and much less organized, than what they had experienced under the Japanese.

Nothing put the new reality of life under the KMT in starker contrast than the incidents of February 1947, two years before Chiang and the remains of his government fled across the Taiwan Strait. In February that year, Nationalist forces retaliated militarily to popular protests which the regime characterized as an insurrection. In what came to be known as the 228 Massacre, Nationalist forces killed and imprisoned thousands of Taiwanese. Using fears of communism in a fledgling Cold War, Chiang's regime declared Martial Law, a period of "White Terror," as it came to be known, that would last thirty-eight years – one of the longest in a twentieth century marked by widespread state repression.

Until Martial Law was lifted in 1987, thousands upon thousands of people in Taiwan would be interrogated, detained, disappeared, exiled, or murdered by the state apparatus. That regime of fear even followed the Taiwanese who lived in exile, in the form of "professional students" employed by the KMT to spy on "agitators" on university campuses.

To an extent that would only become clearer decades later, the White Terror was a foundational development in Taiwan's identity, which over time would come to define itself by *that which we are not,* and *that which we aspire to.* For fifty years, the people of Taiwan struggled against authoritarian rule, contesting a regime that, for much of the Cold War, was regarded by the West as an ally in the "free world's" battle against the ideologues in Moscow, Beijing, and other capitals behind the Iron Curtain. Consequently, while the Taiwanese found allies among civil society and religious groups abroad, their fight for freedom often was treated as an inconvenience to decision makers in Western capitals, who often had no compunction in allying themselves with right-wing regimes as long as they joined the fight against communism.

From the end of World War II until the Korean War, Taiwan existed in a geopolitical limbo, an afterthought for the great powers as the dividing lines of the Cold War were beginning to harden. After the North invaded the southern part of the Korean Peninsula, the Truman administration came under pressure – both from Republicans and members of the Truman administration, including Dean Rusk, Louis Johnson, and General Douglas MacArthur – to include Taiwan within the U.S. "defense perimeter" in East Asia. The move was intended to prevent both an invasion of the mainland (China) by Chiang Kai-shek and an attack by Mao's communist forces upon Taiwan at a time when the U.S. and the U.N. were distracted with the crisis in Korea. Truman also agreed to dispatch the 7th Fleet to the Taiwan Strait to prevent any escalation.[3] More than seventy years later, that U.S. "defense perimeter" remains in place.

In a presage of future tensions, the Taiwan Strait became one of the Cold War's most dangerous flashpoints during the Second Taiwan Strait Crisis of 1958. The crisis was sparked by the shelling of the Taiwan-controlled outlying islands of Quemoy (Kinmen) and Matsu by the PLA.[4] As it rushed to support its ally, the U.S. began drawing up plans to use nuclear weapons against the People's Republic of China (PRC). Such plans were never activated, nuclear strikes were not launched against the communists, and the crisis stabilized into a low-intensity conflict, with the PLA shelling the islets until 1979.

From 1966 until Mao's death in 1976, China descended into the chaos of the Cultural Revolution, a period during which the PRC went into self-imposed isolation.

And yet, at some point during the Cold War, and as the threat of nuclear annihilation loomed, the American government decided it needed to pull Beijing away from Moscow's sphere of influence. Secret meetings were held, and little by little, the PRC was brought in from the cold. This inevitably came at the expense of the ROC, which in 1971 lost its seat at the United Nations. There could have been a chance for recognition of "two Chinas" at the U.N., one seated in Taipei, the other in Beijing, but Chiang, who still believed he ruled all of China and aimed some day to "retake" the mainland, shut the door on that possibility. The U.N. General Assembly passed Resolution 2758, which stated that the PRC is the only legitimate government of China, replacing the ROC with the PRC as a permanent member of the Security Council in the United Nations. Years later, Beijing would encourage the fallacy that Resolution 2758 underscores its "one China" principle and therefore argue that U.N. member states, in signing the resolution, recognized PRC sovereignty over Taiwan. In reality, Taiwan's status remained to be decided, and the resolution made no mention of Taiwan.[5] Subsequently, several governments established diplomatic relations with Beijing and abandoned Taipei.

Then, in 1979, came an even more severe blow. The United States announced it had established official diplomatic ties with the PRC and was now *acknowledging* Beijing's *claim* that there is only "one China."[6] In response to the abandonment of its longstanding Asian ally, U.S. Congress the same year passed the Taiwan Relations Act (TRA), which, among other things, committed the U.S. government to providing security assistance to Taiwan, and used language that committed to the resolution of the conflict in the Taiwan Strait by peaceful means.

Several other agreements would follow, from the Three Communiqués to the Six Assurances, which in the aggregate formed the basis for the "status quo" as it exists today: no official recognition of Beijing's sovereignty claims over Taiwan, the provision of defensive equipment to Taiwan, and a posture of "strategic ambiguity" that was meant to keep Beijing guessing on whether the U.S. would involve itself militarily in an armed conflict in the Taiwan Strait. The year 1979 was a pivotal year, one that has echoes to this day.

Except that today, Taiwan is a vibrant democracy, while China, after decades of gradually opening up to the international community, is a deeply authoritarian state again, one that, furthermore, is armed with a military that, unlike in 1979, is very close to being capable of taking Taiwan by force.

The U.S.'s "abandonment" of Taiwan in 1979 made the regime in Taipei realize that the clock was ticking. By then Chiang had died and his son, Chiang Ching-kuo, was in charge. Seeing the writing on the wall, among other things recognizing that "retaking" the mainland was no longer an option, the younger Chiang decided to gradually loosen the party-state's grip on Taiwanese society. The continued repression of democracy was becoming a handicap for Taipei.

With a global wave of democratization just around the corner, Chiang realized that repression could cost whatever support he was still getting from the U.S. The last major act of state repression against Taiwanese civil society had occurred on December 10, 1979. In what came to be known as the Formosa Incident, the government cracked down on an event commemorating human rights day. Several activists from the *dangwai* ("outside the party"), who would later become key figures in the Democratic Progressive Party (DPP), were among the individuals who were arrested and sentenced to years-long prison sentences. Nearly seven years after the Formosa Incident, the Chiang regime allowed the DPP to register as an opposition party, ending decades of single-party politics in Taiwan.

Then, on July 14, 1987, Chiang signed the documents promulgating the lifting of Martial Law. On January 13 the following year, the younger Chiang followed his father to the grave. Chiang's vice president, the native Lee Teng-hui, assumed the presidency, a post he would hold until May 2000. Lee's inclusion into Chiang's inner circle had been part of a program to allow more ethnic Taiwanese into government and thereby improve the KMT's image with the public (and presumably to co-opt them).

It soon became evident that the Cornell-educated Lee, a man of deep Christian beliefs, was a leader in a very different mold from his predecessor. Always more comfortable speaking Japanese or Holo (Taiwanese), Lee launched Taiwan on the fitful road to democracy. That journey was a serrated one, as Lee sought to dismantle a party apparatus that had ruled over all of society for more than four decades. In 1989, Cheng Nan-jung, founder of the *Freedom Era Weekly*, committed self-immolation at his office in Taipei's Songshan District as law enforcement attempted to arrest him on charges of insurrection for advocating for a constitution for a Republic of Taiwan.[7]

Two months later, the Chinese government launched its bloody crackdown at Tiananmen Square and across China, killing hundreds to thousands of unarmed protesters. This was a major setback for then-leader Deng Xiaoping, who had been wooing the West. The bloody crackdown resulted in brief suspensions of trade and investment in China by Taiwan and Japan, two countries that greatly contributed to the early stages of China's future economic miracle.

The following year, back in Taiwan, student-led protests were held calling for direct elections of the president and against abuses of power by the National Assembly. The movement, known as the Wild Lily Movement,[8] would over the next three decades re-emerge under different names and new leadership to hold the government in check on a variety of issues pertaining to Taiwan's democracy. As some activists would say during student protests in May 2024, at a time when opposition parties which formed a majority in the Legislative Yuan were attempting to pass potentially unconstitutional reform bills, it seemed that every generation of Taiwanese was forced to step up to protect their rights and the sovereignty of their country.

Triggered by Lee's visit to his alma mater in 1995, Beijing staged military exercises near Taiwan that sparked the Third Taiwan Strait Crisis.[9] The following year, as the people of Taiwan were preparing to vote in their country's first direct presidential election, Beijing bracketed Taiwan with ballistic missiles – arguably the first overt attempt by the Chinese side to use military intimidation to influence electoral outcomes in Taiwan. The gambit backfired, and the Taiwanese elected Lee, whom Beijing by then regarded as its nemesis due to his pro-Taiwan independence tendencies, by a wide margin. In that election, Lee defeated his DPP opponent, the former political prisoner Peng Ming-min, and two independent candidates.

China's belligerence also led the Clinton administration to dispatch two carrier battle groups near Taiwan to deter further escalation.

The following year, Hong Kong was returned to China after long negotiations with the British government under "one country, two systems." Under that agreement, Hong Kong's freedoms and system of governance were to be respected even if the former British colony was absorbed by the PRC – hence the Special Administrative Region designation, or HKSAR. That formula had first been envisioned for Taiwan, Beijing hoping that the former British colony could serve as a successful example with which to woo the Taiwanese. Toward the end of his last term, in 1999 Lee told an interview with German media that relations between the ROC and the PRC were "special state-to-state relations" (the "two-state theory"), a formulation that alarmed Beijing, which remained adamant that there was only "one China."[10] That same year, the U.S. Air Force accidentally bombed the Chinese embassy in Belgrade during Operation Allied Force as the North Atlantic Treaty Organization (NATO) sought to end Serb leader Slobodan Milošević's ethnic cleansing in Kosovo. For years afterwards, Beijing would use this incident to demonstrate the U.S. government's bad intentions.

The following year, Taiwan experienced its first power transition when Chen Shui-bian of the DPP defeated Lien Chan of the KMT and James Soong, an independent candidate. A former defense lawyer for the victims of 1979's Formosa Incident, Chen was a native of Tainan, regarded as the "heartland" of Taiwanese independence. Many regarded him as a firebrand. His vice president, Annette Lu, was among those who had been sentenced to jail following the Formosa Incident, serving five-and-a-half years of a twelve-year sentence.

Things got off to a rather promising start for the Chen administration, when U.S. President George W. Bush vowed in April 2001 that the U.S. would do "whatever it took to help Taiwan defend herself" against an attack by China. Earlier the same month, a U.S. EP-3 reconnaissance aircraft flying in international waters along China's southern coast collided with one of two J-8 aircraft dispatched by the PLA to intercept the American aircraft, which was forced to perform an emergency landing at the Lingshui airfield on Hainan, where the crew was detained.[11] The incident was a first glimpse of things to come. Two decades later, the PLA would conduct daily naval and air intrusions across the "median line" in the Taiwan Strait and into Taiwan's Air Defense Identification Zone (ADIZ), a strategy that greatly increased the risks of collision between Chinese, Taiwanese, and American aircraft and navy vessels.

Relations between Taipei and Beijing quickly soured under Chen, whose Taiwan-centric approach and proclamations of *yi bian yi guo* ("one country on each side") caused concerns that Taiwan was moving toward a declaration of *de jure* independence, despite Chen's "four noes and one without" commitment in his inaugural speech. Among other things, Chen had vowed to not declare independence or change the country's name from the Republic of China to Taiwan – in effect distancing himself from Lee's "two-state theory."[12] Wary of Chen, Beijing spurned his olive branch, a theme that would continue years later with China's refusal to meet Taipei halfway when two future presidents from the DPP, Tsai Ing-wen and William Lai, also extended a friendly hand to the Chinese leadership in their inaugural speeches.

The geopolitical context in which Chen served as president was a highly sensitive one. At the time, the U.S. had just suffered a catastrophic terrorist attack by al-Qaeda on September 11, 2001, and had embarked on a "global war on terrorism" with an invasion of Afghanistan to dislodge the Taliban and hunt the al-Qaeda leadership, followed by a misguided invasion of Iraq to unseat Saddam Hussein. Preoccupied with those two contingencies, the Bush administration feared that adventurism by Chen could spark a crisis in the Taiwan Strait at a time when the U.S. military was waging two simultaneous wars.[13] Further complicating things, Washington needed Beijing's acquiescence at the U.N. as it sought a vote on the invasion of Iraq. In that context, reports emerged that Bush had called Chen a "troublemaker" – comments the U.S. Department of State claimed the president never made[14] – and the Chinese propaganda apparatus intensified its efforts to promote the view that Bush did not support Taiwanese independence.

Chen and Lu were re-elected by the slimmest of margins in the 2004 elections, in the lead-up to which the Taiwanese president used rhetoric that was meant to mobilize the "deep green" – pro-independence – base of his party. For example, in November 2003 Chen had proposed to hold a referendum on the sovereignty question concurrently with the 2004 elections, but pressure from Taiwan's Legislative Yuan and the U.S. government forced him to abandon that plan. In response to Chen's "provocations," in March 2005 China's National People's Congress (NPC) enacted the Anti-Secession Law, which provided a list of conditions that could justify the use of force against Taiwan.

Throughout Chen's two terms in office, the KMT held a solid majority of seats in the legislature, and used its votes to block several bills and budgets sought by the government, including for national defense. This occurred just as Beijing was making major investments to modernize the PLA. As a result, for the first time since 1949, the balance of power in the Taiwan Strait shifted in Beijing's favor, a balance that would be fueled by several consecutive years of double-digit growth in official defense spending and further widen after Xi Jinping assumed power in late 2012.

Chen ended his second and last term in 2008 under a dark cloud, his party in shambles, support by the U.S. and the international community lukewarm at best. Meanwhile, by turning itself into the "world's manufacturer," China seemed unstoppable and succeeded in convincing many in the international community that its economic development would eventually lead to a loosening of political controls in China. Things got worse for Chen, who was accused of various financial crimes and was eventually jailed during the administration of Ma Ying-jeou, a rising star in the KMT. Ma, like Chen a former Taipei mayor with the advantage of being highly popular among female voters, had easily defeated his opponent from a deflated DPP in the 2008 elections.

The prospects for a resurgence of the DPP seemed bleak. People had given the party eight years, during which the economy had mostly stagnated while tensions with China continued to rise. They wanted change, and many believed that Ma had the solution: improve ties with Beijing, and reap the economic benefits. For the next eight years, Ma's KMT, which controlled both the Executive and Legislative branches of government, seemed well positioned to deliver on that promise.

We briefly interrupt this narrative and will pick up where we left off in the next chapters. As Chapter 1 demonstrates, during the Ma Ying-jeou presidency (2008–16), rapid rapprochement with China sparked fears of the potential cost for freedom and democracy in Taiwan and underscored the values that unite the people of Taiwan and their resistance *to that which they are not*. This period served to reaffirm the *civic* nationalism that lies at the heart of Taiwan, which clashes with the *blood* nationalism that fuels the PRC's worldview and sovereignty claims upon Taiwan. This definition of what it means to be a Taiwanese[15] has been a continuous process involving both generational change and developments in the PRC. It is like two lines that, while initially running in parallel, have over the years accelerated in different directions.

This chapter also looks at the key role that Taiwan's civil society plays in Taiwan's politics, demonstrating that active civic engagement *between elections* is an essential element of a healthy, fully realized democracy. This chapter explores Taiwan's identity politics and the impact of democratization on the emergence of a shared national consciousness and opposition to annexation by the authoritarian PRC. Using reliable surveys, it shows how generational change has eroded the lingering attachment to the "mainland" even among the descendants of Chinese immigrants (*waishengren*). It then shows how democratization and Taiwan's liberalism, strong tradition of active civil society, and openness to external influences have deepened an identity that increasingly contrasts with the political system that has developed in China, particularly since Xi Jinping assumed power in 2012.

Finally, this chapter also demonstrates how the recent crackdown in Hong Kong has torpedoed the appeal of Beijing's formula for the "reunification" of Taiwan under "one country, two systems." The chapter offers a granular assessment of what it means to be a Taiwanese or citizen of the ROC. In doing so, it avoids the facile characterizations of a "pro-Taiwan separatist DPP" and "pro-China KMT," showing that, despite some disagreements over history, culture, and origins, the main camps in Taiwan's society nevertheless tend to agree upon, and would defend, their way of life, liberal democracy, and increasingly define themselves by that which they are not – the PRC. This, in turn, leads to a discussion on the two forms of nationalism that are clashing in the Taiwan Strait: the bloodline-civilizational ultranationalism espoused by the CCP versus the more multicultural, civic, and Western-styled nationalism that has developed in Taiwan.

Continuing the discussion in the preceding chapter, Chapter 2 opens with one hard conclusion: notwithstanding Beijing's claims that it seeks "peaceful reunification" with Taiwan, such an outcome will be nearly impossible without use of coercive measures. In other words, "reunification" would in reality be *annexation*. And yet, the CCP, and Xi in particular, have staked their legitimacy and historical legacy on achieving the "great rejuvenation of China," of which the "reunification" of Taiwan is a key component. By encouraging an increasingly belligerent narrative on Taiwan, the CCP has painted itself into a corner, with dangerous ramifications: the Party must show strength and determination, as any compromise on Taiwan would be interpreted as a sign of weakness, something that, throughout history, has proven catastrophic to authoritarian regimes.

The chapter places the Chinese leadership's ambitions, particularly Xi's, in the context of longstanding CCP narratives regarding Taiwan with a look at policy pronouncements, and shows why domestic developments in China, from a slowing economy to an aging society, added to developments in Taiwan, may have led Xi, arguably the most impatient and ambitious Chinese leader since Mao, to conclude that the clock is ticking on "reunification."

Chapter 3 details Beijing's "grey zone" or "sharp power" strategies, which aim to undermine Taiwan's democratic firewall and the people's attachment to and belief in liberal democracy. Also known as political warfare, those measures intensified markedly after the DPP's Tsai Ing-wen's election in 2016, and have become even more aggressive after her successor, William Lai, assumed office on May 20, 2024. Unlike Tsai, Lai will have to contend with a Legislative Yuan that is controlled by the opposition, which is bound to make his ability to govern all the more challenging. The chapter looks at Beijing's "carrots" and "sticks," the punitive instruments and various incentives aimed at Taiwanese society, the outreach to substate actors, the uses of mis/disinformation, cognitive warfare, PLA "grey zone" activity in the Taiwan Strait, the use of a maritime militia near Taiwan's outlying islands, the co-optation of political figures in Taiwan, and various efforts to isolate Taiwan internationally.

It also shows how Beijing is exploiting – and exacerbating – political polarization in Taiwanese society to further its objectives. Despite all the talk of imminent war in the Taiwan Strait, this "nonkinetic" option ("everything short of war") presumably remains Beijing's preferred strategy given the high uncertainty surrounding an attempt to seize Taiwan by force. While the "carrots" have proved insufficient to win the hearts and minds of a wary Taiwanese public, Beijing continues to hope that the "sticks" will ultimately provoke a breakdown in Taiwan, or compel its people to give up and negotiate a surrender.

Chapter 4 discusses Russia's invasion of Ukraine in 2022, which serves as a reminder that the type of leadership and political system involved in transnational conflict is a determinant factor in whether a state will engage in aggression, even if doing so has a high risk of proving catastrophic to the aggressor. Like Moscow in the months leading up to its aggression against Ukraine, Beijing would conceivably depict an invasion of Taiwan as a necessary response to provocation, a defensive move that may also coincide with the need to ensure regime survival.

This chapter assesses how Russia's travails in Ukraine – a war Putin hoped would be won in a matter of weeks – are likely to have forced Beijing to reassess its military strategy toward Taiwan, including (1) how not to telegraph its intentions with large-scale deployments; (2) reorganizing its economy to mitigate the effects of international sanctions; and (3) damping the belief that it could win a quick and decisive war against Taiwan and therefore concluding it needs to explore other, more limited, contingencies, including "hybrid war," decapitation of the leadership, destabilization by substate actors, and so on.

For decades, Beijing never abandoned the option of using force against Taiwan. However, until recently, it lacked the material strength to act upon that threat. This could soon change, with Xi having ordered the PLA to have the capability to do so, if called upon, by as early as 2027, the year of the PLA's centennial.

Chapter 5 analyzes the possible major military contingencies in the Taiwan Strait, including a quarantine or naval blockade to throttle Taiwan, accidents leading to escalation, and an invasion of Taiwan. It discusses the military capabilities of both sides, as well as the additional forces that would likely become entangled, chief among them the U.S. and Japan, with other regional allies playing a supportive role. It also looks at how the Taiwanese military has modernized and transformed its defense posture in response to the PLA's expansion and increasingly threatening behavior. The chapter dispels some of the common narratives criticizing Taiwan's commitment to its defense and the nation's resilience, while exploring the difficulties the PLA would encounter in launching an amphibious assault against Taiwan, not to mention the bloody pacification that would be necessary after a successful landing. It explores the various ways in which deterrence has contributed to Taiwan's security, and makes the argument that Ukraine's fate – whether it succeeds in expelling Russian invaders or is forced to negotiate a surrender – is linked to Taiwan's. It also argues that Beijing's best strategy to counter deterrence may be to wait until American isolationism, distraction, and overstretch, combined with transatlantic divisions, reach a point where use of force against Taiwan may offer the best promise of victory.

The chapter ends with an evaluation of the costs of major armed conflict in the Taiwan Strait to the global economy and the destabilizing impact this would have on regional security – from the loss of a vibrant democratic partner to a more emboldened authoritarian China whose expansionist ambitions would likely have been fueled by its success against Taiwan.

Chapter 6 returns to deterrence, with a series of recommendations on how Taiwan and the international community can reduce the likelihood of an armed attack by China. Among other things, it evaluates Taiwan's military preparedness and reform; the viability of the U.S.'s longstanding policy of "strategic ambiguity" in the Taiwan Strait, as well as fledgling American efforts to forge new alliances in the Indo-Pacific. It also discusses the many nonmilitary measures that can be used to complicate Beijing's calculations, including whole-of-society preparedness and state resilience; strategic communication; the exploitation of China's weaknesses and cultivation of forces in China that oppose Xi's destabilizing trajectory; more open immigration and naturalization policies; a revamped investment environment to internationalize Taiwan; as well as pragmatic foreign policy initiatives Taiwan can utilize to bolster its strategic relevance. The chapter argues for the proper balance between preparedness and alarm, positing that failure to do so would increase the risks of an unfavorable outcome for the people of Taiwan.

Chapter 7 takes a step back from the Taiwan Strait and places Taiwan in the context of what is arguably a new ideological cold war (or a series of cold wars occurring simultaneously) that will set the tone for the rest of the century. It looks at the two principal axes, or camps: the U.S.-led democratic world order, with much of the EU, Japan, Australia, South Korea, and Taiwan on one side, and the revisionist/authoritarian axis comprising China, Russia, Iran, North Korea, and a handful of others in Europe and Central/Latin America. It shows how the revisionist camp has colluded to challenge and overwhelm the prevailing order, weaken democracy's appeal, and use force to accomplish its objectives. It argues that we are currently in a period that shares many similarities with the years just before World War II. The chapter concludes with the argument that every contested tinderbox is a link in the same narrative, and that defeat in one (Ukraine or Taiwan) will have serious repercussions for the democratic camp's ability to hold the line on other fronts.

1

The Unbridgeable Divide

The election of the KMT's Ma Ying-jeou in 2008 was a turning point in Taiwan's modern history, although not for the reasons the new president had expected. After eight years of DPP rule under Chen Shui-bian, a new leader was at the helm, elected on the promise of repairing ties with China. Less than six months after Ma's inauguration, Chen was handcuffed and taken into custody on embezzlement charges. In the elections earlier that year, the KMT had not only secured the presidency, with Ma obtaining 58.45 percent of the total vote, against the DPP's Frank Hsieh, with 41.55 percent, but also a firm control of the Legislative Yuan, with eighty-one seats, to the DPP's twenty-seven. Four other seats went to smaller parties ideologically allied with the KMT. The DPP seemed deflated and had run a lackluster campaign in what many saw as a preordained KMT victory. Worse, the DPP's finances were in shambles, and its leadership seemingly directionless.

Unlike Chen, whom Beijing regarded as a "separatist," Ma, the former Taipei City mayor, was regarded as Beijing-friendly and in a much better position to restore stability in the volatile Taiwan Strait. He had also vowed to resurrect Taiwan's stagnant economy, largely by – you guessed it – bringing

Taiwan closer to China. The results of the elections earlier that year led many, both in Taiwan and abroad, to conclude that after eight years of high tensions, the Taiwanese people also wanted rapprochement with China. Beijing, not for the first time in its entanglement with Taiwan, also read the results of the elections as a signal that the Taiwanese were finally amenable to dialogue on "reunification." In his inaugural address, Ma stated that his government would hold "consultations with mainland China over Taiwan's international space and a possible cross-strait peace accord. Taiwan doesn't just want security and prosperity." Ma told a press conference a day later that his administration would endeavor to "achieve peace and co-prosperity with mainland China by resuming the interrupted negotiations with the mainland on the basis of the '92 consensus."

The so-called "1992 consensus" would become a pillar of Ma's cross-Strait policy and a point of contention long after he stepped down in 2016.[1] More construct than actual consensus, the term, coined by KMT legislator Su Chi (who later would become Ma's secretary general of the National Security Council), stemmed from a series of meetings, held in a third country, between representatives from the KMT and the CCP starting in 1992. At the heart of the so-called consensus was the premise that there is "one China, [with] respective interpretations." Lee Teng-hui, who was president at the time, denied there ever was a consensus. From Ma's presidency onward, the CCP and the KMT would insist that dialogue between the two sides could only happen if their governments embraced the "1992 consensus." When future administrations in Taipei refused to do so, Beijing slammed the door shut on dialogue.

The Civic Factor

It didn't take long for the Ma administration to launch negotiations with China. In November 2008, Chen Yunlin, head of the semiofficial Association for Relations Across the Taiwan Straits (ARATS), visited Taiwan, sparking large protests by members of the public who feared that the Ma administration was making too many concessions to Beijing. Such concessions, they argued, would come at the price of their freedoms and democracy.[2] Ma's references to a "peace accord" in May had also fueled anxieties that he did not know what the implications would be.

Amid tight security during Chen's visit, some protesters, if perhaps hyperbolically, claimed that law enforcement was adopting measures that recalled Taiwan's Martial Law era. Police action preventing the display of the ROC flag or the playing of popular Taiwanese songs encouraged the perception that the Ma administration, in its desire to avoid offending the Chinese official, was willingly forsaking the country's sovereignty. A student-led movement, the Wild Strawberries,[3] also emerged amid the protests, chiefly over the uses of the Assembly and Parade Act that law enforcement agencies had utilized to control the protests.

Many saw a direct link between the Wild Strawberries and the Wild Lily Movement of 1990 as a new generation of Taiwanese were standing up to defend their democracy. Several of the student leaders who emerged during Chen's visit would participate in many of the social movements that mobilized throughout the Ma administration.

The large protests over the visit by the head of ARATS did not put a damper on the Ma administration's desire to liberalize cross-Strait ties. President Ma had vowed to improve the economy, and his strategy for doing so focused heavily on the expansion of trade and investment with China. After months of negotiations between China's ARATS and its Taiwanese counterpart, the equally semiofficial Straits Exchange Foundation (SEF), on June 29, 2010, Taiwan and China signed the Economic Cooperation Framework Agreement (ECFA) which reduced commercial barriers and tariffs on a variety of products across the Taiwan Strait.[4] Convinced that economic concessions would win hearts and minds in Taiwan, Beijing's side of the agreement was designed to appear as more generous: while under the ECFA's "early harvest" list Taiwan agreed to lift tariffs on 267 products from China, a total of 539 Taiwanese products saw tariffs lifted by the Chinese side. The two sides also agreed to lift longstanding restrictions on various service sectors, including banking, insurance, securities, accounting, and hospitals.

Much of the optimism at the time stemmed from the hoped-for economic benefits for Taiwan and, abroad, the theory that further economic entanglement would help reduce the likelihood of war in the Taiwan Strait.[5] This optimism also made it more difficult for those in Taiwan who warned about the consequences of overreliance on China to get people's attention. Such people became the "troublemakers," people who opposed peace. Ma was turning the Taiwan Strait into an "avenue of peace,"[6] and very few foreign capitals, struggling to cope with the aftereffects of the 2008 financial crisis, wanted to hear otherwise. China, which in 2008 had successfully hosted the Summer Olympics in Beijing, had emerged largely unscathed from the systemic shock to the global economy. More than ever, the appeal of its ever-growing economy convinced world leaders that it would be imprudent to anger China by insisting on such small matters as freedoms in Taiwan, Tibet, Hong Kong, or Xinjiang. Furthermore, the belief that China's integration into the world economy, with a larger middle class, would eventually liberalize its political environment, still had a lot of traction in academic and government circles. Taiwan, therefore, was an inconvenience, and as the risks of armed conflict in the Taiwan Strait seemed to recede with the two sides talking, investment flourishing, and millions of Chinese tourists visiting the other side, the island therefore became less newsworthy.

Amid retrenchment and tough business decisions by major news outlets around the world, news bureaus in Taipei were trimmed or closed altogether, and their staff relocated to cities like Beijing, Shanghai, and Hong Kong, where the story of our time – the Chinese economic miracle – was unfolding. Thus, very few voices remained within Taiwan to tell its side of the story to a global audience that saw this democracy's struggle to defend its freedoms as a mere inconvenience. What little reporting there was about Taiwan tended to be limited to natural catastrophes like typhoons and earthquakes, of which there are many in Taiwan. And increasingly, even the reporting on those incidents was datelined Beijing, Shanghai, or Hong Kong, meaning that almost all the coverage about Taiwan came through the lens of China.

Viewed from the outside, therefore, everything seemed to be on the right track in the Taiwan Strait. During the two four-year terms of the Ma presidency, Taiwan and China signed a total of twenty-three agreements.[7] While most agreements normalized exchanges in areas such as trade and countering crime, there was no doubt that, in the background, Beijing was aiming to tighten the ties between the two societies until Taiwan could no longer offer resistance to Beijing's political aspirations. For those in Taiwan who were close to the action, it was clear that a storm was brewing and that civil society would play a major role in the eventual pushback. As with the protests surrounding Chen's visit in 2008 and the signing of the ECFA in 2010, China's "black hand" was the trigger.

Starting in 2011, a series of protests occurred over an attempt by the Want Want China Times Group to acquire a major cable distribution system as well as Next Media Group, one of its competitors.[8] At the heart of the controversy was the billionaire Taiwanese businessman Tsai Eng-meng, who three years earlier had acquired the China Times Group. Tsai had made a fortune selling food products in China and ranked as one of the wealthiest individuals in Taiwan. Soon after his acquisition, the group's news outlets, including the *China Times* newspaper and the CtiTV television channel, adopted a Beijing-friendly editorial line, a shift that many concluded was the result of pressure from Tsai and his close associates, who sought to ingratiate themselves with the CCP. The protests warned against media overconcentration and the failure of regulatory agencies to properly review the matter. However, the real cause was the fear of China's "black hand" in Taiwan's media, the byproduct of both financial interests in China and the CCP's uses of the greater access to Taiwanese society to spread propaganda, disinformation, and censorship. Exacerbating the fears were various collaborative projects and media delegations involving Tsai's media group. As with the Wild Strawberries in 2008, many of the future Sunflower Movement leaders cut their teeth during the 2011 protests.

Shifting Identities

The period from 2011 until 2014 was an extraordinarily active one for Taiwan's civil society.[9] Through a process of cross-pollination, a mass movement with an ever-shifting leadership coalesced into an instrument by which the opposition challenged the Ma administration on various policies, from urban renewal projects to mistreatment of young men in the military to the construction of in-shore wind turbines in urban areas. In almost every case, activists pointed out lapses in procedure, oversight, consultation, or implementation. And in many cases, the victims of those government policies were the downtrodden: elderly former soldiers and their families in military villages targeted for eviction, Aboriginal communities upon whose ancestral lands investors sought to erect hotels to cater to foreign (Chinese) tourists, farmers apprehensive about a wind turbine project that skipped proper consultations and environmental impact assessments, a young conscript who died while being punished on a military base, same-sex couples who sought legal recognition of their unions, and so on. This civic force, led by students, nongovernmental organizations (NGOs), journalists, professors, and entertainers, also demonstrated that Taiwan was gradually shedding the old framing of Taiwanese politics, in which the ethnic Taiwanese (*benshengren*) were locked in contest with the KMT's mainlanders (*waishengren*).

For decades after 1949, Taiwanese society was split down the middle by ethnicity-based politics, with both sides regarding the other with suspicion. As democratization approached and Chiang Ching-kuo permitted the participation of opposition political parties, ethnicity continued to mostly define politics, with *benshengren* mainly associating with the DPP and *waishengren* with the KMT or other smaller parties in the "blue camp." This ethnic divide gradually weakened as new generations of Taiwanese came of age.

By the time Ma had assumed office, it mattered much less whether one identified as ethnically "Taiwanese" or "Chinese," or whether a victim of perceived government injustice was an old Nationalist soldier who came over from China in 1949 or the Hakka wife of a Taiwanese man whose home faced demolition. Many young activists were themselves from "mainlander" families, and for many of them, their parents continued to vote for the KMT and their grandparents, if they were still around, might even continue to hope for a return to the "mainland," if not "reunification."

Increasingly, ethnic-based identity was being replaced by a form of patriotism that was defined by a *positive* set of values — liberal democracy — and a *negative* one, or *that which they are not*, that is, governed by authoritarian rule, or the PRC. Under this new model, a person could still identify as ethnically

"Chinese" and yet regard him or herself as a citizen of Taiwan or, to use its official name, the ROC. Those who, for family or other reasons, gravitated toward the KMT and regarded their country as the ROC while opposing Taiwan independence, saw no contradiction in joining hands with civic organizations that were mobilizing against the Ma administration over local issues or controversial trade agreements with China.

By blurring longstanding ethnic distinctions, newer generations of Taiwanese were eroding the divide that, for far too long, had weakened Taiwan's ability to unite against the external, existential threat posed by an annexationist China. Whether they regarded their country as Taiwan or the ROC (or both), these young people were willing to set aside those differences for the sake of defending a set of values that united and defined them. As a result, the argument could be made that the CCP is confronted by not one but two independence movements in Taiwan: those who advocate for Taiwan independence (*taidu*) and those who support ROC independence (*huadu*).

This evolving definition of Taiwanese identity has been accompanied by growing support for de facto independence (the "status quo") or Taiwan independence. In tandem with this momentum, people's identification as Chinese, as well as support for unification, has dwindled. This is a reflection of demographic shifts. Older generations of people who were born in and identify with China are dying and replaced by people who were born in Taiwan, who therefore identify more closely with its land. The younger Taiwanese, those who were born after the 1980s, also only have the experience of living in a democracy, a norm that is part of their self-identification. Meanwhile, developments in the PRC, which has trended toward stricter authoritarianism and an angry ethnonationalism cultivated by the CCP, have also highlighted the contrast between the two sides of the Taiwan Strait.

The Election Study Center at National Chengchi University in Taipei has been reliably tracking trends in identification and political preferences since 1992. Its graphs clearly demonstrate the trends over three decades of polling. Beijing and its allies in Taiwan have long argued that such trends are the result of DPP attempts while in power to "brainwash" the people of Taiwan by downplaying their Chinese ancestry in school textbooks. We should note, however, that even during the eight years of the Ma administration, during which the government re-emphasized the "shared ancestry" of the people on both sides of the Taiwan Strait, promoted the Chinese cultural industry and facilitated contact between young Taiwanese and their counterparts, and even as China "played nice" as it sought to win the hearts and minds of the people in Taiwan, momentum toward self-identification as Taiwanese and against unification continued. In 1992, only 17.6 percent of people identified as "Taiwanese only," 46.4 percent as "Taiwanese and Chinese," and 25 percent as "Chinese only." By 2023, those figures were 61.7 percent, 32 percent, and 2.4 percent respectively.

Data on support for independence, the "status quo," or unification over the same period have tended to trend similarly. According to the same polls, which were first conducted in 1994, 38.5 percent of respondents supported maintaining the "status quo" and deciding on a future status at a later date; 15.6 percent wanted the "status quo" while moving toward unification; 9.8 percent wanted the "status quo" to be maintained indefinitely; 8 percent wanted the "status quo" with a move toward independence; 4.1 percent wanted unification as soon as possible; and 3.1 percent wanted independence as soon as possible that year. By 2023, 33.2 percent wanted the "status quo" (de facto independence) to be maintained indefinitely; 26.9 percent wanted the "status quo" and to decide at a later date; 21.5 percent wanted the "status quo" with a move toward independence at a later date; 6.2 percent wanted the "status quo" for now with a move toward unification at some point; 3.8 percent wanted independence as soon as possible; and only 1.2 percent wanted unification as soon as possible.

By combining support for the "status quo" and support for independence, we get a figure of 92.6 percent of respondents who basically *oppose* unification now. Moreover, most respondents who support the "status quo" for now and to decide at a later date or move toward unification, predicate their response on China having become a democracy, which under current conditions is a nearly impossible prospect. Support for immediate independence or the "status quo" now and toward independence in the future would conceivably be higher absent Beijing's threat to use military force against Taiwan should it declare *de jure* independence. At gunpoint, most Taiwanese for the time being appear to be satisfied with a de facto independence under the "status quo." Still, overwhelming support for the "status quo" and de facto independence does not necessarily translate into more votes for the Taiwan-centric DPP. Rather, the electoral balance reflects the perception, at specific periods, of which party is believed most suitable to navigate the complexities of the relationship with China.

Democracy Between Elections

Nobody who wants to understand Taiwan today can afford to ignore its vibrant and activist civil society, which has contributed to a deepening of the nation's democracy. Far more than being limited to the holding of regular elections, a fully developed democracy also empowers civil society to engage in a consultative relationship with government, and to take remedial action when a government and political parties fail to fulfill their responsibilities or threaten to violate the rules of governance. When needed, Taiwan's civic groups took action that, while inconveniencing the public at times, raised public awareness and forced a discussion on a variety of issues at the national level.

The "narrow" or "minimalist" definition of democracy, as the Austrian political economist Joseph Schumpeter explains, is a political system "for arriving at political decisions in which individuals acquire the power to decide by means of a competitive struggle for the people's vote."[10] This is what most people tend to think of whenever they ponder the meaning of democracy. By this definition, political parties are elected (or not elected) based on a plebiscite conducted on a set of policy proposals; once a party is in power, it is expected to implement those policies within a system of fixed rules, with the next elections serving as a referendum on whether the public determined the government to have met its goals or not.

But what happens if, between elections, a government goes beyond its proposed policies in a way that potentially violates the rules of the game? Or, worse, endangers the viability of the state? The latter question is a particularly salient one in the context of Taiwan's existential dilemma and will inevitably arise whenever a government (or political party) collaborates with the CCP. This is where more extensive definitions of democracy come into play. "Thick" democracy, what Jonathan Schell describes as "enlarged freedom," posits that beyond merely voting in regular elections, society is also empowered *between* elections. This, he states, includes demonstrating and even rebelling against the government.[11] Admittedly, such definitions run the risk of being taken to an extreme, which can end up destabilizing society. Therefore, a mature, fully consolidated democracy needs to have the capacity to strike a proper balance between "narrow" democracy and "enlarged freedom" that, in extreme cases, can justify remedial or retributive action by civil society.

And that is exactly what happened on August 18, 2013. On that day, thousands of people launched a brief but unprecedented occupation of the Ministry of the Interior (MOI) in Taipei. The issue that sparked this drastic move was a series of land expropriations that had been orchestrated by the Ma administration since it came to power.[12] Rather than a spontaneous or irrational act, as some critics at the time claimed, this extreme act occurred after several months of snowballing and cross-pollinating protests, along with perceived indifference to their mounting grievances.

Besides putting the government on notice, the occupation was a trial run for a much more significant occupation the following spring, this time over a highly controversial services trade agreement with China. According to critics, the agreement had been negotiated in a "black box," without sufficient transparency, and had been expedited at the Legislative Yuan. Like the protests over land expropriation issues, the mobilization against the proposed Cross-Strait Services Trade Agreement (CSSTA) occurred over several months. During that period, academics and civic groups sounded the alarm about the potentially harmful effects of the agreement, which would open Taiwan's service industry to Chinese labor and services, while exposing various industries in the cultural sector to Chinese censorship and propaganda. The government reacted with indifference, if not contempt, to the protests, and the KMT-controlled legislature passed the agreement in a matter of minutes. This gave rise to the Black Island Nation Youth Alliance.

Exactly seven months after the overnight occupation of the MOI, hundreds of young activists repeated the act. This time, on 18 March, they occupied the nearby Legislative Yuan. This action, launched by what would eventually be known as the Sunflower Movement,[13] was a defining moment in modern Taiwanese – and cross-Strait – politics. The occupation grew to nearly 1 million people gathering around the parliamentary building on March 30, and lasted for three weeks, until the leadership's decision to vacate the legislature on April 10, 2014. It would ultimately compel the government to mothball the CSSTA until proper review mechanisms were implemented (they never were and the CSSTA never came into force).

And that is where long traditions of civic activism came into play, with veterans sharing their experience with a new generation of leaders. The Sunflowers benefited from guidance by the leaders of earlier social movements, including the 1990s' Wild Lily and the Wild Strawberries. Academics also participated, joining hands with hundreds of participants from the many other movements that emerged during the Ma administration.

Instrumental in the Sunflowers' success was also the personality of the politician who was Legislative Speaker at the time, the ethnically Taiwanese Wang Jin-pyng. Although he was a member of the ruling KMT, Wang had harbored a longstanding feud with President Ma. Wang, who doubled as chairman of the Taiwan Foundation for Democracy (TFD), refused calls by members of his party that he ask law enforcement to forcefully evict the members of the protesters from the legislative building, who had barricaded themselves inside its main chambers.

A week later, a splinter group from the Sunflower Movement nearly derailed the entire affair with a move that could have cost them public support. On the evening of March 23, hundreds of protesters broke into the Executive Yuan, the center of government located a few hundred meters away from the Legislative Yuan. This escalation prompted a rapid and forceful response by the police force. Late into the night, anti-riot police cracked down on protesters, causing several injuries, and many were taken into custody. The images that emerged from this arguably disproportionate response, with dozens of young men and women suffering head injuries after being hit with truncheons, quickly shifted popular support back to the Sunflower Movement. The images of young men and women being beaten by anti-riot police were too much for a public that does not countenance violence. That same night, as water cannons dispersed the thousands of protesters who remained on the streets around the Executive Yuan, groups of lawyers mobilized to provide pro bono legal aid to those who had been taken into captivity.

Seeing trouble brewing, pro-China groups in Taiwan did not sit idle. A week after the bloody incidents at the Executive Yuan, on April Fool's Day, Chang An-le, a former leader of the Bamboo Union crime syndicate and founder of the Beijing-allied China Unification Promotion Party (CUPP), mobilized hundreds of his members in a counterprotest. Many of the participants had links to organized crime. And their aim was to expel the Sunflower Movement from the Legislative Yuan. If the government wouldn't do it, China's proxy would. Chang was a fugitive who spent ten years in a U.S. federal prison for drug trafficking, and who had once been on Taiwan's most-wanted list. After retiring to Taiwan in 2013 following more than a decade on the run in China, Chang, whose nickname was "White Wolf," launched his party into a promotion of Beijing's "one country, two systems." Many senior CCP officials were also visiting Taiwan at the time for meetings and summits with their counterparts from the KMT, and Chang played a role in those, too, by mobilizing his members to provide extra security for the Chinese visitors. On many occasions, Chang and his army threatened violence against President Ma's critics.

The involvement of organized crime in politics had been seen before. In Hong Kong, the CCP was known to be relying on an underground network to move money and weapons around and do the Party's dirty work. This arms-length relationship gave Beijing plausible deniability. While its violent proxies threatened civil society and engaged in various illicit activities to further Beijing's interests on the ground, the Chinese government could claim that it had no knowledge of the matter.[14]

Investigative journalists later showed that Chang had likely been groomed by China's "princelings," the children of former top CCP officials, while he was a fugitive in the country (Chang and his son operate a sports apparel company in China).[15]

Chang created the CUPP during his exile in China, and the party was registered in Taiwan, which gave it the right to field candidates in elections. Taiwan's democracy had matured enough that it could countenance the existence of political parties that espoused a wide range of positions – in this case unification with China. Needless to say, this permissiveness contrasted starkly with the one-party system in China, where the advocacy of any policy that went counter to the CCP's wishes was the surest way to send someone to jail.

Chang's plans to evict the Sunflowers on April 1 were foiled by the deployment of anti-riot police, which made sure to keep the two groups separated. Despite this failed attempt, the CUPP and its affiliates would continue to haunt politics and young activists for years to come.

By April 10, when the Sunflower Movement leadership decided to vacate the Legislative Yuan, the CSSTA was, for all intents and purposes, a dead letter. No further agreement would be signed between the occupation and the end of President Ma's second term in May 2016. In fact, the movement derailed Beijing's plans to use various agreements to further drag Taiwan into China's sphere of influence. Furthermore, the movement reverberated across time to the 2016 presidential and legislative election, creating momentum for the DPP, which eight years earlier had seemed to have lost its way. In nationwide local elections held in late 2014, the KMT suffered a major setback, losing many cities and counties to the DPP. In Taipei, Ko Wen-je, who ran as an independent candidate with the DPP's blessing, defeated his opponent from the KMT, a rare defeat for the party in Taipei. The CSSTA debacle, combined with high dissatisfaction with the Ma administration's inability to deliver on his vow to revive Taiwan's economy by fostering closer ties with China, largely accounted for the KMT's heavy losses in the 2014 elections. With only two years left to his second and last term in office, Ma had been a victim of retribution from both the "thin" and "thick" elements of a vibrant democracy – at the polls, and on the streets.

No sooner had the Sunflower Movement dispensed with the CSSTA and Ma's ambitions to expand ties with the PRC than another group of students – high school students, this time around – launched a series of protests outside the Ministry of Education (MOE), located in the same district as the Legislative Yuan and the MOI. For several days, the protesters, again supported by academics and various civic organizations, occupied the grounds of the ministry.[16] This time, the occupation was triggered by attempts by pro-Beijing academics affiliated with the KMT to change the guidelines for textbook curricula in ways that de-emphasized civics and placed greater focus on Taiwan's Chinese heritage. Those attempts were regarded with suspicion by young Taiwanese, who saw the move as a conspiracy to "brainwash" them and erase their identity. Partly as a result of the protests and because the Ma administration ran out of time, efforts to make Taiwan's textbooks more China-centric came to naught.

China's Frustrated Aims

Throughout the eight years of the Ma administration, even at times when things seemed to be going in Beijing's favor, with cross-Strait talks, bilateral agreements, deepening investment, and rising tourism, Beijing continued to invest heavily in military modernization and preparations for war against Taiwan. Still, the Ma administration chose to play down the threat posed by China. At one point, President Ma stated that nature, rather than China, was Taiwan's No. 1 enemy. His administration also stopped intelligence collection in China by Taiwan's military intelligence agency.

Why, one could ask, was Beijing remaining on a war footing at a time when the government in Taiwan appeared to be giving it what it wanted? Why did the PLA continue to prepare for war against Taiwan amid indications that unification could be achieved by peaceful means? While this may seem contradictory, it was not so for the CCP, whose Marxist-Leninist ideology allowed for the simultaneous existence of two seemingly opposed actions. Whether in times of war or peace, the CCP is in a state of perpetual struggle, or continuous warfare. Every effort, incentive, and act of coercion, is put to the service of an overarching objective – in this case, the "reunification" of Taiwan. For the CCP, there was no contradiction in, on the one hand, signing agreements with Taipei, increasing investment in Taiwan, and allowing large numbers of tourists to visit the island, and continued belligerence on the other. Therefore, while President Ma spoke of Taiwan as an "avenue of peace," state-run media in China publicized military exercises simulating an assault on what appeared to be a replica of Taiwan's Presidential Office – President Ma's office – while the PLA continued to acquire and manufacture various military platforms that would be used in a war on Taiwan.

These two dynamics, the sticks and carrots, existed simultaneously, and the CCP calibrated them in response to developments in Taiwan. Depending on the context, the Chinese leadership emphasized one over the other. But it never abandoned either. Beijing will always keep all its options open. Besides the PLA, China continued to conduct aggressive espionage against the Taiwanese government, military, and private sector. In one prominent case, a senior Taiwanese military officer who had been recruited by China received a life sentence after his spying activities were uncovered. Beijing also used front organizations, "united front" tactics, businesses and various economic incentives, such as preferential treatment, access to experimental free-trade zones and so on, to penetrate, reward, and co-opt individuals across Taiwan.

By late 2015, it was clear that President Ma's efforts to consolidate the gains made in cross-Strait relations had come short. The general elections were set for January 2016 and Ma, whose popular support had dropped significantly, could not, under constitutional rules, seek a third consecutive term. He was running out of time to achieve his main political objective.

And things went downhill for his party. The KMT's initial choice for presidential candidate in the 2016 elections, Hung Hsiu-chu, was like the DPP's candidate, Tsai Ing-wen, a woman. This was a first for both parties. However, in what came to be regarded as a stunningly misguided decision, the KMT candidate ignored, or perhaps misread, the mood across Taiwan in the wake of the Sunflower Movement. Rather than take those setbacks into account, Hung began campaigning on a policy platform that proposed to go beyond what President Ma had done in terms of rapprochement with China. The DPP's Tsai, meanwhile, was capitalizing on the aftereffects of the spring of 2014's dramatic events at the Legislative Yuan and, much better at reading the public mood, sought to empower the young Taiwanese who had mobilized to defend their democracy. As the elections approached, it became clear that Hung stood no chance against Tsai, and that Hung's Beijing-friendly rhetoric compromised the party's chances in the legislative elections that would be held concurrently with the presidential one.

In a surprise move, on October 17, less than three months before election day, the KMT decided to switch out its presidential candidate and to replace her with party chairman Eric Chu.[17] The eleventh-hour decision was unlikely to turn things around in the presidential race, as Chu did not have enough time to articulate his campaign platform. Still, the KMT hoped that by reducing the tone-deafness of the party on Taiwan's relations with China it could mitigate the damage in the legislative elections.

The following month, on November 7, President Ma and Xi Jinping met in Singapore for a historic summit. This was the first by the leaders of the two sides of the Taiwan Strait since the conclusion of the Chinese Civil War in 1949. In his opening remarks, Ma, who like Xi was there representing his party rather than his country, declared that "Cross-strait relations are at their most peaceful and stable since 1949." Ma elaborated on five points – "consolidation of the 1992 Consensus and the maintenance of peace," "reduction of hostility and peaceful handling of disputes," "expansion of cross-strait exchanges and mutual benefits," "establishment of a cross-strait hotline to handle important or urgent matters," and "joint cooperation for cross-strait prosperity." Those five points, he said, "are not aimed at achieving selfish goals or unilateral gains, but a better future for coming generations. Both sides should accord great importance to the values and way of life that our people cherish, maintain cross-strait peace, and ensure mutual benefits and success for both sides with the wisdom embedded in Chinese culture."[18]

However groundbreaking and "historic" the meeting, which included an eighty-second handshake between the two leaders, its effects were mostly symbolic. Six months from then, Ma would no longer be in office, and there was little doubt that his remaining days in the Presidential Office would be as a lame-duck president – an unpopular one at that, with only 23 percent of respondents in an opinion poll conducted by a pro-KMT media outlet expressing satisfaction with his policies. Ma was no longer in a position to direct the future course of cross-Strait policy. Whoever assumed the presidency after him – and by then very few people doubted that the DPP's Tsai would do so – would be in charge of the relationship with China. It also became clear that Xi's remark to Ma, that there is "no problem that cannot be talked through," would be put to a serious test after the next president entered the Presidential Office in Taipei.

A New Era

On January 16, 2016, the people of Taiwan elected Tsai Ing-wen, the DPP candidate, with 56.1 percent of the votes cast, against the KMT's Eric Chu, at 31 percent. The third candidate, James Soong of the People First Party, came last with 12.8 percent. In the same election, the DPP won 68 legislative seats, to the KMT's 35, with 9 seats going to three smaller parties. The results represented a gain of 28 seats for the DPP and a loss of 29 for the KMT. For the first time in Taiwan's democratic history, the DPP had a majority of seats in parliament, where 57 seats were needed to secure a majority. Tsai, Taiwan's first female president, had been given a strong mandate, one that in many aspects would depart from her predecessor's policies. The big question was: How would Beijing react to this protégé of former president Lee Teng-hui, who had served as chairperson of the Mainland Affairs Council (MAC) and top negotiator for her country's World Trade Organization affairs?

After eight years under a president who had vowed to reduce tensions in the Taiwan Strait and to use this "peace dividend" to secure economic benefits for Taiwan, the Taiwanese voters had picked a new president, and a new legislature, that was much more Taiwan-centric and skeptical of Beijing. In picking Tsai, voters knew full well that Beijing was unlikely to respond to this reversal with equanimity. Over the next eight years, President Tsai actively sought to deepen Taiwan's liberal practices and to consolidate its young democracy. Those efforts further highlighted the contrast between the two societies as China under Xi descended deeper into authoritarian rule.

The crackdown on pro-democracy advocates in Hong Kong, and the passage of national security laws in China that coincided with the Tsai presidency, torpedoed whatever appeal the "one country, two systems" formula may still have had with the Taiwanese public.[19] The eight years under President Ma had served as a window during which the two sides could test how far they could venture in rapprochement. The effort fell well short of Ma's ambitions and Xi's hopes to compound China's influence on Taiwan. Taiwan's democratic firewall had frustrated Ma's efforts to tighten Taiwan's bonds with authoritarian China.

This was a point of no return. The eight years of the Ma presidency had been the one chance for the two sides to find a peaceful resolution to decades of conflict in the Taiwan Strait. In the end, they did not even come close. At best, the two sides succeeded in normalizing various aspects of the bilateral relationship that should have been addressed a long time ago. But those were the low-hanging fruit. On the more controversial and sensitive aspects of that relationship, chief among them the status of Taiwan, negotiators from both sides never came close to reaching an agreement. Talks went on, and at some point Ma suggested a peace agreement but almost immediately shelved it amid a strong domestic backlash and fears of its impact on future elections. Peace, real peace, therefore, had been an illusion. The two societies had grown so fundamentally different that the contradictions made a political union impossible. It was also clear that even a more "generous" offer than the "one country, two systems" would nevertheless result in an unequal relationship, in which Beijing would be the center and Taiwan merely a peripheral entity, province, or Special Administrative Region. Such an arrangement, furthermore, would inevitably come at a cost to Taiwan's hard-earned freedoms, liberal values, freedom of speech, and democratic institutions.

By electing Tsai and giving her DPP a majority in parliament, voters also sent a strong signal to Beijing that the Taiwanese were cognizant of China's intentions and that they did not buy the idea of "peaceful unification." That is not to say that they refused to acknowledge the legitimacy of the PRC, or even its attractiveness as a destination for business, tourism, or education. Most did not oppose normalized ties per se, but they wanted relations to be among equals, a precondition that the incoming president would insist upon over and over again during her two terms in office.

Tsai came into office with an ambitious reform agenda. In addition to overhauling the pension system, something no president before her had been able to accomplish, the Tsai administration took important steps to address transitional justice over the authoritarian era, and legalized same-sex marriage, making Taiwan the first country in Asia to do so. During the same period, Taiwan regularly ranked among the freest societies in Asia and often at the top in freedom of the press. Through civil society exchanges, Taiwan also became a partner to many countries in their struggle to balance their efforts in countering authoritarian influence in ways that do not violate democratic principles.

The Tsai administration's desire to turn Taiwan into a hub for international civic organizations also bore fruit. After revising antiquated laws, several organizations involved in media freedom and democracy promotion, such as Reporters Without Borders (RSF), the National Democratic Institute (NDI), the International Republican Institute (IRI), Freedom House, the Westminster Foundation for Democracy, the Friedrich Neumann Foundation, and others, opened regional offices in Taipei. Other organizations and journalists also began relocating to Taiwan amid tightening repression in China and Hong Kong. Taiwan also hosted important global events, among them the Religious Freedom Forum and the World Movement for Democracy (WMD), further positioning the island as an essential partner in efforts to build democratic solidarity and resilience amid authoritarian resurgence.

The government also empowered several dozen Taiwanese civic organizations, often with the government-funded Taiwan Foundation for Democracy (TFD) as a bridge. Such initiatives helped give a voice to a constellation of Taiwanese NGOs by helping them connect with foreign partners. Organizations like DoubleThink Lab, the Information Operations Research Group, Cofacts, gov, and many others gained prominence worldwide for their pioneering work on identifying and countering disinformation and other forms of authoritarian influence. At a time when civic groups and foreign governments were finding it increasingly difficult to engage with Chinese NGOs, Taiwan was opening its doors and advertising itself as a willing partner. On the security side, government-funded organizations like the Institute for National Defense and Security Research (INDSR) and the Prospect Foundation also deepened their relationships with think tanks, academic institutions, and NGOs worldwide, including parts of Europe where the threat from Russia loomed larger than ever following its invasion of Ukraine in 2022.

Taiwan also expanded its participation at various security forums such as the Halifax International Security Forum (reserved for democratic countries only); the Shangri-La Dialogue in Singapore; the Raisina Dialogue, India's premier conference on geopolitics and geoeconomics; the Munich Conference; Forum 2000 in the Czech Republic, founded by former president Václav Havel; the Copenhagen Democracy Summit; and others. Taiwan was also invited to participate in President Biden's Summit for Democracy. The Taiwan-Asia Exchange Foundation (TAEF), meanwhile, held various events and exchanges with counterparts across South and Southeast Asia as part of the Tsai administration's New Southbound Policy (NSP). The NSP was an essential component of the administration's efforts to reduce Taiwan's economic dependence on China.

Audrey Tang, Taiwan's first digital minister and a transgender woman, also gained international prominence and was invited by several countries to share her experiences in the digital sphere. Tang, who at 35 was the youngest-ever Taiwanese to be made minister, designed the contact-tracing application that was used by the Taiwanese government to successfully monitor and contain the spread of the coronavirus, striking a balance between state intrusiveness and respect for privacy that many countries were struggling to emulate.

During the Covid-19 pandemic, Taiwan demonstrated how a democracy can successfully use big data and technology to protect its population without violating people's rights and privacy. It also donated millions of facial masks to countries in need. Through such efforts, Taiwan increased its visibility despite relentless attempts by Beijing to isolate it internationally.[20]

As more and more countries recognized the challenges posed by China's growing influence in their regions, governments often turned to Taiwan for advice. They knew that, as a democracy, Taiwan had needed to carefully balance its national security requirements while cohabiting with an authoritarian neighbor that accounted for approximately 40 percent of its exports and with which it shared linguistic and cultural affinities. President Tsai's clear-eyed foreign policy strategy, combined with Taiwan's renewed soft power, market diversification, and active civil society helped Taiwan to shine on the international stage in ways it never had before.

The greater role that Taiwan was playing in the global supply chain and as a top producer of the most advanced semiconductors also encouraged foreign multinationals to open regional offices in Taiwan. This success was in large part due to its own efforts and the vision of the Tsai administration. All this received a major boost from Beijing, at a time when China was cracking down on dissent, passing far-reaching national security laws, further restricting freedom of the press, clamping down on the LGBTQ+ community, tightening controls over civic and academic exchanges with the outside world, smothering Hong Kong, and violating international law in its territorial dispute with the Philippines. Taiwan saw an opening, and seized it.

Incompatibilities Deepen

While Taiwan under President Tsai deepened and embraced civic nationalism, in which people of various ethnic backgrounds are united in belief in and support for a shared polity (laws, way of life, a defined territory), China was defining nationality strictly in terms of blood. Regardless of where a Chinese person was, China would always exert a gravitational pull that defies borders, nationality, and allegiance. In other words, once a Chinese, a person was always a Chinese with duties to the motherland. Taiwan's concept of the nation is much more akin to how it is understood in the West, particularly immigrant societies, where despite being of multifarious origins and ethnic stock, the citizen is defined by, and united in, a shared sense of responsibility toward and protections by a political unit.

Taiwan's system, its existence as a sovereign entity, is an affront to the CCP. It directly contradicts Beijing's narrative on "reunification" and the entire architecture of its posture vis-à-vis Taiwan. To recognize the validity of the Taiwanese model would risk undermining the foundations upon which the PRC is based. By refusing to change its narrative on Taiwan, and in fact hardening it during the Tsai administration, the CCP has backed itself into a corner. Under Xi, any admission that the Party is wrong about Taiwan is inconceivable, as this could be perceived as weakness. In the system that has been cultivated by Xi, any individual who questions the legitimacy of China's position on Taiwan, or who proposes alternative approaches to how Beijing should handle the Taiwan "question," is bound to lose his job, or worse. For many of the ultranationalists who have adopted a hawkish position on Taiwan, the refusal of the people of Taiwan to join "the motherland" is an offense against their pride, something inconceivable in their aspirations to superpower status and China's rightful place under the sun. They cannot conceive that people could choose safety, freedom, and civility, even at the cost of a lower "status" in the hierarchy of nations, over national greatness.

For most people in Taiwan, particularly younger Taiwanese, China is a foreign country. They do not deny its legitimacy, nor do they ignore the opportunities that may exist there for them. But China is to them what the United States is to Canadians, notwithstanding the similar culture and shared languages. It is also true, however, that KMT and DPP supporters tend to differ in their assessment of the extent to which Taiwan and China should interact. In general, the DPP and its supporters are more wary of China, and are therefore more inclined to support candidates and policies that emphasize national security. Their KMT counterparts, meanwhile, favor closer ties and greater economic engagement, with less focus on national security. The DPP tends to favor a closer alliance with the United States, Taiwan's security guarantor, while the KMT hews to a policy of accommodation meant to reduce tensions with the PRC.

With Beijing closing the door to dialogue with Taiwan after Tsai assumed office in 2016, the KMT has used this as an opportunity to position itself as the party that is best equipped to negotiate with Beijing and thereby reduce the risks of war in the Taiwan Strait, a specter it has used to its advantage among its supporters. In turn, such a policy has often led to accusations that the KMT is colluding with Beijing in its efforts to annex Taiwan. While some KMT members could indeed be described as pro-Beijing, the picture is far more complex. The KMT will use any opportunity that presents itself to counter the DPP or complicate its efforts. That is politics, not the result of ideological affinity with Beijing. (Such practices can nevertheless inadvertently assist Beijing by weakening unity and institutions.) The political battles can get fierce, as shown by the many confrontations at the legislature, resulting in shoving, fist fights, and even the lobbing of pig entrails at one's political opponent, practices that no Taiwanese should be proud of. Additionally, those antics tend to engender the perception that Taiwan is split down the middle and that the DPP and KMT cannot agree on anything. That is not the case. On the essentials – freedom, democracy, and way of life – the majority of them tend to agree. And with few exceptions, all are opposed to the idea of Taiwan being governed by the PRC.

Through the choices that peoples and governments on both sides of the Taiwan Strait have made in recent decades, this dispute has nevertheless taken the characteristics of a battle of values. In so doing, Taiwan and China have joined different ideological camps in the battle for how the international system should be run (and by whom). By deepening its attachment to and practice of democracy, Taiwan has joined, and is increasingly being embraced by, the group of nations that seeks to sustain the liberal democratic world order that was created at the conclusion of World War II. Revisionist powers such as China and Russia, on the other hand, regard this system as unfair, incompatible with their histories, and defined by rules, values, and norms that are not suitable for current and future challenges.

In the end, all this charade about Taiwanese "compatriots" being of the same blood as the Chinese, members of the same nation awaiting "reunification," has been institutionalized to mask a much more prosaic ambition: China's annexation of land that happens to stand in the way of its naval expansion into the West Pacific. Beijing's greater aim (after Taiwan) is to expel the U.S. from what it regards as its rightful sphere of influence. Thus, even though the CCP insists that Taiwan is an "internal matter," "unfinished history," and a "family feud," the implications of China's territorial designs upon Taiwan are regional and possibly global. How the matter is settled, if ever, will have consequences for the entire international community.

2

Xi's Unbridled Ambitions

It would be wrong to argue that China's threat against Taiwan is anything new and the result of a single man – Xi Jinping. After all, China launched missile attacks and held military drills simulating an invasion of the island in 1995 and 1996, when Jiang Zemin was president. Jiang's successor, Hu Jintao, never abandoned China's territorial claims on Taiwan and, under him, the Chinese military continued to conduct exercises simulating an assault on Taiwan while modernizing its forces to meet that goal. Much of China's military activity during that period, however, was theater, as China did not have sufficient capabilities to undertake an actual invasion. The threat grew by leaps and bounds after Xi, whose ambitions and leadership style introduced a much more bellicose stance against Taipei and its partners in Washington, D.C.

Historians and political scientists have long debated whether individuals or invisible forces drive history. Xi's emergence as CCP party secretary and president of the PRC in 2013 made it clear that strong leaders have the power to change history – often not for the greater good. Throughout its history since its foundation in 1949, the PRC's claims of sovereignty over Taiwan, or the urgency with which it treated the cause, have waxed and waned. In times of domestic crisis, such as the Great Leap Forward (1958–62), the Cultural Revolution (1966–76), and the Tiananmen Massacre (1989), China was simply too distracted domestically to care much about Taiwan. The first two crises had been caused by China's strongman, Mao, with catastrophic results during which China isolated itself from the international community. And of course, as long as China was weak economically and militarily, it could ill afford to threaten a war that it had no hope of winning.

By the time the relatively unknown Xi assumed power in 2013, all the elements that would fuel greater assertiveness by the PRC – a stabilized domestic front, a strong and globally connected economy, and a much more formidable military – were in place.

In authoritarian systems, a small circle of elites decides on war and peace, and the public has little if any say on the matter. That is particularly the case in authoritarian systems where an ultra-personalistic, or megalothymic, leader is in charge. Which is the case of China under Xi. The political scientist Francis Fukuyama describes megalothymia in a leader as one who "thrives on exceptionality: taking big risks, engaging in monumental struggles, seeking large effects, because all of these lead to recognition of oneself as superior to others."[1] From the founding of the PRC, perhaps with the exception of Mao, decision-making tended to be made by a cabal of CCP cadres who arrived at various policy decisions by consensus. Even Deng Xiaoping, China's paramount leader from 1978 until 1989 and arguably the strongest leader after Mao (before Xi), avoided concentrating power around his person, largely because of the Great Leap Forward and the Cultural Revolution, which future leaders blamed on Mao's excessive powers. Following Deng, every Chinese leader therefore ruled by consensus, which ensured that the leader received, and took into account, input from a variety of influential experts within the CCP. Deng, the architect of China's economic rise, counseled that it was best, as China remained relatively weak, to "hide your strength, bide your time, never take the lead."

All this changed with Xi's coming to power. After some speculation among China watchers that Xi could be the hoped-for reformist that many saw as necessary for China to fully integrate into the international community, the new leader made it clear that his governance style would be characterized by assertiveness. Unlike his predecessors, Xi inherited a China that was far wealthier and influential, with a military that was on the cusp of launching one of the most extraordinary periods of military modernization in the past century. Moreover, unlike the typical technocratic cadres who had traditionally run the CCP, Xi quickly accumulated new powers. And he launched an ambitious anti-corruption campaign that, conveniently, allowed him to rid himself of any would-be challenger within the Party.

The historian Sulmaan Wasif Khan notes, "Jiang [Zemin] and Hu [Jintao] had gone about grand strategy quietly, not altering much, trying, when possible, to be conciliatory. They sought simply to keep China on the course Deng had set – continue with reform and opening, seek a balance of power in a multipolar world, modernize the military, and keep China whole. There was something dull and uninspiring about their ways."[2] Over the next decade, the regime implemented and amended sets of laws that further tightened controls over information, the political space, civil society, and exchanges with the outside world. For Xi, the outside world was increasingly seen as hostile, while democratic ideals were "pollution" that threatened China's system.

Xi accumulated immense powers, eliminated potential challengers, and broke with tradition by abolishing the ten-year term limits for Chinese presidents in 2018, making himself president for life. His ambitions for the country became quasi-messianic. Xi's Chinese Dream, as Carl Minzner observes, was "a sweeping attempt to shift the ideological basis of Beijing's rule away from the Marxist framework that the Communist Party has embraced since the 1949 revolution to a more explicitly ethnonationalist vision rooted in 'traditional Chinese culture.'"[3] Those sweeping ambitions were centered around Xi himself. Like Russia's Vladimir Putin, Xi, who also heads the Central Military Commission (CMC), substantially narrowed his circle of advisers on matters of war and peace. When strongmen do this, there is a high likelihood that the leader is not listening to the advice of other influential figures within the party or government. Or the advisers may become reluctant to provide the leader with views that contradict a leader's pre-established notions. This kind of hubris and reluctant councils increase the risks that a leader's folly will drag an entire country into catastrophe.

As Cai Xia, a former professor at the Central Party School of the CCP, wrote in the influential journal *Foreign Affairs*, "[a]s Xi's rule becomes more extreme, the infighting and resentment he has already triggered will only grow stronger. The competition between various factions within the party will get more intense, complicated, and brutal than ever before." This, he warns, could lead China to "experience a vicious cycle in which Xi reacts to the perceived sense of threat by taking ever bolder actions that generate even more pushback. Trapped in an echo chamber and desperately seeking redemption, he may even do something catastrophically ill advised, such as attack Taiwan."[4]

Xi's visions of grandeur – the great rejuvenation of China – inevitably pass through Taiwan. "Reunification" has been a pillar of CCP doctrine for decades. Under Xi, China has intensified activities on every front to bring Taiwan to heel.

There is great danger, however, in staking the China Dream – and therefore Xi's and the CCP's legitimacy – on the basis of a lie. China's claim of sovereignty over Taiwan and the alleged historical inevitability of its "reunification" with "the mainland" is based upon a highly selective reading of history. It is only logical if we ignore (and erase) historical facts. It also depends on the refusal to acknowledge that most Taiwanese, despite Beijing's claims to the contrary, oppose unification. Most, as we have seen, favor the "status quo," which is tantamount to de facto independence.

On one side a proud people, united in their opposition to absorption by an external entity; on the other, a regime that countenances no opposition, stubbornly insists on a single model for unification ("one country, two systems"), and which has made the "reunification" of Taiwan a cornerstone of its grand ambitions.

With this rigidity, Xi has painted himself and his party into a corner. His refusal to listen to contrary advice from his experts, or their fear of contradicting him, have blinded Xi to the reality that the "peaceful reunification" of Taiwan is a pipe dream, or that his approach to the matter has been counterproductive. And there doesn't seem to be a way out of this dead-end: no authoritarian leader, especially one who has ruthlessly sought to eliminate competitors, critics, and rivals, will ever admit to being wrong on a core policy. For this could signal weakness and result in removal from office – a particularly plausible scenario given Xi's abolition of the presidential term limits. Instead, a leader in such a difficult position, as Cai asserts, will have every incentive to double down. And in this case, rather than "peaceful reunification," the desired end goal will either be Taiwan's (coerced) capitulation or more belligerent measures to bring the whole affair to a satisfactory (for Beijing) conclusion.

The Fujian Factor

Xi's decision to make Taiwan a key element of his policy stems from his sense of destiny and primary role as *the* orchestrator of the great rejuvenation of China. His past functions at lower levels of the party-state also played a role in fueling those ambitions. Key to this are the seventeen years he spent as a party official in Fujian Province, located immediately opposite Taiwan in the Taiwan Strait. Transferred there in 1985, Xi would spend the next seventeen years occupying various administrative positions and rising through the ranks. During that period, Xi served as mayor of Xiamen, secretary of the Ningde Prefectural Party Committee, secretary of the Fuzhou Municipal Party Committee (MPC), deputy secretary of the Fujian Provincial Party Committee (PPC), acting governor and governor of Fujian Province.[5]

Xi's seventeen and, by most accounts, rather unimpressive years in Fujian also bolstered the self-image that he, above anyone else, best understood Taiwan. This was because exchanges between Taiwan and Fujian at the cultural, linguistic, and trade levels have historically been extensive. As Taiwan's economy boomed in the 1980s and 1990s, Fujian became a major investment destination for Taiwanese manufacturers, which made a substantial contribution to the PRC's own economic takeoff, something that Beijing would only reluctantly acknowledge. Those interactions, and the interdependence that developed over the years, helped create many of the channels that Beijing used to increase its leverage and political influence on Taiwan. Given the roles he played in Fujian, Xi was therefore keenly aware of the possibilities.

Xi became governor of Fujian at a time when relations between Taipei and Beijing were becoming more tense, particularly after the election of the DPP's Chen Shui-bian in 2000. As governor of the frontline province facing Taiwan, Xi was in charge as the PLA held exercises across from Taiwan. During those years, Xi developed an ability to enact two seemingly contradictory concepts simultaneously, something that would characterize his approach to Taiwan after he became party secretary general and president: On the one hand, the adoption of a "conciliatory" tone toward Taiwan, emphasizing trade, investment, cultural, and other exchanges with Taiwan, while on the other presenting an iron fist with military maneuvers, threats of the use of force, and ideological inflexibility. In Xi's mind, these two approaches could coexist seamlessly; in fact, they were meant to reinforce each other with the aim of accomplishing the inevitable: Taiwan's "reunification."

All this experience familiarized Xi with Taiwan, and during that time he came to know many Taiwanese officials and businesspeople. And yet, like many CCP officials, Xi has exhibited an inability to fully understand the impact that democratization has had on Taiwanese identity. This tone-deafness has repeatedly resulted in policies and a discourse by Xi that have been self-defeating, leading to the further alienation of the Taiwanese people. It has also made the lives of those within Taiwan who espouse unification much more complicated. Xi's misguided self-assurance and belief that he knows best has led him down a road that has reduced the likelihood that the two sides could reach an agreement on "peaceful unification."

The fact that Xi likely isn't listening to his advisors, who may know a bit more about Taiwan, is not only the result of his immense power. He may also have an anti-intellectual streak. Xi's upbringing and, in the words of one Xi biographer, "lackadaisical" achievements,[6] certainly suggest that this is the case. As the journalist Chun Han Wong observes in a recent book, Xi, who often misreads in his public addresses, may have a "deep-seated insecurity about his lack of a formal education – particularly in contrast with Mao, who wrote poetry, and even Jiang Zemin, who spoke several languages and sang and played music alongside foreign leaders."[7] Xi, Wong writes, "took power as a relative unknown" and came to power on a myth-making campaign that portrayed him as a book lover, claims which he used to impress foreign leaders.

What has made it even more difficult for Beijing to understand Taiwan is the decision by Xi in 2016 to suspend dialogue with Taiwan following the election of Tsai Ing-wen. During that same period, Xi also tightened the ideological line across all aspects of Chinese society. Therefore, academic exchanges with Taiwan (and Western countries) suffered, often limiting contact with like-minded intellectuals and politicians. Thus, the Chinese side's ability to have a more nuanced and realistic picture of the situation within Taiwan became a victim of Xi's ideological rigidity and refusal to hear contradictory assessments.

Xi's Miscalculations

Xi's obstinacy and misreading of Taiwan has undermined earlier successes, such as his summit in Singapore with the outgoing Taiwanese president Ma Ying-jeou in late 2015. From May 20, 2016, when President Tsai Ing-wen was inaugurated in Taipei, Xi orchestrated a campaign to isolate Taiwan internationally while using various "sharp power" instruments to coerce, confuse, and weaken Taiwanese society. This assault on Taiwan, punctuated by growing military intimidation, served to highlight Xi's misguided approach. By the time President Tsai ended her second and last term in May 2024, Taiwan was more connected internationally, and better positioned as an ally in the democratic camp. Its society, meanwhile, refused to allow intimidation, disinformation, and cognitive warfare to dictate their choices at the polls. Nor did it alter how they identified, or the depth of Taiwanese attachment to a free, democratic way of life. Rather than embrace a more benevolent approach to Taiwan that offered a more pragmatic and realistic blueprint for coexistence, Beijing stubbornly stuck to the same failed formula.

One salient example of Xi's inability or refusal to understand the mood in Taiwan occurred on January 2, 2019, when he delivered a 4,254-character speech marking the 40th anniversary of the "Message to Compatriots in Taiwan."[8] The speech occurred less than two months after President Tsai's DPP had suffered a major setback in nationwide local elections, following which Tsai stepped down as party chair. Xi completely misread the significance of the electoral outcome by regarding it as a sign of public disfavor for the Tsai administration in general (including its foreign and cross-Strait policy) and renewed support for the KMT's more China-amenable stance.[9] He therefore decided to go on the offensive with a message to the people of Taiwan that sabotaged any gains it may have made following the KMT's success at the polls. In his remarks, Xi closed the door on the "different interpretations" that had allowed Beijing and Taipei, when the KMT was in power, to use the "1992 consensus" as a baseline for cross-Strait dialogue. It was no longer possible to argue that the two sides would agree to disagree. Xi made it clear that negotiations would be on China's terms. Worse, by doing so, Xi was erasing the ROC, whose continued existence was the KMT's guiding light. If the KMT had gone along with this, it would have betrayed many of its members and the people who vote for it, people who, though they oppose "Taiwan independence," nevertheless regard themselves as citizens of the ROC.

And it got worse. In the same address, Xi equated the "1992 consensus" with the "one country, two systems" formula. The timing could not have been worse, with Hong Kong descending into chaos. Xi's remarks forced the KMT to openly state its opposition. After all, as a party in a democracy, its official positions need to reflect the wishes of a large enough number of voters if it is to have a chance to win in elections. That's a lesson that small, pro-unification parties like Chang's CUPP quickly learned when they ran candidates in elections. They won nothing. Zilch. What Xi was proposing was unpalatable, toxic for the KMT. Xi's hardened line on Taiwan, at a moment of weakness for Tsai, was an unintended lifeline. It gave her an opportunity to retake the initiative. Although her party had suffered a major setback in the local elections, Xi's address allowed her to reclaim the moral high ground by re-emphasizing that which unites the people of Taiwan: their opposition to "one China" on Beijing's terms, and the "one country, two systems." Once again, China under Xi had shown its tendency to shoot itself in the foot. Perhaps its inability to understand the workings of democracy was the main reason.

Mere Rhetoric or Signal of Intention?

Taiwan and countries that are seeking to avert catastrophe in the Indo-Pacific and elsewhere have had a hard time predicting the behavior and intentions of leadership in authoritarian systems. Even more challenging is doing so when the leadership is driven by an ideology that is not fully understood by Western democracies. When it comes to matters of war, a state's willingness to engage in warfare depends to a large extent on its military capabilities. A leadership's decision to go to war is predicated on *intent* and *capabilities* as well as other variables including domestic stability and the international context. As we have seen, for several decades, although China maintained its sovereignty claim over Taiwan, it did not have sufficient capabilities to launch a major military offensive against Taiwan, especially if doing so risked dragging the U.S. into the conflict. Thus, while the CCP leadership underscored its claim over Taiwan, its threats sounded hollow.

Xi's coming to power coincided with the emergence of the People's Liberation Army (PLA) as a much more formidable fighting force. The PLA was approaching the point where it could legitimately claim to have the ability to use force against Taiwan and to complicate U.S. plans to intervene on its behalf.

The stage was therefore set for a highly ideological leader to present himself as the Chinese leader who could finally accomplish the long-sought dream of "reunifying" Taiwan. Yes, his predecessor, Hu Jintao, had passed the Anti-Secession Law of 2005, which technically gave China the "right" to use force against Taiwan under certain conditions. But even then, few believed that China had sufficient military capabilities to take on Taiwan, especially if this ran the risk of prompting a U.S. intervention.

Xi is now close to having such capabilities. This makes predicting his future behavior even more challenging than before, all of which is further complicated by his personality, ideological inclinations, and the closed nature of decision-making within the CCP. On this, experts and government assessments have wildly differed, with some analysts arguing that Xi is merely blustering, aiming to force Taiwan to bend to his will, while others are warning that he means business and that his warnings should be taken seriously. Analysts in the first group expect policy continuity and "rational" decision-making based on the cold calculations of the costs and benefits of taking military action against Taiwan. Those in the second group, conversely, believe that Xi and the CCP are telegraphing their intentions. They put greater emphasis on how ideology and personality drive decision-making, and believe that a leader like Xi will not be dissuaded by the potentially catastrophic costs of an attempt to bring Taiwan to heel.

Xi's inner thoughts are unknown to all but himself. We can nevertheless analyze his various speeches regarding Taiwan for signs of intent, continuity, and indications of departure from the CCP's longstanding policy toward Taiwan. Throughout his tenure, Xi has maintained that he remains committed to "peaceful reunification," the same position held by his predecessors. Still, China's stance regarding Taiwan has inarguably hardened under him.

Before Xi came to power, on nine key policy issues on Taiwan, there was surprising continuity in the speeches made by the CCP secretary general at the 16th, 17th, and 18th National Party Congress, in 2002, 2007, and 2012, respectively. During his first three years or so, as he gained his footing, Xi's messaging on Taiwan tended to reflect that of his predecessor,

Hu Jintao. This was largely because the Taiwanese president at the time, Ma Ying-jeou, was aiming to improve ties with China by signing various cross-Strait agreements with Beijing. Even the highly ideological Xi knew then that aggressive signaling would risk derailing rapprochement with Taiwan. Thus, even the highly ideological Xi could be softer when it was necessary for him to be so and when the conditions were right.

However, Ma's miscalculation over the Cross-Strait Services Trade Agreement and the rise of the Sunflower Movement derailed those plans. This was a hard lesson for the CCP: a seemingly unstoppable process, with a KMT in control of both branches of government, had run into the firewall erected by Taiwan's democratic forces and vibrant civil society. Within two years, the edifice of collaboration across the Taiwan Strait had crumbled. This was a slap in the face for Xi that contributed largely to the resentment that fueled many of his policies toward Taiwan from 2016 onward. From that moment on, there would be very few carrots.

The first signs of the CCP's hardening stance on Taiwan emerged at the 19th Party Congress in October 2017. As Richard Bush of the Brookings Institution observed at the time, China's Taiwan policy, as stated in the secretary general's speech to the Party Congress, had included nine key elements over time:

1. The guiding principle of peaceful reunification of Taiwan according to the "One Country, Two Systems" formula and the eight-point proposal enunciated by Jiang Zemin in 1995.
2. Adherence to the "One China" principle, the key point of which is that the territory of Taiwan is within the sovereign territory of China.
3. Strong opposition to separatism and Taiwan independence.
4. Willingness to have dialogue, exchanges, consultations, and negotiations with any political party that adheres to the One China principle.

5. Stress on the idea that the people on Taiwan and people on the mainland are "brothers and sisters of the same blood."
6. Establishing a connection between unification and the cause of "the great rejuvenation of the Chinese nation."
7. Placing hopes on the Taiwan people as a force to help bring about unification.
8. A promise that progress toward unification, and unification itself, will bring material benefits to Taiwan.
9. An expression of "utmost sincerity" by Beijing toward the unification project.[10]

As Bush and others noted at the time, the last three points were not mentioned in Xi's speech. More importantly, by not mentioning "Placing hopes on the Taiwan people as a force to help bring about unification," Xi appeared to be signaling that Beijing would no longer take the desires and preferences of the Taiwanese people into account. In other words, rather than consult the Taiwanese side to find an acceptable solution to the Taiwan "question," it now seemed that Beijing intended to dictate the terms under which "reunification" would be accomplished. It also suggested that the Chinese side would work more closely with partners and proxies within Taiwan to undermine the Tsai administration.

Turning to Taiwan independence, Xi's language became even harsher, stating that China "will resolutely uphold national sovereignty and territorial integrity" and "never tolerate a repeat of the historical tragedy of a divided country." Any effort to split the motherland, he added, "will be resolutely opposed by all the Chinese people." Xi concluded by saying that China has the "firm will, full confidence, and sufficient capability to defeat any form of Taiwan independence secession plot. We will never allow any person, any organization, or any political party to split any part of the Chinese territory from China at any time or in any form."

The next major speech by Xi that signaled a hardening posture toward Taiwan was the one he gave marking the 40th anniversary of the "Message to Compatriots in Taiwan," given less than two months after the DPP's poor showing in nationwide local elections. As we saw earlier, Xi and the CCP grossly misinterpreted the causes and effects of the DPP's poor performance in those elections. Emboldened, the CCP then attempted to influence Taiwan's presidential election campaign the following year, with Xi's remarks appealing directly to the Taiwanese to embrace their destiny by agreeing to "reunification" under "one country, two systems." In a united effort to oppose Taiwan independence, Xi said, "all political parties and all sectors of society on both sides [will] recommend representatives who will engage in extensive and in-depth democratic [*sic*] consultations on cross-Straits relations and the future of the nation and work toward institutional arrangements for promoting the peaceful development of cross-Straits relations." If the two sides abide by the "one China" principle, Xi continued, then Taiwanese compatriots would benefit. However, should they deviate from his program, he warned, "cross-Straits relations will become strained and volatile, and the interests of our compatriots in Taiwan will be harmed."

Xi then suggested that the Taiwanese people bypass their government, while pointing out that China reserved the "right" to use force. Speaking directly to Beijing's would-be allies in Taiwan, "regardless of political affiliation, religious belief, social status, or origin of birth, whether civilian or military," Xi said that Taiwan independence "will only bring disaster." Consequently, Taiwanese patriots "should resolutely oppose 'Taiwan independence' and join hands with us to pursue the bright prospects of peaceful reunification. We are willing to create vast space for peaceful reunification; but we will definitely not leave any room for separatist activities aimed at 'Taiwan independence' in any form." In the event that all this failed, he threatened, "We do not renounce the use of force and reserve the option of taking all necessary measures. This is to guard against external interference and a tiny number of separatists and their separatist activities for 'Taiwan independence.'"[11] There it was again, the reference to a "tiny" number of "separatists," a claim that flew in the face of all evidence.

The aggressive tone and refusal to recognize that the "one country, two systems" formula held little appeal for the people of Taiwan, left little doubt that Beijing only had one "offer" for Taiwan: an arrangement largely discredited by the disaster in Hong Kong, or else – war.

Over the next few years, Xi's rhetoric on Taiwan continued to harden, with endless references to the need to "resolutely fight 'Taiwan independence' separatism" and "further grasp the strategic initiative to achieve the complete unification of the motherland." Observers noted in 2024 that on some occasions the CCP's language dispensed with earlier references to the need to "oppose" Taiwan "separatism," using instead the more combative "resolutely fight."[12]

In one statement, Defense Ministry spokesman Wu Qian, referring to the "handful" of people in Taiwan who seek independence, said that "We warn those 'Taiwan independence' elements: those who play with fire will burn themselves, and 'Taiwan independence' means war."[13] Those warnings coincided with a more threatening PLA presence around Taiwan, with patrols by PLA aircraft and navy vessels becoming more frequent. They also occurred as Beijing unilaterally decided to no longer abide by a tacit agreement, observed for decades, to respect a "median line" separating the Taiwan Strait that had helped reduce the risks of accidents.[14] From then on, PLA aircraft crossed the invisible line at sea with greater frequency, increasing tensions. PLA aircraft also began entering Taiwan's Air Defense Identification Zone (ADIZ),[15] making the strong rhetoric that was emerging from Beijing a felt reality for the Taiwanese people.

The somewhat conciliatory language that had characterized Xi's first years in power, when his counterpart in Taipei was a more amenable partner, was over. From then on, the tone of the CCP's rhetoric was consistently belligerent, replete with warnings and appeals to would-be ideological allies in Taiwan to bypass their government, institutions, and the wishes of the majority.

During that same period, the CCP's belief in the KMT's ability to serve as a partner for "reunification" was seriously questioned. Officials began lamenting that KMT officials only crossed the Taiwan Strait to eat food and drink wine in China while doing nothing to achieve Beijing's political objectives. The KMT's losses in the 2016 and 2020 elections, in which it failed to secure both the presidency and a majority in the Legislative Yuan, was further evidence that its would-be partner could not – or was unwilling to – deliver. At home, the KMT seemed to have lost its footing and was unable to garner sufficient votes. The 2024 presidential election, moreover, served as additional evidence that President Tsai had not been an aberration. Her vice president, William Lai, won the election against two other candidates who had campaigned on a platform of lowering tensions with China. Regarded as even more pro-independence than the generally cautious Tsai, Lai won the election amid renewed warnings by Beijing. The result demonstrated that China's carrots and sticks had both failed to win over or coerce the Taiwanese into making choices that went against their interests, particularly when it came to their country's status vis-à-vis China.

In June 2024, one month after President Lai's inauguration, the Chinese government signaled that it was going to play hardball with the new administration in Taipei. It did so by unveiling its "Opinions on Punishing Crimes of Separatism and Inciting Separatism by 'Taiwan independence' Die-hards in Accordance with Law."[16] The Opinions drew upon the already existing Anti-Secession Law, the Criminal Law of the People's

Republic of China, and the Criminal Procedure Law. They sought to "severely punish Taiwan independence diehards for splitting the country and inciting secession crimes in accordance with the law, and resolutely defend national sovereignty, unity and territorial integrity." The section of the Opinions titled "Accurately Determining Crimes" identifies five types of activities that Beijing regards as independence work warranting punishment. It is worth quoting the passages in full:

1. Initiating or establishing a "Taiwan independence" secessionist organization, planning or formulating a "Taiwan independence" secessionist action platform, or directing individuals to engage in secession activities or activities that undermine national unity.

2. Attempting to alter Taiwan's legal status as part of China by developing, amending, interpreting, or repealing relevant provisions, holding a "referendum," or using other methods.

3. Attempting to create "two Chinas," "one China, one Taiwan," or "Taiwan independence" in the international community by promoting Taiwan's membership in international organizations restricted to sovereign states, engaging in official external exchanges or military contacts, or using other methods.

4. Using power to distort or tamper with the fact that Taiwan is part of China in education, culture, history, media, or other areas, or suppressing political parties, groups, or individuals that support peaceful cross-strait development and national reunification.

5. Engaging in other actions that attempt to separate Taiwan from China.

The relatively loose language in the Opinions, as well as the lack of clarity with regards to which law would be used to punish "wrongdoers," left many wondering whether foreign nationals could also be dragged into the net. Soon thereafter, Taiwan's

Mainland Affairs Council warned against travel to China. The inclusion of efforts promoting Taiwan's right to join multilateral organizations in the list of punishable "crimes" was also highly problematic, and many pointed out that several KMT politicians over the years had advocated for Taiwan's meaningful participation at U.N. bodies. Would KMT politicians, supposedly Beijing's allies, also be subjected to the new laws? The penalties stipulated by the Opinions allowed for trials in absentia, with sentences ranging from several years' imprisonment to the death penalty for "crimes" considered "especially serious or . . . vile."[17]

Then in August, the Taiwan Affairs Office (TAO), the organ in charge of handling cross-Strait relations (the MAC's counterpart), updated its website with a section that, besides providing the documents related to the "Opinions," included a top-ten list of Taiwan diehard separatists. The TAO had named the so-called separatists in 2021 and 2022, a list that included Vice President Hsiao Bi-khim, Defense Minister Wellington Koo, and National Security Council Secretary-General Joseph Wu. Moreover, a "mailbox" was added to the TAO webpage, inviting Chinese citizens to report "crimes" and provide evidence against "separatists." Analysts regarded this new effort as a decision by Beijing to wage "lawfare" against Taiwan. The new tactic reflected the hardening line that top CCP leaders like Xi, Wang Huning, chairman of the Chinese People's Political Consultative Conference (CPPCC) and Xi's top theoretician, as well as TAO director Song Tao, were taking against Taiwan. Little by little, the dangers facing the Taiwanese people seemed to be growing as Beijing ran out of patience with them.

Deepening Authoritarianism Under Xi

The dispute over Taiwan's status is also related to Xi's growing authoritarian rule in China. Xi's strongman tendencies and cult of personality have resulted in an unprecedented concentration of power, centered around Xi. The crackdown launched by the domineering "strict disciplinarian" across Chinese society, which has targeted NGOs, journalists, academics, and ordinary citizens, has reduced the space wherein policy can be debated. From Xi Jinping Thought on just about every aspect of Chinese society to Xi dispensing with longstanding term limits for president, the CCP secretary general, president, and head of the Central Military Commission was increasingly all-controlling. In Australian Sinologist Geremie Barmé's apt description, Xi became "Chairman of Everything," appointing himself head of various CCP committees on matters including economic reform, internet policy, national security, and military reform, among others.

Xi, furthermore, tended to avail himself of powers that normally were the remit of the premier, and had the Central Committee name him as a "core" of the Party's fifth-generation leadership.[18] More and more, the mythology that surrounded Xi, the "great leader," positioned him at the center of all things, equal only to, if not even above, Mao Zedong. Xi and only Xi could guide China's destiny and make its dream of Great Rejuvenation a reality. Another sign of Xi's further descent into dictatorship – no would-be successor to Xi has appeared from within the CCP ranks. History, it seems, will be written by, and will end, with Xi, who sits at the pinnacle of the Party's "hierarchy of guidances."[19]

According to Party historians interviewed by the American political scientist Susan L. Shirk, Xi has destroyed Deng's legacy by dispensing with the longstanding collective political leadership of China, a regular turnover of the top leadership, and restraint in China's foreign relations.[20] In this environment, party members have been conditioned into regurgitating Xi's views on matters of policy, or to prove their mettle by becoming even more radical on China's "core interests,"[21] such as Taiwan's "reunification." Consequently, the more moderate voices within the CCP, in academia and the media, went silent, ceding the space to more hawkish elements. Such dynamics help explain the rise of China's so-called "Wolf Warrior" diplomats. Those diplomats, including ambassadors abroad, went on the offensive. They spewed vitriol against local journalists and academics, or top officials physically assaulted protesters outside diplomatic missions. Such behavior, needless to say, ended up alienating the host countries and proved highly counterproductive. The decision to persevere in such, shall we say, *undiplomatic* diplomacy, can be explained by the fact that the diplomats' principal audiences were not the countries to which they had been posted, but rather their CCP masters back in Beijing. Hardline stances on "core issues" were a ticket for promotion; one contradicted Xi at the risk of a demotion, if not worse.

China's deepening authoritarianism under Xi was also in sharp contrast with developments in Taiwan, which during the same period continued to consolidate its democracy and improve its ranking on various democracy indexes.[22] For the people of Taiwan who cherished and participated in the expansion – and protection – of their rights, developments across the Taiwan Strait served as a reminder of the dangers of proximity to China. In China proper, in Hong Kong, Tibet, and Xinjiang, the CCP was cracking down on dissent and ethnic minorities, with reports that as many as 1 million Muslim Uyghurs had been imprisoned in one form or another.

For most people in Taiwan, their flourishing democracy contradicted the claim, promoted by China and other icons of purported "Asian values," that Western democracy is incompatible with Asian societies. Taiwan's success as a democracy, while celebrated abroad, came to be regarded by Beijing as a threat. For one thing, there was the risk that the Chinese people might find Taiwan's freedoms appealing. In late 2024, reports emerged that many young Chinese were sharing former president Tsai's inaugural address on their social media, particularly the parts of her speech where she detailed her policies to look after the welfare of young Taiwanese.

Taiwan's successful handling of the Covid-19 pandemic, furthermore, also dispelled the notion that democracies are less well-equipped than their more regimented authoritarian counterparts to deal with emergencies. Taiwan became an example to the world on how to respond to the pandemic, while China, besides denying that the virus had originated on its territory, bungled its response with rigid lockdowns (during the entire pandemic, Taiwan never went into lockdown).

For Xi, who has no intention of lifting his and his party's controls on society, the continued existence of Taiwan as a vibrant and successful democracy is a threat to the CCP's governance model. Thus Beijing's constant efforts, through disinformation, to discredit Taiwan, its government, and democracy, often describing it as a dictatorship. This fear of democracy right next door, moreover, creates an additional incentive for Beijing to "resolve" the issue of Taiwan's status once and for all. In other words, Taiwan's democracy needs to be extinguished. The notion that Beijing would somehow allow Taiwan to keep its democracy after unification is based on a complete misreading of the CCP's objectives and paranoia. Instead, as in Hong Kong, the rights and freedoms of the Taiwanese would gradually be eroded by the center – Beijing.

And there's another reason why Beijing would kill democracy in Taiwan after unification. The Chinese themselves could rightly ask why Beijing would make such concessions as allowing democracy for a "Taiwan Province" or Special Administrative Region while denying similar freedoms to Chinese citizens in other parts of China. Xi is not a man of concessions. Not for the Chinese people, and certainly not for the Taiwanese.

Other Factors Pushing Xi on Taiwan

Xi may also believe that he is running out of time to accomplish his objectives toward Taiwan. Facing a growing military threat, Taiwan has not been sitting still. Rather, it has embarked on its own program to modernize its defenses. It has done so with the acquisition of more advanced defense systems from the U.S. and the production, at home, of various weapons systems as part of an asymmetrical defense posture. U.S. sentiment has also turned against China, with both Democrats and Republicans deepening ties with Taiwan while strengthening the security relationship with Taiwan's neighbors. Over time, this threatens to erode the edge that the PLA currently has in the Taiwan Strait.

Even greater trouble is brewing at home which may lead Xi to conclude that he needs to achieve his goals sooner rather than later. The three key challenges are demographics, economics, and the environment. A rapidly aging society and a slowing economy suggest that China's composite power may be about to peak, with a subsequent period of decline. China, furthermore, may be facing a looming demographic implosion. According to Chinese government statistics, China's population dropped by 850,000 in 2022, the first decline since the early 1960s.[23] That decline is expected to continue, with a projected population of just 766 million by 2100, nearly half as large as it is today. China's previous "one child" policy is believed to have made a substantial contribution to this rapid decline.

But that's only one half of the story. As China's population drops, it is also aging rapidly. According to projections by the Chinese government, approximately 30 percent of China's population, or 400 million people, will be above the age of 60 by 2035.[24] The U.N. Population Division estimates that 40 percent of the Chinese population will be above the age of 60 by 2050, and nearly 50 percent around 2080.[25] Combine this with China's inability to sustain the levels of economic growth it enjoyed over the past two decades, and the Chinese leadership will soon – very soon – have to make extremely difficult decisions. Inevitably, a larger share of the total budget will have to go toward healthcare, and this will be at the expense of other areas – including defense. Moreover, unlike other aging societies in Asia and elsewhere, where rapidly aging societies are relatively prosperous, China will join the club at a time where it has yet to achieve high-income status. A massive segment of the population will therefore claim an ever greater share of the country's resources. Meanwhile, China's fertility rate slipped to below 1.1 in 2022, less than the replacement rate of 2.1, a trend that is likely to continue as an economic slowdown and pessimistic outlook within China drags down adults' willingness to have children.

For similar reasons, China's high-net-worth individuals are voting with their feet and moving abroad, mainly to the U.S., Canada, Singapore, and Japan. In 2023, a record 13,800 wealthy Chinese individuals moved abroad, a figure that was surpassed the following year, when 15,200 millionaires did so.[26] The investment migration firm Henley & Partners attributes the exodus to "uncertainty over China's economic trajectory and geopolitical tensions." The International Monetary Fund (IMF) says that China faces "high uncertainty" due to the real estate turmoil, higher unemployment, and an economic downturn. The situation has resulted in an unprecedented exodus of Chinese millionaires. Xi's targeting of wealthy individuals, along with an increasingly restrictive environment and discontent with the government's handling of the Covid pandemic, are also believed to have fueled the desire to leave China. The IMF projects that China's economic decline will continue for the next four years, expecting economic growth to drop to 4.6 percent in 2024 and down to 3.4 percent by 2028.[27]

Due to all this, China's window of opportunity to resolve the dispute over Taiwan – a combination of economic strength and military might – will soon peak. Xi, who is 72 years old as this book goes to print, is aware of all this and could decide to accelerate his efforts to accomplish this objective before he steps down (or dies). Therefore, while a patient or more lenient approach to Taiwan could create conditions that have a higher chance of lowering tensions in the Taiwan Strait, Xi is pushing his country's Taiwan policy in the opposite direction. And this, in turn, only further alienates the Taiwanese people. The Gordian knot tightens, with little if any potential for a truly peaceful resolution to the dispute.

3

Attacking Taiwan's Democracy

President Xi's response to the escalating tension between his country and Taiwan, the United States, and other countries in the Indo-Pacific has been to build a strong military and to modernize the PLA, fit to meet a number of twenty-first century needs. This, it is believed, includes having the capability to use force against Taiwan by as early as 2027. Despite this, the CCP leadership remains ostensibly committed to a policy of "peaceful reunification" with Taiwan – at least for the time being.

While Xi has made numerous references to keeping the military option on the table – rhetoric that Chinese military commentators have willingly amplified whenever the PLA has held large-scale exercises near Taiwan – China continues to emphasize nonmilitary options to resolve the sovereignty dispute over Taiwan. Much of this comes in the form of what is known as "sharp power," "political warfare," or "united front work." All involve efforts by state and front organizations to achieve political objectives through subversion, co-optation, and other methods. This "toolkit" also includes dis/misinformation and "cognitive warfare," or efforts to affect how people view and understand the world around them.

The CCP's approach to Taiwan is twofold, involving two apparently contradictory policies simultaneously. China's strategy features incentives ("carrots") and punitive/deterrent ("sticks"). Depending on the situation in Taiwan, including the nature of its government, Beijing calibrates its approach by emphasizing or de-emphasizing the "sticks" and "carrots." When the Beijing-friendly Ma Ying-jeou administration was in power and the KMT enjoyed a majority of seats in parliament, for example, Beijing prioritized incentives, with a focus on highlighting the economic benefits that accrued from a closer union with the PRC. This strategy gave preferential access to Taiwanese businesses seeking to invest in China and promoted the cultural similarities between the two sides of the Taiwan Strait in the entertainment industry, schoolbooks, and various cross-Strait exchanges.

Still, even in times of rapprochement, Beijing never completely ceased using the more coercive elements of its strategy. Cross-Strait agreements were signed, cross-Strait tourism was booming, and the government in Taipei was talking about an "avenue of peace" in the Taiwan Strait. But as this was unfolding, Beijing continued to equip and train its military for a Taiwan scenario. It also ramped up its efforts to develop an Anti-Access/Area Denial (A2/AD) strategy to complicate any involvement by the U.S. in a Taiwan scenario. It held regular live-fire exercises simulating an amphibious assault against Taiwan. It deployed and modernized its ballistic missile force with missiles of greater reach and precision. It even publicized, on state media, a simulated assault by PLA soldiers on a replica of the Presidential Office in Taipei.[1] This dual approach to Taiwan overlapped between the Hu and Xi administrations. Both leaders saw an opportunity to exploit goodwill from the KMT government. Toward the end of President Ma's second term, Xi even agreed to a summit with his counterpart in Singapore.

All this came to a crashing end when the KMT lost both the presidential and legislative elections in 2016. The newly elected president, the DPP's Tsai, extended an olive branch to Beijing early on. She acknowledged the historical framework of the "1992 consensus" and referred to the "constitutional ROC framework," suggesting a step back from her party's past commitment to *de jure* independence. Despite this overture, Beijing accused Tsai of an "incomplete test answer" after her inaugural speech on May 20, 2016, and unilaterally closed the door to dialogue.[2] Interestingly, in the months prior to the election, many Chinese commentators had argued that the two sides could reach a modus vivendi even if the new government in Taipei did not fully recognize the "1992 consensus." But this kind of flexibility was no longer possible under Xi, and such comments were never made again, at least publicly.

Following Tsai's election, Beijing recalibrated its two-pronged approach to Taiwan, this time by putting a premium on the coercive elements of its strategy while de-emphasizing the inducements. Whatever inducements were offered were meant to split Taiwanese society by creating winners and losers. Municipalities that were governed by the opposition and whose politicians stated their adherence to the "1992 consensus" reaped the benefits of Chinese tourism and other forms of largesse, while those that were governed by the ruling DPP were removed as destinations by China. Municipalities that were governed by DPP politicians were denied Chinese tour groups while China also imposed sanctions on sectors that are important for the local economies (chiefly agricultural products), often after claiming that inspectors had found "bugs" or other pollutants at the border.

Throughout the Tsai presidency, China weaponized tourism (4.1 million Chinese arrivals at its height in 2016, the year Tsai came to power) to punish the administration for its China policy and turn tourism-related industries, including hotel and restaurant operators, against the government. While small protests were organized by members of the industries that were negatively affected, the movement never gained momentum, and the effects of Beijing's punitive policy were largely mitigated by the Tsai administration's efforts to attract tourists from other countries, primarily in Asia and Europe. Taiwan eventually saw record numbers of tourist arrivals, thus overturning the sector's overreliance on China and ensuring greater resilience through diversification. Taipei applied similar strategies to counter the effects of China's sectoral sanctions by exploring new market destinations for its export products, which contributed to greater resilience by reducing the economy's dependence on the Chinese market.

Economic inducements continued to be used, with the goal of capturing specific groups of people within Taiwan, among them businesspeople and Taiwan's youth. Through this, Beijing hoped to create a brain drain in Taiwan and to generate positive publicity about China. Thus, in February 2018, China announced its thirty-one incentives program, which targeted Taiwan's youth, talent, and businesses with tax cuts, investment capital, and relaxed rules on certification for 134 sectors.[3] All this was part of Beijing's "social fusion" policy, which sought to bypass politics and create a sense of unity between the two sides of the Taiwan Strait.

However, by 2019, amid rising tensions in the Taiwan Strait, the crackdown in Hong Kong, and escalating competition between the U.S. and China, the policy had little to show for it. Economic opportunity still wasn't enough to dilute emotional elements such as one's self-identification and attachment to democratic governance.[4] Or at least it wasn't able to persuade a large enough group of people to have the desired effect. The Taiwanese government also implemented countermeasures in response to the thirty-one incentives program, which aimed to create a better environment for young Taiwanese entrepreneurs and thereby dilute the appeal of Beijing's incentives.

In addition to shutting down the official communication channel between the State Council's Taiwan Affairs Office and the Mainland Affairs Council after Tsai's inauguration,[5] Beijing also resumed its campaign to poach Taiwan's official diplomatic allies. During President Tsai's eight years in office, Beijing succeeded in luring ten of them, leaving Taiwan with only twelve. China also used its growing clout within the U.N. system to prevent Taiwan securing meaningful participation, or observer status, at specialized U.N. bodies such as Interpol, the World Health Organization (WHO), and the International Civil Aviation Organization (ICAO). The folly of excluding Taiwan from such institutions became clear during the Covid-19 pandemic, and yet no progress was made on that front, despite appeals by a number of influential U.N. member states.

While China was deploying its entire "sharp power" toolkit against Taiwan, it also ramped up the military pressure to give the impression that Beijing was readying to use force. Much of this constituted psychological warfare, which aimed to reinforce notions of inevitability and the futility of resistance among the Taiwanese public. Through this form of intimidation, Beijing hoped to scare the Taiwanese, who in turn could feel that they had to elect more Beijing-friendly governments in future. Large-scale military exercises, accompanied by belligerent rhetoric by Beijing, became more frequent and threatening over the years. Often, they coincided with developments that were favorable to Taiwan, such as U.S. arms sales, visits to Taiwan by senior American government officials (such as House Speaker Nancy Pelosi in August 2022), or statements on Taiwan by multilateral groupings such as NATO or the G7. The rhetoric was as direct as it was simple: nothing would go unpunished.

United Front Work and Taiwan Under Xi

In May 2015, two years after Xi assumed the leadership, the CCP convened a national united front work conference, the first in nine years. Titled "CCP Central Committee's Conference on United Front Work," the meeting resulted in the creation of a Leading Small Group (LSG) on United Front Work (Central United Front Work Leading Small Group), signaling a greater role for the United Front Work Department (UFWD) under Xi.[6] It's now big business. According to the China analyst Gerry Groot, the number of cadres within the UFWD expanded by as many as 40,000 staff in recent years.[7] Alex Joske, an expert on Chinese intelligence, has noted that the UFW LSG created a "'Great United Front' that characterises the United Front's direction under Xi by increasing the party's leadership over united front work, ensuring all relevant agencies are involved and their activities coordinated."[8] At the 19th Party Congress in 2017, Xi described united front work as a "magic weapon" to bring about the "rejuvenation of the Chinese nation."

Five years later, during the 20th Party Congress in October, Xi stated that

> The people's support is of the utmost political importance, and the united front is an effective instrument for rallying the people's support and pooling their strength. We will build a broad united front to forge great unity and solidarity, and we will encourage all the sons and daughters of the Chinese nation to dedicate themselves to realizing the Chinese Dream of national rejuvenation.[9]

At that same event, Xi appointed Wang Huning, who is widely regarded as Xi's top political theorist and ideological guru, to head the united front system.

Wang's influence on Taiwan affairs cannot be overstated. In 2023, *Nikkei Asia* referred to Wang as China's "top brain in charge of Taiwan unification strategy," adding that Xi had tasked him with creating an alternative to the "one country, two systems" formula.[10] According to Neil Thomas, a Chinese politics fellow at the Asia Society Policy Institute's Center for China Analysis, Wang "is a political survivor who loyally served Jiang Zemin and Hu Jintao but found his greatest supporter in Xi Jinping. Wang's neo-authoritarian intellectual project is a perfect complement to Xi's centralising political project."[11] Wang became chairman of the National Committee of the Chinese People's Political Consultative Conference (CPPCC) in 2023, a position that further expanded his role supervising Taiwan affairs. After William Lai's election in January 2024, Wang revealed his hawkish stance on Taiwan by calling for a "tough crackdown" on Taiwan independence and "interference from outside forces."

UFW efforts against Taiwan are coordinated by the CCP's Central Leading Group for Taiwan Affairs, headed by Xi, with Wang Huning and Foreign Minister Wang Yi as his deputies. Those three individuals are widely regarded as the "Big Three" on guiding policy toward Taiwan. The Central Leading Group for Taiwan Affairs has final say over the strategy of the State Council's Taiwan Affairs Office, which since December 2022 has been headed by Song Tao. Among many positions over the years, Song headed the CCP's International Liaison Department (ILD) from November 2015 to June 2022.[12] The ILD coordinates the CCP's relations with foreign political parties, international political organizations, and overseas political elites. It is also believed to be involved in intelligence collection and political work against foreign political parties.

Song's past involvement with the ILD suggests a greater role for behind-the-scenes contact with, and political work against, political parties in Taiwan. Upon being appointed director of the TAO, Song released an 1,800-character New Year message titled "Work Together, Create Great Achievements Together" in the *Relations Across Taiwan Straits* magazine. In it, he stated that China would "carry out extensive and in-depth discussions on cross-Strait ties and national reunification with people of foresight from all walks of life of Taiwan society." This indicated his intent to reach out to ideological supporters on the Taiwan side. Former KMT legislator Alex Tsai, who is known to have close contacts within the CCP, once observed that of all the TAO directors over the years, Song has the best understanding of the DPP.

China's "Sharp Power" Toolkit Against Taiwan

The American political scientist Joseph S. Nye Jr. describes "soft power," a term that he coined, as "a country's ability to influence others without resorting to coercive pressure." It does so by "projecting [its] values, ideals, and culture across borders to foster goodwill and strengthen partnerships."[13] By such a yardstick, China's "soft power" largely failed to win over the Taiwanese people – mostly due to the fact that the ideas and ideals it proposes are wildly incompatible with those that have emerged in democratic Taiwan.

Recognizing those shortcomings, China has relied on various other, nonmilitary tools. This toolkit, a mixture of coercive, divisive, and attractive instruments, aims to erode Taiwan's democratic firewall to compel unification. In doing so, China's political warfare apparatus uses democracy, and the permissiveness and openness inherent to it, against itself. Sharp power also exploits the blind spots in targeted societies – corruption, lack of transparency, and so on – to further its objectives.

The U.S. National Endowment for Democracy (NED) coined the term "sharp power" in a landmark 2017 report. It defined it as "the attempt by Beijing and Moscow to wield influence through initiatives in the spheres of media, culture, think tanks, and academia." "Sharp power," it continues, "is neither a 'charm offensive' nor an effort to 'win hearts and minds,' the common frame of reference for 'soft power' efforts. This authoritarian influence is not principally about attraction or even persuasion; instead, it centers on distraction and manipulation."[14]

While the world is now a target of China's "sharp power," many governments still struggle to implement the necessary countermeasures, legal frameworks, and capabilities to mitigate its corrosive effects on their societies. For Taiwan, the threat of "sharp power" has been a fact of life for decades. In recent years, several countries have turned to the Taiwanese government, along with its civil society, for help with understanding China's "sharp power" – as well as the related realm of cyberattacks – and how to counter it. Taiwan, for example, has provided assistance to other countries via the Global Cooperation and Training Framework (GCTF) organized by Taiwan's Ministry of Foreign Affairs and the U.S. Department of State.

China's sharp power mobilizes its entire society as part of a coordinated attempt to subdue Taiwan. Various bodies within the CCP and the state apparatus, such as the Central Leading Group for Taiwan Affairs, the Taiwan Affairs Office, the International Liaison Department, the People's Liberation Army, the United Front Work Department, the China Council for the Promotion of Peaceful National Reunification (CCPPNR) and others are involved in implementing this strategy. A constellation of state agencies, "civic" groups, front organizations, media outlets, and others also play various roles in this endeavor.

This strategy also needs partners on the Taiwan side. Those "proxies" can be found in political parties, civic groups, religious organizations, the media, the business sector, and crime syndicates. Most of them have agreed to do China's bidding after being co-opted. Their conscious decision to enact, facilitate, finance, or amplify the CCP's political efforts in Taiwan is the result of an agreement, with financial gain, preferential access to lucrative markets in China, or an "in" for journalists and academics, as a reward. While some proxies act out of ideological alignment with the CCP (the China Unification Promotion Party comes to mind), many others do so for purely selfish reasons. Consequently, not every proxy of Beijing is necessarily committed to unification for ideological reasons; many do so out of greed. But in the end, the result is the same, with various individuals and organizations seeking to weaken Taiwan.

Co-opted business leaders, religious figures (local temples), and politicians also play a role in influencing elections in Taiwan. They do so by engaging in vote-buying, intimidation of opponents, and "bloc voting" to give an advantage to candidates who are favored by Beijing. Ahead of the 2024 elections, party members co-opted by Beijing (including a member of the pro-unification CUPP) helped organize all-expenses-paid trips to China for Taiwanese who in return were expected to help Beijing's preferred candidates. Those candidates supported "peace" and opposed Taiwan independence. They were also treated to banquets under the theme "cross-Strait is one family." Seventeen individuals were taken in for questioning in December 2023 in connection with this effort.

Beijing also aims to co-opt political figures from both the ruling and opposition parties. It does this in Taiwan and in other countries. Politicians from the DPP and KMT, including current and former legislators, are believed to have been co-opted by Beijing. Some of them have appeared on party-controlled media in China and regurgitated CCP propaganda. Others have visited China and met senior party officials, including Xi. One example of this is Lin Kuo-ching, a former DPP legislator who was running as an independent candidate in the 2020 elections. Lin once said that "nobody loves Taiwan more than Xi Jinping."[15] Soon after he made the controversial comments, investigations revealed that members of Lin's family, including his son, had ties to the CCP and were running a business in the Pingtan Free Trade Zone, where he promoted cross-Strait tourism and the creative industry. Lin also said that one of his motivations for running in the election was the coming "economic collapse in Taiwan," a collapse that never came close to happening. Lin's wife, daughter, and daughter-in-law also all ran businesses in China.

Ahead of the 2024 elections, Ma Chih-wei, an independent candidate with close ties to the smaller Taiwan People's Party (TPP), received illegal funding from the PRC during her campaign. It was later revealed that Ma had received funds in return for passing on "Taiwanese intelligence and other election-related information to her benefactors" in China.[16] The CCP also targets outliers and populists within traditional parties, as well as independent candidates, for co-optation.

The CCP uses various exchange programs, summer camps, forums, cultural events, and other cross-Strait initiatives to co-opt Taiwanese youth, scholars, and others. It does so through all-expenses-paid trips, during which participants will meet top CCP officials in charge of Taiwan and united front affairs. Much of these activities are run by "front" units of the CCP to cover the actual intentions of the organizers, banking on a lack of awareness within the targeted public and benign-sounding names to lower suspicions. The effectiveness of such initiatives is in doubt, however. Young Taiwanese and academics interviewed by this author have all affirmed they were aware of what "Beijing was up to." Many of them said they would be foolish to turn down a free trip, while emphasizing that they had refused to repay Beijing by doing what was expected of them. Still, others, including a number of prominent influencers and YouTubers, willingly join Beijing's campaigns and enjoy the perks.

Some of the largest media conglomerates in Taiwan are headed by businesspeople who made fortunes in China selling various products. The most prominent of those is the Want

China Times Group, headed by the billionaire Tsai Eng-meng. Outlets from this conglomerate have been complicit in spreading Chinese propaganda or disinformation aimed at undermining confidence in the Taiwanese government while tending to avoid stories that depict the CCP and China in an unfavorable light. While the group, which controls print, TV, and other outlets, denies the accusation that it is "red media" (i.e., pro-China), it has been fined by the National Communications Commission (NCC), and its television outlet, CTiTV, saw its cable license suspended for several months for spreading disinformation.

Many senior managers of other Taiwanese media outlets, as well as management at PR firms, producers, chief editors, film producers, and film distributors, have also participated in annual cross-Strait media forums held in Beijing and Xiamen. During those gatherings, Taiwanese participants are given instructions by senior CCP officials on how to report on cross-Strait relations. Influencers on platforms such as YouTube, TikTok, Facebook, Instagram, Little Red Book, and others, whom Beijing refers to as "island netizens," have also been lured by the prospect of fortunes in China in return for spreading and amplifying disinformation about Taiwan while generating content that supports "reunification." Others are simply asked to portray China favorably. Online personalities with as few as 3,000 followers (known as "nano" influencers) have been recruited by China to spread CCP narratives, with additional perks including all-expenses-paid trips to China. Beijing has also used public relations firms to spot and recruit influencers for various campaigns, including work opportunities in the PRC. Beijing's heavy investment in Taiwanese influencers appears to be a long-term endeavor, with cognitive warfare slowly influencing perceptions with the goal of convincing the Taiwanese that it is in their interest to elect politicians who are more amenable to Beijing's ambitions.

Members of the entertainment industry have also come under pressure by the Chinese government, compelling them to spread a pro-China ideology in return for their ability to access the Chinese market. Since 2016, several actors and popular singers were forced to state their allegiance on their social media accounts or to participate in propagandistic videos supporting "one China" and opposing Taiwan independence. While this ruffled some feathers back in Taiwan, most reacted with their usual pragmatism, understanding that partaking in such activities is the cost of doing business in China.

Beijing has also relied on "content farms" to spread disinformation and propaganda. Many of those were financed by Taiwanese businesspeople. Also known as "content mills," "content farms" claim to be legitimate online news sites, and often look like them. However, dispersed across articles on seemingly innocuous subjects (health, food, travel, and so on) one will find disinformation about the Taiwanese government or tropes supporting Beijing's claims. Like social media, where CCP organs and "little pinks" – as China's internet army is known – operate, the "content farms" are part of the ecosystem of disinformation. Pro-Beijing traditional media often repost or repackage material from "content farms" to "legitimize" their content and to ensure the spread of disinformation. Other platforms used by Beijing to target Taiwan include Facebook fan pages, instant messaging applications such as Line, and bulletin board systems.

Once disinformation has entered Taiwan's media bloodstream, co-opted pro-Beijing politicians and talking heads on political talk shows amplify the information and pro-Beijing narratives, thus extending the content's shelf-life. This, in turn, often forces government authorities to spend time and resources debunking the false claims.

The Chinese united front apparatus has depended on crime syndicates, or triads, to threaten civil society and officials. The use of gangsters has the advantage of plausible deniability, with little to prove that orders were given by Beijing. In Taiwan, the Bamboo Union, one of the main crime syndicates active in the country, has a symbiotic relationship with the pro-Beijing CUPP. The founder of the CUPP, Chang An-le, is a former head of the Bamboo Union and served a decade in federal prison in the United States for drug trafficking. Chang is believed to have been recruited by the CCP when he was on the run in China. He is also believed to be close to the TAO and China's "princelings" – the powerful scions of the CCP's founders. It was while he was in exile in China that Chang founded the CUPP. In recent years, CUPP officials hired "muscle" from the Bamboo Union and other local factions to protest against the Tsai administration. During the Ma years, members of other triads active in Taiwan, such as the Four Seas Gang, also provided physical on-site security for visiting senior Chinese officials. Their members also intimidated and assaulted members of civil society from Taiwan and Hong Kong, including democracy activists and protesters. In 2017, Chang's son, Chang Wei, violently assaulted a young Taiwanese protester. Pro-Beijing civic groups, such as the Concentric Patriotism Association (CPA),[17] also orchestrated protests against visiting pro-democracy advocates from Hong Kong. Chang's son and nine colleagues were also charged in a visa scam reportedly used by more than 1,000 PRC nationals to enter Taiwan between 2017 and 2019. This reportedly included Chinese government officials.

CUPP cadres and the chairman of the New Party, another pro-unification party, have also taken their politics overseas, linking up with like-minded organizations there. To give just one example, in 2017 their members participated in the "Cross-Strait Development Forum" hosted by the National Association for the Promotion of China's Peaceful Reunification in New York City.[18] The forum was co-sponsored by the New York chapter of the CCPPNR, one of many overseas organizations that are part of China's united front.

Taiwan has strict gun laws, but triads are heavily involved in arms trafficking, using regional networks to move various types of firearms around. It is therefore feared that triads, acting on directives from the CCP, could cause serious civil unrest, possibly including assassination, sabotage, and other acts that could be committed to weaken state institutions prior to military action by China. In recent years, Taiwanese border officials and law enforcement have seized several major shipments of firearms – enough to fuel a militia, as a former minister of the interior observed – orchestrated by the Bamboo Union. Triads are also involved in other areas of criminal activity, including drug and human trafficking, prostitution, debt collection, garbage collection, and construction. All this creates opportunities to raise funds that can be put to political work, including co-optation and vote-buying. The Taiwanese government has actively investigated the potential for illegal funding to the CUPP, such as funds coming from China. In late 2024, the government began looking into the possibility of deregistering the party, claiming that it represented a threat to Taiwanese society. This is a move that, arguably, should have been made a long time ago.

Cognitive Warfare, Taiwan, and the International Community

Attempts by Beijing to shape perceptions about Taiwan deserve their own section. The term cognitive warfare has been bandied about frequently in recent years, often with its users not fully understanding what it means. The North Atlantic Treaty Organization (NATO) provides an apt definition, saying it is a strategy which uses "activities conducted in synchronization with other instruments of power, to affect attitudes and behaviors, by influencing, protecting, or disrupting individual, group, or population level cognition, to gain an advantage over an adversary." Cognitive warfare is "designed to modify perceptions of reality," it says, adding that "whole-of-society manipulation has become a new norm, with human cognition shaping to be a critical realm of warfare [focused] on attacking and degrading rationality, which can lead to exploitation of vulnerabilities and systemic weakening."[19]

The media often uses cognitive warfare interchangeably with disinformation. In reality, disinformation is one of many elements of cognitive warfare, which uses several tools to alter the way in which the citizens of a targeted society regard, and respond to, reality. Just as important, like other elements of "sharp power," cognitive warfare is waged by Beijing along a continuum of peace and war. Thus, even when relations between Taipei and Beijing are cordial, the party-state apparatus is always waging political and cognitive warfare, calibrating its efforts to better suit existing conditions.

China's cognitive warfare strategy against Taiwan operates on two levels: the global front and inside Taiwan. The first reinforces key elements in Beijing's narrative about Taiwan, chief among them the claim that the Taiwan "issue" is a *domestic* matter and an "unfinished civil war" that is being waged among the Chinese people. Any effort by outside forces to support Taiwan is therefore treated as "meddling," "interference in China's internal affairs," and a conspiracy to "split" China. Related to this strategy are efforts to overturn international law (the United Nations Law of the Sea Treaty) by claiming that the Taiwan Strait is an "internal water" of China rather than international waters as affirmed by international law. The distinction has major implications for freedom of navigation in what is one of the most important channels in the world. One hundred and seventy-seven kilometers long and 130 kilometers wide at its narrowest point, the Taiwan Strait is a major shipping corridor, accounting for 44 percent of the world's container traffic in 2022.[20]

China also relies on its extensive influence at the United Nations to ensure that the world body, along with its specialized agencies, continue to exclude Taiwan. Since 2016, Beijing has redoubled its efforts to prevent Taiwan joining U.N. agencies such as ICAO, the WHO, Interpol, and others as an observer. By doing so, China has helped create dangerous blind spots in global monitoring of epidemics, transnational crime, and civil aviation. Furthermore, using its influence at the U.N. General Assembly, China has leveraged most member states in the developing world to engage in "bloc voting" on the Taiwan issue. Consequently, any motion by one or a few U.N. member states calling for Taiwan's participation in U.N. agencies is blocked by a plurality of votes. Most if not all of the countries that vote in Beijing's favor on the matter are either the recipients of infrastructure investment from China, as part of the Belt and Road Initiative, or autocratic states.

Similar pressure has made it possible for China to condition the U.N. system into erasing Taiwan and its citizens. As a result, holders of a Taiwan passport are denied entry at all U.N. buildings. And this is not just Taiwanese diplomats: journalists and even school children have been barred entry on U.N. premises.

China has also insisted – falsely – that U.N. General Assembly Resolution 2758, adopted in 1971, states that the U.N. abides by the "one China" principle and recognizes that Taiwan is part of China, which disqualifies Taiwan from membership. In reality, the resolution makes no mention whatsoever of Taiwan or its status. Nevertheless, through repetition and pressure on U.N. member states, China has often succeeded in using that resolution to "legally" support its sovereignty claims over Taiwan, while arguing that Taipei does not deserve a seat at the U.N. table.[21] After all, if the U.N. says so, who could argue otherwise?

Besides the U.N., China also endeavors to erase Taiwan and any suggestion of its statehood by pressuring organizers of cultural and sports events worldwide to ban Taiwan's participation or national flag. Several incidents have occurred over the years in which Chinese coaches or officials ripped the ROC flag from the hands of Taiwanese participants. At the Paris Olympics in the summer of 2024, Chinese officials were caught on camera guiding security staff who actively removed ROC flags at Olympic venues as well as any other symbols that merely suggested Taiwan. Taiwan, whose athletes are forced to compete under the name "Chinese Taipei," therefore found itself in the same category as Belarus and Russia – two major human rights violators – as well as regions with major separatist movements such as Quebec, Basque, and Tibet.

Chinese nationals acting as public servants in foreign countries, as well as co-opted officials and politicians, have also promoted China's interest while preventing contact between their governments and Taiwan. In September 2024, the FBI revealed that Linda Sun, a former aide to New York Governor Kathy Hochul, had acted as an agent of China. According to a Department of Justice filing,

> Acting at the request of PRC government officials and the CCP representatives, Sun engaged in numerous political activities in the interests of the PRC and the CCP, including blocking representatives of the Taiwanese government from having access to high-level New York State officers; changing high-level New York State officers' messaging regarding issues of importance to the PRC and the CCP; obtaining official New York State proclamations for PRC government representatives without proper authorization; attempting to facilitate a trip to the PRC by a high-level New York State politician; and arranging meetings for visiting delegations from the PRC government with New York State government officials.[22]

Footage shows that Sun joined pro-PRC groups – some of them tied to or funded by the United Front Work

Department – that protested President Tsai's visit to New York in 2019.

In late 2024, the FBI also warned that China may be using disinformation to discredit members of Congress who support Taiwan through claims that they are receiving bribes from the Taiwanese government.[23] Such efforts aim at undermining the confidence of the American public in the true purposes behind continued U.S. support for Taiwan, particularly in times of potential retrenchment and isolationism.

The Chinese government has also put pressure on foreign governments to no longer recognize the Taiwanese passport. In 2023 and again in 2024, Taiwanese tourists seeking to enter Cuba were turned away. In one incident, Cuban immigration officials informed them that the refusal was "due to the strained relations between Taiwan and China" and because Cuba does not recognize the ROC passport due to the "one China" principle.[24] In a move that also undermines Taiwan's jurisdiction and sovereignty, Chinese authorities have also pressured governments to send Taiwanese telephone fraud suspects to the PRC to face prosecution rather than back to Taiwan. According to a report by Safeguard Defenders, between 2016 and 2019, more than 600 Taiwanese nationals held on criminal charges around the world were sent to China to face prosecution. Some countries, however, have refused to extradite the Taiwanese suspects, citing the likelihood that they will not receive a fair trial or could face torture.[25]

In similar fashion, China has put immense pressure on international firms to remove any information from their websites that may suggest statehood for Taiwan. This includes having Taiwan as an option on drag-down menus, or maps of China that fail to include Taiwan. In recent years, apparel firms, hotels, and airlines, among others, have been pressured to comply with local Chinese laws.[26] Failure to do so can result in fines, the suspension of market access in China, boycotts by members of the Chinese public, and harassment. Fearing the economic repercussions, many international companies have complied with the requirements, with changes to their websites referring to Taiwan as "Taiwan, Province of China."

Chinese media have also signed various content-sharing agreements with counterparts around the world, and used this as a conduit to promote Beijing's line on a variety of core issues, including Taiwan. Some of the principal narratives include the depiction of Taiwan's DPP as a "separatist" and "troublemaker" backed by a U.S. that seeks to "split" China,[27] all of which "compels" China to retaliate "defensively." Through co-optation of business owners behind media conglomerates (many of whom depend on access to the Chinese market to make their fortunes) China has also succeeded in censoring news that is critical of China. It has also successfully pressured editors, producers, journalists, content creators, and opinion makers to echo its propaganda regarding Taiwan. Social media, including platforms such as TikTok, Little Red Book, YouTube, Weibo, X, and others, also play an important role in saturating the information ecosystem with a pro-Beijing perspective on Taiwan while harassing the owners of pro-Taiwan accounts.

The second part of China's cognitive warfare strategy is aimed at Taiwan itself. The principal narrative is that only a few "separatists" from the DPP refuse to acknowledge the "inevitable" and "historical trend" of "reunification with China." This implies that the majority of the people in Taiwan are in fact amenable to unification, which is pure confabulation. Beijing and its allies in Taiwan have also used cognitive warfare to promote the view that the DPP's "separatist" work will drag Taiwan into a catastrophic war with China. They have also spread the claim that the United States is an unreliable security partner, that Washington is using Taiwan as a pawn in its contest for supremacy with China, and that Taiwan is a client for overpriced and antiquated weapon systems from the U.S. All this seeks to cultivate the view that it is futile to resist "historical trends."

China's cognitive warfare uses influential figures in the entertainment industry, influencers on YouTube, and co-opted politicians to erode confidence in the Taiwanese government, Taiwan's democratic system, and the viability of the state in the face of China's claims. There is mounting evidence suggesting that China's sustained cognitive campaign is having some effect on political polarization in Taiwan and thereby turning Taiwanese against each other. China may not be able to win the hearts and minds of the Taiwanese, but at least it can aim to divide them and in doing so to weaken their ability to work together.

Boiling the Proverbial Frog, Chipping Away at the "Status Quo"

Another essential element of China's "sharp power" against Taiwan involves the attempt to change the status quo in the Taiwan Strait. And China wants to achieve this by means other than war. It has already had success using this strategy elsewhere in the region: the South China Sea. There, over years, China has "boiled the frog" by incrementally building up its presence. Locked in a territorial dispute with several other countries (including Taiwan), China claims the entirety of the South China Sea. Rather than fight to seize the entire area, however, it has used propaganda, disinformation, patrols using its coast guard and fishing boats, and built artificial islands, some of which it eventually used to deploy military assets, including airstrips.

China has been boiling the proverbial frog against Taiwan for several years, and such efforts intensified after Xi assumed power. The aim in all this is to gradually erode Taiwan's sovereignty, narrow its room to maneuver, and constrain its ability to counter Chinese pressure. To do so, Beijing has constantly moved the goalposts, created new facts on the ground (and at sea), all of which put Taiwan at a disadvantage, while refraining from using force.

One early move by Xi was to put an end to the charade whereby the two sides could "agree to disagree" on what "one China" meant. Before Xi, the KMT had gotten away with claiming that "one China" meant the ROC. Beijing disagreed, but nevertheless permitted the flexibility as long as it created opportunities for dialogue. Under Xi, the very idea that anyone could argue that "one China" meant anything other than the People's Republic of China was treasonous. The ROC had died with the CCP's victory in the Chinese Civil War in 1949. Thus, China was the PRC, and Taiwan was an inalienable part of it. Xi didn't seem to be particularly bothered by the fact that his rigidity on the subject ended up complicating the KMT's life back in Taiwan.

Xi also quickly moved against countries that were seeking to deepen their unofficial relationships with Taiwan. Before him, Beijing bristled at the idea of Taiwan establishing official ties with other states, but as long as relations were at the unofficial level it tended to look the other way. Now, aiming to deepen Taiwan's international isolation, even unofficial ties were unacceptable. It didn't help that, under President Tsai, Taiwan's unofficial ties with other countries were often expanding the areas where Taiwan collaborated with its partners. China therefore ramped up its pressure on governments to coerce them into avoiding any contact with Taiwan.

Things came to a head when Taiwan opened a representative office in Lithuania in late 2021. To add insult to injury, the office used the name "Taiwan" rather than the usual "Taipei Trade Representative Office." Beijing, which seemed to have completely missed preparations for the opening of a Taiwan office in the Baltic country, reacted with fury, downgrading relations between the two countries and imposing trade sanctions on Lithuanian firms, among other moves. Meanwhile – and this is where China changes the status quo – Taipei was allowing countries with which it has official diplomatic relations to deepen their ties with China, often on matters of trade and investment. Eventually, Taipei would learn to its detriment that Beijing was using deepening trade (or the promise thereof) as part of a strategy to force those governments to switch diplomatic relations from Taipei to Beijing. China did that with great success in Panama.

However, nowhere has China endeavored to change the status quo more than in the Taiwan Strait itself. As mentioned earlier, China undermined longstanding agreements when, in 2020, the PLA stopped respecting the "median line" in the Taiwan Strait. The move allowed Chinese military aircraft to penetrate the side of the Strait that had hitherto been controlled by Taiwan and to get closer to Taiwan's airspace. Additionally, the Civil Aviation Administration of China unilaterally introduced new flight paths, including the M503 flight route and the W122 and W123 flight paths connecting M503 to Fuzhou and Xiamen. The lack of consultation and international arbitration undermined Taiwan's sovereignty, spelling out Beijing's opinion that, as a subsidiary of the PRC, Taipei simply had no say on the matter.

China had first announced the M503 route in 2015, when President Ma was still in office. Showing some flexibility after Taipei criticized the move, Beijing agreed to move the M503 path 11 kilometers west of its intended location, which at its nearest came within 7.8 kilometers of the median line. However, after bilateral ties soured, Beijing overturned that decision and canceled the 2015 offset, bringing M503 back to its original location. China launched the W122 and W123 paths in April 2024, a mere month before Lai's inauguration. Taiwan's Civil Aviation Administration has stated that the new flight paths pose a safety risk due to their proximity to airspace over the outlying islands of Kinmen and Matsu.[28]

At sea, PLA Navy (PLAN) and China Coast Guard (CCG) vessels have also increased their presence nearer to the median line. CCG vessels, "fishing boats," and dredgers began repeatedly violating longstanding agreements on restricted waters around Kinmen and Matsu, two islands in the Taiwan Strait controlled by Taiwan.

The CCG has taken over "grey zone" operations in the Taiwan Strait, with the PLAN moving to areas in the West Pacific and in waters between Taiwan and Japan and Taiwan and the Philippines. In February 2024, the Taiwan Affairs Office upped the ante by denying the existence of "prohibited" and "restricted" waters in the area. Those had been part of the rules of engagement under the old status quo. Around the same time, agencies including the Chinese Ministry of Transport's Fujian Maritime Safety Administration and the East China Sea Rescue Bureau launched patrol and law enforcement operations aimed at creating new facts at sea to consolidate China's control over the median line.[29]

China has also used cognitive warfare and disinformation following incidents at sea, such as an accident in February 2024 in which two Chinese men, purported fishermen, drowned after their vessel capsized.[30] Throughout the political storm that followed, Beijing retaliated with the dispatch of patrols in the same waters and briefly held passengers on a Taiwanese ferry boat. Beijing also insisted that Taiwan's Coast Guard Administration (CGA) was at fault, even though the Chinese vessel had entered Taiwan's restricted waters. Meanwhile, politicians in Taiwan, some of them believed to be in China's pocket, amplified China's propaganda over the crisis by portraying the Taiwan side as the culprit in the matter. The dispute was eventually concluded when the Taiwanese side agreed to apologize (for the coast guard officers not having body cameras during the operation, and not for their law enforcement) and to pay reparations (from private sources) to the families of the two Chinese. A high-placed intelligence source in Taiwan confirmed to this author that the Chinese involved in the incident were not fishermen, and that their boat did not carry fishing equipment.

In China's "grey zone" strategy, many of the actors involved are not what they seem. This applies to the China Coast Guard, which despite its name does not operate in the way it is expected to do in the West. The CCG is not a purely civilian organization. Rather, it acts as a quasi-military force (some analysts have referred to it as "China's second navy") that, since 2018, has been under the People's Armed Police (PAP), which itself is overseen by the Central Military Commission (CMC) headed by Xi.[31]

The ostensible civilian nature of the CCG, along with that of its "maritime militia," poses challenges for the law enforcement units and navies of neighboring countries like Taiwan, Japan, Vietnam, and the Philippines, which all have territorial disputes with China.[32] Some CCG vessels have extremely large displacement and weaponry on board that qualify them as military vessels. The maritime militia, meanwhile, acts as a paramilitary unit and also reports to the Chinese military establishment. Its fishing vessels have all the appearance of innocuous civilian ships, but they are anything but.

The blurring of the lines creates a force asymmetry, as has been evident in clashes in the South China Sea between Chinese and Philippine vessels. Furthermore, it creates an additional challenge for China's competitors, who must make hard decisions on how to respond to what seemingly are provocations by civilian actors. If a country responds using military assets, Beijing could turn around and accuse it of disproportionate response under international law (this is what is known as "lawfare").

During the large-scale Joint Sword-2024A military exercises near Taiwan in May 2024, CCG vessels operated alongside PLAN vessels, underscoring the coordination – and blurring of the lines – between China's military and civilian assets.[33] In October 2024, China launched the Joint Sword-2024B military exercises around Taiwan, this time in "response" to President Lai's remarks during "Double Ten," the ROC's National Day, earlier that month. Another large-scale exercise was held between December 9 and December 11 following stopovers by Lai in Hawaii and Guam on his state visit to three diplomatic allies in the Pacific. In all three exercises, Beijing used a mix of navy and civilian vessels (more than ninety in the December drills, the largest number in three decades). The major military exercises were also part of Beijing's changing the status quo, this time by using displays of force in retaliation for developments that had hitherto been deemed acceptable.

While the PLAN, CCG, and China's maritime militia tightened the noose around Taiwan at sea, aircraft from the PLA Air Force (PLAAF) and PLAN, including long-range bombers, fighter aircraft, electronic warfare aircraft, and unmanned aerial vehicles (UAVs), have intensified their activity around Taiwan. Taiwan now sees daily incursions across the median line and into Taiwan's Air Defense Identification Zone (ADIZ). Although the ADIZ and the Taiwan Strait are over international waters, the sustained activity by the PLA has forced the Taiwanese military to activate air-defense systems and to scramble interceptors. PLA aircraft and vessels have also begun operating closer to Taiwan's 24-nautical-mile contiguous zone. On some occasions, they even approached Taiwan's 12-nautical-mile territorial seas boundary. Since 2020, PLAN vessels have also deployed almost permanently at four locations around Taiwan: close to Japan's Yonaguni Island; between Yonaguni Island and the Philippines; and in northern and southwestern waters off Taiwan.

All this activity aims to constrain Taiwan's ability to control its surroundings, and to create a sense of embattlement among the Taiwanese public. Besides tightening the noose around Taiwan, this activity greatly increases the risks of collisions or miscommunication. It is not difficult to imagine that Beijing would use an accident to its advantage. Chinese authorities would almost certainly launch a disinformation and cognitive warfare campaign to portray Taiwan as the cause of an incident. This, in turn, would force China, the victim, to retaliate.

The nationalism that the CCP has encouraged in recent years would also create incentives for Beijing to respond, as failing to do so could be perceived as weakness. This is what in fact occurred at the height of the Covid-19 pandemic in June 2021. At the time, U.S. Senators landed at Taipei International Airport (Songshan) onboard a USAF C-17 Globemaster III aircraft. Chinese commentators described such a precedent as a "red line" that justified a military response.[34] When China failed to react, nationalists reacted with fury online and blamed Beijing for cowardliness. Beijing's lack of initial reaction to the landing of a USAF aircraft in the Taiwanese capital is believed to have created the pressure to escalate in August the following year, when U.S. House Speaker Nancy Pelosi visited Taiwan, sparking days of major live-fire military exercises around Taiwan.[35]

China's military "grey zone" activities around Taiwan are an essential part of its "sharp power" strategy to win without fighting. The civil–military composition of the actors and agencies involved represents a great challenge to Taiwan. The Taiwanese government must inform the Taiwanese public about what the Chinese side is up to without sparking a panic that could destabilize society or lead to the election, out of fear, of politicians whom Beijing prefers. Amid all this, the Taiwanese have shown great resilience and have not panicked, even when the Chinese military launched aggressive maneuvers around Taiwan (in fact, during the Joint Sword-2024A in May 2024, Taiwan's stock market reached a new high). Still, the government must ensure that the public doesn't descend into apathy, which could have major ramifications for preparedness and the will to fight. Striking a proper balance, and finding the best ways to communicate this information to the public, is an ongoing challenge for the Taiwanese government.

Exploiting Taiwan's Political Polarization

If you can't win them over, divide them. The one area where Beijing's sharp power has arguably yielded the most promising results is in Beijing's ability to exacerbate political polarization in Taiwan. Through this, Beijing hopes to weaken the unity that is essential to Taiwan's ability to withstand Chinese pressure. As the Russian experience in Europe has demonstrated, authoritarian regimes are especially keen on dividing societies in the enemy camp.

It's not easy to establish a direct correlation between political warfare and rising polarization in a targeted society. Still, there is much evidence to suggest a link. Campaigns to polarize one's opponent are carried out over extended periods of time, through the gradual solidifying of opposite camps. This is done using disinformation, social media, and pundits to fuel constant bickering and animosity. Any issue, however anodyne, will do. Pension reform, the legalization of same-sex marriage, the death penalty, food security, corruption, and the coronavirus pandemic have all been used by different camps and Beijing to increase polarization in Taiwan.

Little by little, this undermines the social and political cohesion that are essential for a society's ability to counter an existential threat. The key ingredient in this strategy is the ability to bring political polarization to such a pitch that one camp comes to regard an opposition or ruling party as the main enemy above all else.

In Taiwan's case, this means that competing political party is of greater concern, and deserving of greater contempt, than the CCP. As Timothy Snyder observes in *The Road to Unfreedom*, "This level of partisanship, where the enemy is the opposing party and the outside world is neglected, creates a vulnerability that can be exploited by hostile actors in the outside world."[36] In this kind of political environment, the political discourse becomes such that parties will do just about anything to undermine their opponent. And in many cases, this may end up creating opportunities that can be exploited by Beijing.

One of the most salient examples of the CCP's exploiting controversy and division in Taiwan was its decision, in September 2024, to weigh in on a major graft investigation against TPP Chairman Ko Wen-je. Ko was a former Taipei mayor and presidential candidate in the 2024 elections.[37] Ko's party obtained eight seats in Taiwan's legislature, where it immediately collaborated with the KMT on various policies aimed at weakening the Lai administration.

As prosecutors closed in on Ko and a business conglomerate involved in the scandal, TPP politicians began promoting the narrative that President Lai had abused his authority as president to personally target Ko. At various rallies, TPP members referred to Ko as a "martyr" while referring to the DPP as a "new party-state apparatus" and the investigation against Ko as a "green terror" (the color green is associated with the DPP, and the term was intended to bring to mind the period of "White Terror" during Taiwan's Martial Law period). They also warned that Taiwan's democracy was dead, which is rather ironic given that most international watchdog organizations were ranking Taiwan at the top of their indexes.

As a democracy, Taiwan has separation of powers, and the president has no authority to interfere with legal processes. The TPP also conveniently ignored the fact that, a few months earlier, former deputy premier Cheng Wen-tsan of the DPP had been detained and faced several years in prison as part of an investigation into alleged corruption during his time as Taoyuan mayor.[38] Rather than recognize this as proof of judicial neutrality, the TPP claimed that President Lai had again interfered in the case, this time to rid himself – *à la Xi Jinping* – of a potential opponent within the party.

That's when Beijing stepped in. Weeks into the investigation, and with Ko and others behind bars, China's TAO accused

President Lai of "manipulating the judicial process" and "hunting down those who do not support Taiwan independence." Revealingly, TAO spokesperson Chen Binhua also used the term "green terror," alleging that the Lai administration had imposed it "all over the island."[39] This did not prove that the TPP was necessarily colluding with the CCP. Rather, it showed that Beijing was paying close attention to potentially divisive developments within Taiwan and was ready to exploit them to further its own objectives.

Another egregious example of Beijing's tapping into divisive controversies to fuel polarization occurred during the Covid-19 pandemic. Several opposition politicians claimed a locally produced vaccine, Medigen, was unsafe,[40] or alleged government corruption over vaccine procurements[41] to score points against their opponents. Others criticized the government's response to the pandemic (at a time when it was being lauded by the international community). In Taiwan and elsewhere, this type of disinformation directly contributed to "vaccine hesitancy" and thereby may have cost many lives.[42] In a press conference, Chinese Foreign Minister Wang Yi went out of his way and singled out the Medigen vaccine. This was a clear attempt by the Chinese side to weaponize public health to discredit the Taiwanese government and turn the public against it.

According to research by DoubleThink Lab (DTL), a leading research institute on disinformation in Taiwan, there is "significant political polarization in Taiwanese society," with "individuals with different political leanings and ideologies present[ing] starkly polarized viewpoints."[43] A survey conducted by DTL in 2024 found that perceptions of disinformation and information manipulation fell into two camps: "(1) those who believe it comes from the DPP, other parties, or all camps, and (2) those who believe it stems from the KMT, TPP, or PRC." The report then observes that "those who agreed that disinformation and information manipulation primarily came from the DPP were more likely to be aged 30 years or younger, male, and not identify as Taiwanese." This group, it continued,

> tends to be dissatisfied and distrustful of Taiwan's democracy and electoral system and tends to agree with narratives such as the cost of living is increasing drastically, housing prices are too high, Taiwan's judiciary is unfair, the government tolerates scammers, the government provides citizens with subpar vaccines and contaminated eggs, the ruling party is corrupt, and the DPP restricts Taiwan's freedom of speech."

The report added that people in this group tend to believe that the DPP is responsible for tensions in cross-Strait relations.

While serving to disparage the government, these narratives also help consolidate separate camps. Belonging and identification serve as a filter for the consumption and spreading of reinforcing narratives, creating an "echo chamber." Not all narratives that contribute to this state of affairs come from China. In fact, many are produced at home by the Taiwanese themselves – some by China proxies, but by no means all of them. Still, Beijing is more than happy to give those a healthy push, as we saw with the Ko corruption case.

In this volatile political context, the KMT and TPP, which together hold a majority of seats in parliament, have engaged in zero-sum politics, which threatens political stability and the country's institutions. Co-opted opposition politicians are conscious of and willing to engage in this type of behavior. However, most members of the opposition are simply guided by high polarization; their behavior is not the result of ideological alignment with the CCP (most would resent the idea) but rather from a desire to defeat one's principal enemy – the ruling party – at almost any cost. For example, many opposition politicians have threatened to defund important defense projects despite the fact that the impact would undermine everybody's security, theirs, as well as that of their voters. So focused are they on frustrating their enemy that national security, it seems, is not first and foremost on their minds.

Since President Lai assumed office in May 2024, opposition parties have attempted to enact extraconstitutional means, such as "oversight laws,"[44] that could undermine state institutions. They threatened to freeze budgets and block ministerial appointments. In January 2025 they did just that, cutting billions of dollars from the 2025 central government budget.[45] The cuts were wide-ranging, affecting civilian defense preparedness, cyber defense, military procurement, funding for cultural activities, and many other areas (a public backlash forced the opposition to drop more than 2,000 other proposed cuts). This, in turn, further inflamed calls for a recall of all opposition legislators, sparking counterattacks by supporters of the opposition KMT and TPP. Opposition lawmakers have also attempted to water down laws passed during the Tsai administration aimed at countering external interference.[46] Such machinations, in turn, have led to blanket accusations by some in the ruling party that the opposition is a tool of the CCP, which contributes to further polarization. Although there is no information available publicly to prove that the opposition is colluding with the CCP, there are grounds to suspect that some opposition figures are in fact doing so.

Taiwan is not the only country to be facing high polarization. Other democracies, such as the U.S., France, the UK, Canada, Israel, and many others, are also struggling to address this crisis. And in most cases, polarization has been exacerbated by external, usually authoritarian, forces to weaken them. Many European countries have been targeted by Russia before and after the invasion of Ukraine in 2022. In recent years, divisions have also widened due to a backlash against liberalism, with conservative forces fueled by anti-immigration, anti-LGBTQI, and anti-liberal ideals joining forces, domestically, regionally, and globally, to push back against a "liberal agenda" they believe has gone too far. Taiwan's liberalism, especially under the DPP, has created openings for conservative forces, as well as the CCP, to exploit.

Polarization taps into the irrational, using emotions to cultivate a sense of belonging to a certain camp while fueling a sense of alienation from, and fear of, the "other." Once such levels of polarization have been achieved, reality, objectivity, and scientific facts no longer arbitrate one's worldview, decisions, and willingness to be persuaded by the evidence. Claims by the other side, even when supported by solid facts, becomes a matter of opinion – or disinformation, lies by the "deep state" or "state apparatus" that targets you and your favorite politician.

This is an area where the authoritarians may have a major advantage over their democratic rivals. That's because the party-state apparatus in an authoritarian system has the ability to control and censor information, reduce public space, and constrain opposition parties (if they are even allowed). In such an environment, it is much less likely that highly polarized camps that threaten state cohesion will emerge. At the same time, the authoritarians are entirely willing to exploit and amplify these weaknesses inherent in enemy democracies. It's a handicap that the democratic camp has yet to find a satisfying solution to.

4

The Impact of Ukraine

It was a chilly, late November day in Vilnius, the capital of Lithuania, when we entered the Defense Ministry building. A week or so earlier, Taiwan had opened a new Taiwanese Representative Office in the Baltic state's capital, a move that, as expected, had angered Beijing, which threatened retaliation. Not only was Taiwan, under the Tsai administration, establishing new, albeit unofficial, ties with a part of the world with which it had not traditionally engaged, but the Lithuanian government's decision to allow the office to use the name "Taiwan" had caused consternation in Beijing. As we saw earlier, representative offices normally used terms, such as "Taipei" and "economic," that were less suggestive of statehood and official relations.[1] To make matters worse, there were indications that the Chinese government had missed signs of the flourishing relationship between Taipei and Vilnius, an embarrassment that later would compel Beijing to react forcefully, calling the whole affair an "egregious act."

The reason our delegation was in Vilnius in late 2021 was to hold a series of exchanges between officials and academics from both countries. The Lithuanians were visibly nervous, expecting retaliation from China and yet not knowing from which direction, and in what form, the blows would come. One of their main fears was that China could launch cyberattacks. This was an area where Taiwan's vast experience and extensive capabilities could prove handy.

And yet, beyond the concerns about possible Chinese retaliation, a larger shadow and far more immediate threat loomed: as our Lithuanian counterparts told us, countries in the region had solid intelligence from the U.S. that, early the following year, Russia would launch an invasion of Ukraine. At the time, many – including people in government – still believed that Russian President Vladimir Putin was bluffing, that all the bluster and troop deployments along the border with Ukraine were merely a tactic to extract a better deal. Many analysts and officials, while acknowledging the despotic nature of the Putin regime in Moscow, nevertheless predicted that the Russian leader would act rationally and weigh the costs and benefits of launching the largest land war in Europe since World War II. The mere threat of international economic sanctions, many argued, would deter Putin from invading Ukraine, a country that, in the Russian dictator's mind, did not exist. For him, Ukraine was part of "Ancient Rus," as he argued in a 2021 article titled "On the Historical Unity of Russians and Ukrainians."[2]

The intelligence provided by the U.S. to regional allies appeared to be solid, and for our Lithuanian interlocutors, there was no doubt that Putin would make a move against Ukraine, and that it would occur before the following spring.[3] A few months earlier, in the summer, Belarus, an ally of Russia, had initiated efforts to destabilize Baltic states. It sparked a crisis by sending large numbers of migrants from North Africa and the Middle East across the borders with Lithuania, Latvia, and Poland. This was a "grey zone" tactic, presumably coordinated with Moscow to cause instability in countries that were likely to work closely with NATO, the EU, and the U.S., when Russian troops crossed the border into Ukraine.[4]

As we concluded our meetings, Lithuanian defense officials requested that we exit the building using a side door. Outside, a ceremony was being held for a Lithuanian general who had recently died of Covid; several Chinese embassy officials were present, and the Lithuanian government did not want the Chinese to spot the Taiwanese delegation. Once outside, the cold November air seemed laden with presages of incoming doom. Many of us continued to hope that the twenty-first century would not become the stage for the kind of devastating land warfare that had blemished much of the twentieth. Surely, despite his murderous inclinations, Putin – and his advisers – would realize the potential high costs of invading Ukraine and refrain from doing the unthinkable.

For those of us from Taiwan, continued Chinese restraint also was a major part of our calculations over matters of war and peace. Our expectations of continuity were largely based on those assumptions. If Putin did do the unthinkable, how would this influence how Beijing and its own despot, Xi Jinping, assessed the costs of, and potential for, victory in a war against Taiwan? Would Putin unleash a new era, one where deterrence no longer prevailed against the murderous instincts of expansionist authoritarian powers? We did not have answers to those questions. But the future certainly seemed bleak.

The rest is history. Deterrence did not work, and Putin did the unthinkable. On February 24, 2022, the Russian military crossed the border into Ukraine, launching a war that would cause hundreds of thousands of deaths, destabilize the global economy, and bring great powers closer to major, possibly nuclear, confrontation than at any point since the Cold War. All estimates of rational decision-making were thrown out the window, as were assessments of how strong leaders like Putin and Xi arrive at their decisions on matters of war and peace. More than ever, given the potential for catastrophe, governments and security analysts needed to better understand how despotic leaders think as well as the nature of the security apparatus and network of advisers that gravitate around them.

It was later discovered that Putin did not listen to his advisers, or that the sycophants within the Russian security apparatus who could have dissuaded Putin were afraid to contradict their leader. Either they remained silent, or only told the leader what they believed he wanted to hear. Now more than ever, whether similar dynamics existed in Beijing around Xi, and the possibility that he, like Putin, could make decisions based on an incomplete picture of the situation, were questions the answers to which had suddenly gotten much more urgent.

Moscow and Beijing's Grievances

Russia's invasion of Ukraine, along with escalating tensions in the Taiwan Strait amid a major increase in PLA activity around Taiwan, contributed to an unprecedented linkage of the two crises. Increasingly, developments in one theater could potentially influence developments in the other. Many saw Putin's war on Ukraine as an indicator that Beijing could also be preparing to use military force to annex Taiwan. Some analysts warned that the distraction caused by major war in Europe could give China a strategic opportunity to strike against Taiwan. Others, including former chief of the United States Indo-Pacific Command (INDOPACOM), Admiral Philip Davidson, had posited in 2021, and again after the war in Ukraine had started, that China could make a move against Taiwan "in the next six years"[5] – in other words, by 2027. This was the date by which Xi had ordered the Chinese military to be prepared to take action against Taiwan if called upon to do so (this came to be known as the "Davidson Window").

The invasion of Ukraine also sparked debate among security analysts, with one side arguing that the international community should rally to Ukraine's defense and help it defeat Russia.

They assessed that a Russian defeat would further deter China from attacking Taiwan. This was a view shared by Taiwan's Foreign Ministry and President Tsai, among others. The other side posited that the U.S. should not waste its limited resources assisting Ukraine, and that Europe should play a greater role on that front. Instead, they argued, the U.S. ought to allocate the majority of its resources to helping defend Taiwan and upholding stability in the all-important Indo-Pacific.

Whatever the merits of either argument, one consequence of Washington's decision to provide weapons to Ukraine was long delays in the supply of as much as US$18 billion in arms already purchased by Taiwan.

How the war progressed, and how the international community responded to Russia's invasion, would have direct ramifications for the Taiwan Strait and Beijing's calculations. Quick capitulation by Kyiv, or a decision by major powers to abandon Ukraine and perhaps force it to the negotiating table, would risk emboldening Beijing, with potentially catastrophic repercussions for Taiwan.

Narrative also played an important role in both disputes. Beijing and Moscow had long complained that the West, primarily the U.S., were actively seeking to "contain" and "encircle" them to frustrate their regional (if not global) ambitions. For Moscow, and Putin more particularly, NATO expansion after the fall of the Soviet Union was evidence of such a conspiracy against Russia. Never mind that several efforts had been made by NATO to find a modus vivendi with Moscow, including an invitation for Russia to join the Partnership for Peace ([PfP], Russia joined in 1994). The Partnership provided "a framework for enhanced political and military cooperation for joint multilateral activities, such as humanitarian assistance, peacekeeping, and crisis management and enables Partners to improve their interoperability with NATO."[6] It also aimed at "advancing Russia's integration into the new European security architecture."[7] Three years later, the NATO–Russia Founding

Act (NRFA) was also signed, opening the way for the creation of a NATO–Russia Permanent Joint Council (NRPJC), which was replaced by the NATO–Russia Council (NRC) in 2002 "to serve as a forum for consultation on current security issues and to direct practical cooperation in a wide range of areas."[8]

Moscow, however, was not satisfied with participating in the PfP and the NRPJC; rather, Russia briefly sought full membership in NATO and a higher status within the organization than former Soviet satellites (a "Study of NATO Enlargement" by NATO in 1995 did not rule out Russia's admission, and for some time NATO and Russian soldiers served side by side in the Balkans).[9] As the historian Vladislav M. Zubok observed in his excellent study of the collapse of the Soviet Union, "Washington offered Yeltsin a place in the club of world leaders and many plaudits, provided the Kremlin did no funny business in its neighborhood or on the international scene in general. Most Western scholars later concluded this was the best option – to keep Russia in, while at the same time containing it."[10]

A far greater bone of contention, however, was the historical disagreement over whether NATO, and the U.S. more specifically, had promised never to expand NATO eastwards. During negotiations following the collapse of the Soviet Union, Moscow seemed to convince itself that the U.S. (President Bush Sr.'s Secretary of State James Baker, that is) had promised Mikhail Gorbachev, the Soviet leader, that NATO would not expand – "not one inch" – eastward. In his history of NATO, Sten Rynning relates that "neither the offer nor the mutual understanding was put in writing, leaving it open to dispute how solid the Soviet-American understanding was"[11] (the unclear language may also have been deliberate in order to sweeten the pill for Moscow regarding the reunification of Germany, which it looked at with some degree of apprehension).

The desire of Eastern European countries to join NATO in the 1990s was largely the result of mistrust of Russia. And for good reason. From as early as late 1993, Moscow's behavior alarmed many European capitals. This included Russia's first war in Chechnya, and a victory by anti-reform extremists in 1993 parliamentary elections. Then, in 1994, President Bill Clinton stated that the PfP was not "a permanent holding room," meaning that it was no longer about whether NATO would welcome new members, but rather "when and how."[12] Still, Russian President Boris Yeltsin continued to believe that NATO enlargement was not on the agenda. He was wrong. On March 12, 1999, mere months before the Second Chechen War, the Czech Republic, Hungary, and Poland joined as full NATO members, becoming the first three former Warsaw Pact countries to do so. The second wave of NATO enlargement occurred in March 2004, with Bulgaria, Estonia, Latvia, Lithuania, Romania, Slovakia, and Slovenia joining as full members.[13]

Spurred by Russia's military actions in Georgia (2008) and Ukraine (2014), NATO suspended the NRPJC and "all practical cooperation between NATO and Russia."[14] Moscow continued to refuse to acknowledge that its own destabilizing behavior in the years following the collapse of the Soviet Union had been major contributing factors propelling several countries in Europe to seek NATO membership. This development was highly reminiscent of the impact the Soviet intervention in Czechoslovakia in 1968 had had on NATO, which responded by shelving talks of the pact's potential dissolution twenty years after its founding. Instead, the crisis led it to configure itself as an alliance of "indefinite duration."[15] The two sides had entered a vicious circle. By fostering a desire among Russia's neighbors to seek security through alliance, Russian belligerence was fueling Moscow's fears of encirclement, which in turn forced it to take action to prevent further Western encroachment through NATO.

Years later, as war with Ukraine loomed, Putin also played to his domestic audience. As the former U.S. State Department official Michael Kimmage has observed, in 2021 Putin launched a "flurry of diplomacy" to persuade the West to make concessions on Ukraine "neutrality" that was so "off-putting" and "maximalist" that "he had to be unsurprised when his diplomatic threats and ultimatums changed no hearts and no minds in the West."[16] Given this, Kimmage argues that the "crucial audience for Putin's diplomatic onslaught may have been Russian." Using "highly coordinated state media," Putin argued that the West was "yet again saying no to Russia." Western countries had "betrayed Russia after the Cold War, articulating superficial respect for Russian interests." Exploiting "a supine Russia," the Western alliance had extended NATO and the European Union eastward. Kimmage contends that the narrative, replete with ultimatums, was designed to ensure that the West would say no, "not least because this 'no' gave him real political currency at home." For the Kremlin, he adds, "this was the final round of diplomacy in performative terms, a climax to the geopolitical drama that had begun in 1991, a narrative of shame turning to assertion, humiliation turning to pride, territorial loss turning to territorial expansion."

Beijing, also claiming the "moral" high ground, has used similar narratives over Taiwan. It has blamed the U.S. and its allies for alleged efforts to prevent China's "rightful" re-emergence as a regional hegemon. As with Russia, China's grievances followed years of efforts by the West to integrate the country into the international system. In China's case, this included securing its admission into the World Trade Organization (WTO) in December 2001. By doing so, the West hoped to facilitate China's transition to political liberalization.

But that's not how China sees it. Tapping into memories of the so-called "century of humiliation,"[17] the CCP has argued that the U.S., fearing the emergence of another superpower, is endeavoring to "keep China low." Such a narrative gained further currency in China after the Trump administration launched a trade war with China. President Biden's decision to retain many elements of that policy further deepened the view in Beijing of the West's ill intentions. From Beijing's perspective, the continued presence of the U.S. military in the region also constitutes an attempt to deny China a chance to break out of the "first island chain," an imaginary line at sea that extends from Japan to Borneo, with Taiwan located in the middle.

Beijing also saw nefarious Western designs behind every attempt to assist countries with which China has had territorial disputes. This particularly applies to Japan in the East China Sea and the Philippines in the South China Sea, with other countries including South Korea, Vietnam, and India also locked in territorial disputes with their large neighbor. Unlike Russia, China has not engaged in large-scale military action against its neighbors. The last time the Chinese military invaded a country was in 1979 against Vietnam. Still, in the past decade it has deployed various military assets, including PLA soldiers, PLA Navy vessels, China Coast Guard ships and its maritime militia, to enforce its territorial claims. China's vast military budget and rapid modernization efforts, meanwhile, have alarmed countries in the region, with many now convinced that it is only a matter of time before China uses its military to resolve disputes.

Thus, as in Europe, the insecurity generated by the emergence of a revisionist hegemon, the recognition that China's "peaceful rise" has ended, created a desire among countries in the Indo-Pacific to hedge against the China threat. And they have done this even as many of them continue to trade heavily with China. China's gradual militarization of the South China Sea started under Hu Jintao and accelerated after Xi came to power. China's refusal to abide by a 2016 International Court of Arbitration ruling in favor of the Philippines in its territorial dispute in the South China Sea, further fueled regional apprehensions that Beijing would stop at nothing to overturn the longstanding foundations of stability in the region. Without a regional security organization like NATO, most countries in Asia appealed to the U.S. (and later Japan, which the U.S. has encouraged to play a greater role in regional security) for security guarantees and called upon it to deepen its military presence. Such appeals went counter to Beijing's aim of expelling the U.S. from what it regards as its rightful sphere of influence. This gave the Chinese leadership the rationale it needed to continue to build up the Chinese military and to engage in more aggressive behavior.

Like Russia in Europe, China claimed that its actions were purely defensive, a necessary response to external provocations. Moscow's and Beijing's grievance-based historical narratives offer important lessons. The dispute over whether NATO and the U.S. broke a mutual understanding with Moscow at a time of Russian weakness has become a matter of interpretation, selective memory, and overarching narratives. The ambiguous language at the heart of this dispute, with differences on whether NATO expansion would be *geographical* or merely serve a *political function* as a promoter of democratization in the former Soviet republics, was at the heart of the matter. This was made worse in 2008 with NATO's ambiguity on Georgia and Ukraine's possible accession to the organization. All this gave a revanchist regime like Putin's the ammunition it needed to push a narrative of victimhood, grievance, and "justification" for rectification – by force if necessary, as Russia did with the invasion of Ukraine.

Russia effectively used the West's alleged broken vow of never to expand NATO for propaganda purposes, attributing the blame for instability in Europe to the organization's expansion and thereby arguing that Russia's actions were both necessary and defensive. This view was shared by a number of academics in the West and elsewhere, which the scholars John Mearsheimer[18] and Noam Chomsky[19] were willing to amplify.

Similarly unclear language over Taiwan's status following the end of World War II, as we saw earlier, also contributed to the longstanding dispute. The lack of clarity at the United Nations in 1971 after Beijing gained China's seat, and again the lack of precision in countries' "one China" policy (which Beijing conflates with its "one China" principle), has made it easier for Beijing to claim that the West somehow "violated" prior agreements regarding Taiwan's status. China, therefore, is entitled to take any necessary measures to correct this alleged injustice.

In the Russia and China cases, clear language following negotiations could have prevented major headaches – and the risk of war – decades down the line. Without by any means justifying Putin's decision to invade Ukraine in 2022, the seeds of that conflict, and of potential threats against other European countries, were sown in the immediate years following the collapse of the USSR. For Yeltsin in 1995, the eastward expansion of NATO was an "extremely acute" matter that could lead to future confrontation.

Lessons for Beijing

How the war in Ukraine played out and the manner in which the international community reacted to aggression were bound to have a major impact on Beijing's assessments of whether it could prevail militarily against Taiwan.[20] If Ukraine failed to mount a credible resistance to aggression, some analysts observed, Beijing was bound to conclude that it, too, could successfully achieve its political objectives through force at a reasonable cost. According to various sources, the Russian leadership had concluded that Ukraine could last no more than thirty days and that Russian troops could occupy Kyiv within as little as three days. Such a blitzkrieg no doubt would have emboldened the Chinese leadership, as such a quick operation would have made it impossible for other countries to respond. For years, Chinese military analysts and propagandists have also argued that the PLA could occupy Taiwan and seize Taipei within a matter of days. Such a lightning operation would not give sufficient time for U.S. forces deployed in the region to intervene.

As Russian forces pushed into Ukraine and missiles rained down on Ukrainian cities, Moscow's hopes for a rapid victory collided with a Ukrainian population that decided to fight back. Ukrainians were led by President Volodymyr Zelenskyy, who turned down Western offers to seek refuge abroad and launched a global campaign to secure assistance as his country fought on. Not only did Russia fail to occupy the Ukrainian capital, but as weeks turned into months, it became increasingly clear that a Russian victory was becoming less likely, despite the devastation that its more formidable military was inflicting on its enemy's territory.

As the war ground on, with battlefields reminiscent of the battles of attrition that had characterized World War I, EU countries, as well as the U.S., Canada, and other Western partners, began providing Ukraine with the weapons it needed to level the playing field against Russia. Ukraine had also had time to prepare itself against this onslaught. NATO and U.S. security assistance, training, and the provision of defense articles following Russia's annexation of Crimea in 2014 and its shadow war in other parts of the country, such as the Donbas region,[21] ensured that this time around Russian invaders would face a military and society that were much better prepared to defend themselves against aggression.

This whole-of-society effort became a source of inspiration for Taiwan, which closely studied the war and provided financial assistance for reconstruction. Ukrainian defenses had fared poorly in 2014, and much of the country had also been unprepared to deal with the grey zone tactics used by Russia in its special operation. Eight years on, Putin appeared to have concluded that Ukraine had not learned its lessons. This was a costly miscalculation, which cost the lives of countless Russian soldiers and severely undermined morale in the ranks.

With Putin's plans foiled for the time being, Taiwan and its allies sighed in relief as the possibility that Beijing would be inspired by a quick Russian victory in Ukraine receded. There was good reason to believe that Russia's quagmire in Ukraine would make the Chinese leadership think twice about embarking on similar adventurism, as a debacle in the Taiwan Strait could cost Xi and the CCP their ability to stay in power. Beijing also took note of the international response in support of Ukraine, concluding that war against Taiwan could result in similar measures against China. Taiwan's role in the global supply chain and source of most of the world's most advanced semiconductors also gave it the kind of strategic importance that made countries pay attention.

Russia's misadventure in Ukraine likely bought time for Taiwan as Xi and the Chinese military studied the war in Europe and assessed that an invasion of Taiwan could be just as disastrous if it did not go as planned.

Another advantage for Taiwan is its geography, which favors the defending side: whereas the Russian military only had to cross a land border to invade Ukraine, in Taiwan's case the PLA would have to cross the waters of the Taiwan Strait in an amphibious assault. This is a much more formidable endeavor. In fact, as most military strategists will argue, this is the most difficult of any military operation. To successfully invade Taiwan in an amphibious assault, China would need to use various transport ships, which it currently does not have in sufficient numbers, to carry a large number of soldiers. Military doctrine stipulates a ratio of 3:1 for invading forces.[22] In a Taiwan scenario, this would mean a *minimum* of approximately 300,000 soldiers. The actual number of soldiers that China would want to deploy against Taiwan would conceivably be much higher, which would put even greater strain on transport capabilities. To complicate matters even more, Taiwan's topography is such that only a limited number of beaches are suitable for the disembarkment and offloading of troops and armored vehicles. And for decades, the Taiwanese military has built up its defenses to counter landings at such locations.

Another lesson the Chinese leadership is likely to have learned from Russia's war against Ukraine is the importance for the defending side of strategic warning. In Europe, intelligence had given the Ukrainian military and society months to mobilize against an expected attack. Imagery and signals intelligence, much of it provided by the U.S., gave advance warning about troop deployments. As a result, Russia lacked the element of surprise that had given it the advantage in its limited operations in 2014. Thanks to advanced intelligence collection capabilities in the twenty-first century, it was virtually impossible to conceal the estimated 190,000 Russian soldiers that had amassed along the border with Ukraine by February 2022.[23] Given the large-scale mobilization and extensive logistics that would go into months-long preparations for an invasion of Taiwan, Beijing's mobilization for war would not go undetected by Taiwanese intelligence and U.S. surveillance capabilities. That's the problem with large-scale conventional military operations: preparations will inevitably telegraph intentions. There is no element of surprise, which gives defending forces – and their allies – time to strengthen their defenses and mobilize accordingly. Russia's blunder in Ukraine has made this clear. Even with overwhelming force and military superiority, there is no guarantee that the stronger opponent will prevail against a well-prepared, dug-in, and committed opponent.

The use of asymmetrical capabilities by the Ukrainians in their confrontation with a stronger military opponent, particularly the use of armed drones, is another lesson that major militaries such as the PLA may have taken from Russia's experience in Ukraine, and one that could make them think twice about launching an invasion. The size of a military force alone is no longer the sole factor to determine the outcome of war.

New, cheaper, asymmetrical capabilities can now frustrate a stronger opponent.

How, and to what extent, Russia's bogged down invasion of Ukraine has influenced thinking within the PLA and the CMC, and what lessons the Chinese leadership has learned, remains unclear. That is largely due to the opacity of the authoritarian regime. Months into the conflict, Joel Wuthnow, a Senior Research Fellow at the U.S. National Defense University, lamented that "The PLA has made it frustratingly difficult to answer these questions using direct evidence: several months into the conflict, PLA officers have produced almost nothing detailing their views on the implications of the conflict for future Chinese operations and modernization."[24] He added, "It is also doubtful that internal assessments, if they exist, will be available in a way that can substantiate foreign speculation."

Despite this, Wuthnow states that the PLA was already aware of the shortcomings that had undermined Russian efforts in Ukraine. Among them, which in his view the PLA "has already basically internalized," are "perfecting joint operations, decapitating Taiwan's leadership at the outset of an invasion, and prioritizing political work." Many of the lessons learned from Russia's experience in Ukraine could directly influence Beijing's approach to an invasion of Taiwan and its expectations of a more favorable outcome. As Wuthnow notes,

> the PLA could derive other insights from Ukraine that have larger implications: reassessments of the ground force's near-complete shift to a brigade and battalion model that failed for Russia in Ukraine, a stronger focus on strategic deception early in a Taiwan campaign, and preparations for a protracted struggle involving staunch resistance in Taiwan and participation from a larger-than-anticipated set of U.S. allies.

China's observations of the war in Ukraine could therefore help it overcome the strategies that have been effective in the defense of Ukraine, Wuthnow argues. In this case, this includes the use of anti-tank missiles by Taiwan to degrade PLA ground forces, intelligence to deny China's element of surprise and to counter its narrative, or the expansion of the conflict beyond China's capacity, could therefore be much less effective than they were with Russia.

In a June 2024 review of four articles written by Chinese academics on the Russian invasion of Ukraine, experts at the U.S.-based Center for Strategic and International Studies (CSIS) concluded that Chinese scholars refrained from criticizing China's support for Russia or its stated "neutrality" over the conflict.[25] The criticism, instead, focused on "the various mistakes Moscow has made in prosecuting the conflict, especially in the first year," presumably with a view to informing PLA decisions in a future war in the Taiwan Strait. As CSIS points out, there seems to be consensus among Chinese scholars that as a result of the invasion, "the West is more united under U.S. leadership, NATO has expanded, and the world is more divided between democracies and authoritarians," with the four articles translated by CSIS agreeing that "the war has left the world more deeply fractured, competitive, and fraught with uncertainty."

Despite this, the Chinese leadership has only deepened its relationship with Russia, which suggests that, in the CCP's view, a world that is more deeply divided into ideological camps is not necessarily a bad thing. In fact, as much of the international community criticized or imposed sanctions against Russia, and after the International Criminal Court in March 2023 issued an arrest warrant for alleged war crimes against Putin,[26] Xi greeted Putin at the Great Hall of the People in Beijing in May 2024, where the two strongmen agreed to a "new era" of partnership between the two countries. Already in February 2022, mere days before Russian troops crossed the border into Ukraine, the two countries had pledged a "no limits" partnership.[27]

The Chinese authors have taken note of how polarizing the war in Ukraine has been within the American polity and how China could exploit future presidential elections to shape the global environment in its favor. As Ouyang Xiangying and Zhang Yuxin write – again as translated by CSIS – "It will be difficult for Europe to maintain its support for Ukraine in the long term if its politics become more right-wing, populist, and fragmented." Undoubtedly, Chinese and Russian "sharp power" and cognitive warfare can play a role in creating such conditions. There was consensus on how science and technology, and new weapons such as unmanned aerial vehicles (UAVs), now play a greater role in modern warfare. The Chinese authors also pointed to Western efforts to decouple their tech sectors from Russia and China as a result of the war.

Beijing does not want Russia to fail in Ukraine. When it became clear that the expected quick victory would not materialize, Beijing modulated its support for Moscow with financial and quiet military assistance. Just enough to ensure that Russia could remain in the fight, yet still below the threshold where it could stand accused of being a direct participant in the invasion of Ukraine. With a Russian victory in Ukraine elusive, Beijing then aimed for the second best thing: a drawn-out conflict that was bound to sap U.S./NATO capabilities. A protracted conflict in Europe could also distract the West away from the Indo-Pacific, which would certainly be to Beijing's advantage.

European Lessons

Speaking at an annual security forum in Taipei in August 2024, former Slovakian prime minister Eduard Heger told the audience that Europe needed to learn important lessons from the Russian invasion of Ukraine. Many of those lessons, he added, also applied to the Taiwan Strait. According to Heger, who was in office from April 2021 until May 2023, and under whose prime ministership Slovakia deepened its ties with Taiwan, one of the gravest mistakes committed by European countries before the invasion of Ukraine was to allow a high dependence on Russian oil and natural gas. By doing so, he said, Europe was "trading values for economics, which always ends up costing us." In his assessment, had Europe not been so highly dependent on Russia to fuel their economies, its member states would have been less divided, and less risk averse, when the time came to unite against the prospects of major war on the continent.

Instead, dependence on Russian oil made it possible for Moscow to sow divisions, capture elites, engage in blackmail, and ultimately weaken European unity and dilute its response to aggression. Before the war, EU countries sourced 155 billion cubic meters of gas from Russia, approximately 45 percent of total imports, via pipelines operated by the state-controlled Gazprom. Russia was also a major supplier of oil (108.1 million tonnes), petroleum products (91 million tonnes), and coal (51.4 million tonnes).[28] Once the invasion was launched and sanctions were being mulled against Moscow, EU countries learned the hard way that decoupling from the Russian energy behemoth, which turned off the taps in May 2022, and finding alternative sources for their energy security, would be a painful process. And it was costly: between September 2021, with war in Ukraine looming, and January 2023, European countries allocated more than €650 billion to mitigate the impact of the energy crisis on the continent.[29] In most cases, the infrastructure was inexistent or insufficient, resulting in various sectors of the European economy facing widespread disruptions, while diversification caused bottlenecks in other energy markets such as Latin America and Asia. Moreover, in the year after the war began, 14.8 percent of gas imports to Europe still came from Russia, which demonstrated that the "handful of [EU] member states that have not been able to or have not chosen to reduce their dependency remain highly vulnerable to Russia's weaponization of energy imports."[30]

The lessons for Taiwan and its allies – and no doubt for Beijing – could not be starker. Except that this time, the situation is even more complicated. The EU's high reliance on Russia for its energy supply pales in comparison to the world economy's reliance on China. Despite efforts by the Obama, Trump and Biden administrations to decouple from the Chinese economy, China was still a top trading partner to more than 120 countries in 2023 and the largest trading partner to Japan, South Korea, Vietnam, and Taiwan.[31] As with the case of Russia, China has adeptly exploited economic dependency to divide countries, co-opt policymakers, and signal that it is ready to weaponize trade against any state that acts against China's interests. A threat by Beijing to do so would sow divisions within countries in times of war in the Taiwan Strait. Vested business interests could undermine any government policy (such as assisting Taiwan) that put those interests at risk (e.g., retaliation by Beijing).

In his talk in Taipei, Heger also questioned the effectiveness of sanctions against authoritarian regimes, arguing that rulers in such systems, by being less accountable to the public and armed with more formidable means to suppress discontent, are better positioned than their counterparts in democracies to survive the effects of sanctions. This seemed to be the case with Russia. Rounds of international sanctions against Russia's war machine and specific individuals have been imposed since the war started. The U.S., UK, EU, Australia, Canada, and Japan alone have imposed more than 16,500 different sanctions against Russia since February 2022, with approximately 70 percent of assets of Russian banks frozen and some Russian banks excluded from the SWIFT banking system.[32] And yet, all this has failed to convince Putin to end aggression against Ukraine.

The home front has equally been neutralized by Putin. Early in the war, protests by opponents of the invasion across Russia were quickly contained, and the state apparatus shifted gear to censor discontent online. Hopes that crippling sanctions would compel Putin to reverse course, or perhaps lead to his overthrow, did not materialize.

Given the importance of China to the global economy, it is therefore highly doubtful that sanctions on the scale unleashed against Russia could be imposed. More countries would likely sit on the fence or be reluctant to join in the sanctions. Undoubtedly, Chinese officials have scrutinized the sanctions regimes against Russia, their effects, and elaborated various plans to mitigate their impact should such punitive measures be imposed on the PRC ahead of, or following, a move against Taiwan. And as in Russia, the CCP benefits from having a tight grip on information and society across China, meaning that discontent resulting from foreign sanctions could be controlled and prevented from spreading.

As with Putin, therefore, threats to Xi's regime would be limited. Both leaders, furthermore, have already rid themselves of most of their internal opponents.

Like Russia and its apologists, Beijing would also wage a cognitive warfare campaign against countries that provide material support to Taiwan. Since its invasion of Ukraine in February 2022, Moscow has used disinformation to depict the U.S. and other countries' provision of defensive equipment to the Ukrainian military as "provocative" and "destabilizing." In essence, as with its propaganda on NATO expansion, Moscow has sought to convince the international community that the West is responsible for fueling – and unnecessarily prolonging – the war over Ukraine. The reality, of course, is that those countries are providing a sovereign, democratic country with the means to defend itself against external aggression. Russian disinformation on military assistance to Ukraine has nevertheless had traction in some pro-Russia circles and on the left. The provision of defensive equipment to Taiwan by the U.S. has attracted similar criticism by groups that regard security assistance to countries like Taiwan as provocative and destabilizing. Beijing has expressed outrage whenever arms packages to Taiwan are announced. More recently, this has been accompanied by sanctions against the defense firms and individuals involved. Like Russia, Beijing's disinformation machine would encourage the view that the provision of military assistance to Taiwan prior to or during an attack by China is "provocative," "destabilizing," and "interference in China's internal affairs."

Operations Short of War

Moscow's inability to achieve its objectives may have forced the Chinese leadership to modify its timeline regarding the annexation of Taiwan. Consequently, for the foreseeable future, Xi is unlikely to gamble everything on a major amphibious assault against Taiwan. Instead, if and when the Chinese government feels the need to escalate, it will likely resort to operations short of war – grey zone activities that nevertheless have a military or paramilitary component involving the PLA, CGG, the maritime militia, UAVs, substate actors, and the full arsenal of "sharp power" tools.

Until PLA capabilities have reached their optimal level and geopolitical conditions are deemed suitable for major military action against Taiwan, China's strategy is likely to resemble more the kind of "hybrid war" and irregular warfare that Russia successfully used against Ukraine during its operations in 2014, which resulted in the annexation of Crimea. Beijing could seek to emulate – with Taiwan's outlying islands of Kinmen and Matsu in mind – Russia's "nominal integration"[33] of Abkhazia and South Ossetia following its limited incursions into Georgia in 2008.

As the Russian security affairs expert Mark Galeotti has noted regarding Russia's successful annexation of Crimea in 2014, "Military force, armed proxies, disinformation, deception and disruption in combination with the right mix of careful planning and field improvisation worked beyond Moscow's expectations."[34] In late February 2014, Russian forces launched unannounced military exercises that in reality were used to provide cover for Russian paratroopers, which quickly seized control of the airport at Sevastopol. The following day, pro-Russian militias in Crimea (including defectors), backed by Russian military personnel (from the Special Operations Command, or KSO) in unmarked uniforms (the so-called "little green men") seized government buildings, including the parliament in Simferopol.

Soon after a new government was installed, a referendum on whether Crimea should rejoin Russia was announced. At the same time, the Duma in Moscow passed new laws on the absorption of new territories by the Russian Federation without the requirement of consultations with the country to which the territory belonged. Following coercion and machinations, the referendum was held on March 16, with 97.66 percent of voters voting in favor of annexation by Russia from a turnout of 83.1 percent – numbers hard to believe despite the existing pro-Russian sentiment within Crimea at the time.[35]

Russia's annexation of Crimea could serve as a model for similar "hybrid war" tactics against Taiwan, particularly Kinmen and Matsu, which are located close to China in the Taiwan Strait. Due to its proximity to China, with a high influx of tourism and cultural exchanges, a larger segment of residents of Kinmen favors closer ties with China (and have elected politicians who espouse such views). Beijing has used this sentiment to its advantage. Starting in 2024, the Chinese Coast Guard and China's maritime militia began encroaching on Kinmen's restricted waters. During large-scale exercises held later that year, which involved both PLAN and CCG vessels, Chinese activity further challenged the existence of restricted waters around the island chains. Should Beijing decide to ramp up the pressure on Taipei without resorting to all-out war, it could therefore adopt a "Crimea" strategy to annex Kinmen and Matsu using a similar mix of local proxies, disinformation, deception, and disruption. And as with Crimea, China could use the cover of military exercises to launch local military or paramilitary action and overwhelm the limited Taiwanese Coast Guard and military forces deployed on those islands.

Short of military action, the Chinese could also use coercive measures, such as a threat of invasion or an economic embargo, coupled with proxies on the islands, to encourage the holding of a referendum on unification in ways that bypass the central government in Taipei. Such a move would compel Taipei to dispatch a larger number of military and CGA assets to its outlying islands, a move that Beijing, using disinformation, would likely characterize as provocative and escalatory, resulting in higher tensions. Conversely, failure to defend the outlying islands would likely result in accusations by opposition parties that the government in Taipei is incapable or unwilling to defend the ROC's sovereignty.

Beijing could also use accidents, such as the one that occurred in February 2024, in which two Chinese drowned when their boat capsized, to spark a crisis and exploit the ensuing chaos to make a move against the islands. Although such an operation to seize Taiwan's outlying islands would spark international condemnation, as occurred after Russia's annexation of Crimea, and could lead to sanctions, it is unlikely that a sanctions regime would be sufficient to cripple China's economy, let alone force it to overturn its policy. Most countries would also be reluctant to risk their economies over the fate of small islands in the Taiwan Strait.

China could thereby seize one or two outlying islands. But the gains for Beijing would be modest. The potential backlash that such a move would have on Taiwan's perceptions of China, along with U.S. views on Beijing's willingness to alter the status quo through more aggressive action, furthermore would result in greater mobilization in Taiwan and more willingness on the part of the U.S. and other regional actors to provide assistance to Taiwan. In other words, a quick gain for Beijing could have unforeseen consequences that are ill conducive to its ultimate goals. The same applies to any move by the PLAN or CCG to seize islets controlled by Taiwan in the disputed South China Sea.

Besides Crimea-style action targeting Taiwan's outlying islands, China could use fishing vessels to "accidentally" cut submarine internet cables in the Taiwan Strait as part of a larger strategy to disrupt Taiwan's internet infrastructure. Although Taipei stopped short of calling it a deliberate act, in February 2023 a purported Chinese fishing boat severed two undersea cables linking Taiwan to the Matsu islands, resulting in widespread disruptions for the islands' 14,000 residents.[36] In another incident, this one in early January 2025, another cable was cut by the cargo vessel *Shunxin 39*, a Cameroon-flagged Chinese vessel. The twin incidents, added to similar acts against undersea cables in Europe, have raised the specter of a "grey zone" strategy to blockade Taiwan electronically.[37]

There is also great potential for China to cause havoc in Taiwan's critical infrastructure through cyberattacks[38] or sabotage. In recent years, vulnerabilities in Taiwan's energy networks,[39] with a limited number of terminals, insufficient redundancy, negligence, and lack of physical on-site protection at various critical sites have been highlighted, presenting potential targets for attacks by pro-Beijing proxies in Taiwan, including crime syndicates.

Major blackouts that occurred in recent years have also highlighted low public patience for disruptions, not to mention the real impact on activity at science parks, demonstrating the high potential for efforts aimed at sowing public discontent and undermining support for a sitting government. Such operations, which likely would also target banking and telecommunication networks, could be carried out as part of a political warfare campaign coinciding with information manipulation, or as the first phase in major military hostilities in the Taiwan Strait.

Finally, as Ouyang and Zhang observed about EU support for Ukraine, long-term assistance to Taiwan could be difficult to sustain if the political environments of its security partner, the U.S., and other countries "become more right-wing, populist, and fragmented." Therefore, one major lesson that Beijing is bound to have learned from Russia's experience in Ukraine is the need to ramp up political warfare campaigns to shape its opponents' domestic political environments, and to exploit politicians and political parties that are more isolationist, reluctant to get drawn into foreign wars, or insistent that longstanding beneficiaries of U.S. security assistance should bear a greater share of the costs of defense. These are all things that the new Trump administration has insisted upon repeatedly.

While it sought to convince Ukrainians, Russians, and the international community that the Zelenskyy regime was composed of Nazis, Moscow's information operations in the lead-up to the invasion of Ukraine were deficient. Rather than discredit the leadership in Kyiv, Russian actions in 2022 and after turned the former actor into a figure of resistance who was lionized internationally. Whether Beijing could succeed in discrediting and isolating a Taiwanese leader using an information campaign is anyone's guess. The CCP may have concluded from Russia's mishandling of Zelenskyy that a better option would be to decapitate the leadership in Taipei, either by military means or assassination by special forces introduced into the country or proxy groups that are already operating on Taiwanese soil. Incidents in recent years involving Chinese "fishermen" who attempted to enter Taiwan's waters using zodiacs or speedboats[40] may have been part of efforts by the Chinese side to identify blind spots and weaknesses in Taiwan's defenses; such weaknesses could be exploited to introduce special forces into Taiwan.

Both Russia and China have a set of operations in their toolkits that come short of all-out war. In both cases, and as the case of Crimea demonstrated, "hybrid warfare" serves to weaken an opponent at relatively low cost – sometimes without a single shot being fired in anger. Moreover, operations that fall below the threshold of full-scale warfare benefit from an element of surprise (at least in the early phase) compared with the telegraphing of intentions (mobilization) that precedes major contingencies such as an invasion. These types of operations can be used to fuel nationalistic pride, regulate tensions (up or down as necessary, for domestic purposes), and to discredit or weaken an opponent's regime. Moreover, the costs of such operations are limited, both in terms of casualties and the potential for retaliation by the international community, which would not risk major war over territories that are regarded as peripheral and expendable.

However, limited operations of this type are unlikely, in and of themselves, to have a major impact on a country's *strategic* objectives (annexation of Ukraine by Russia, of Taiwan by China) as their repercussions tend to be too limited. Additionally, such moves are bound to cause a backlash in the targeted societies by drawing attention to one's hostile intentions. A limited contingency aimed at Taiwan's outlying islands could have an unintended effect on the government and population of Taiwan by making them more likely to make the necessary sacrifices to ensure preparedness (including military training and civil defense). It would also run the risk of increasing the willingness of partner countries like the U.S. and Japan to help Taiwan strengthen its defense capabilities in preparation for major war in the Taiwan Strait.

5

The Catastrophe:
War in the Taiwan Strait

For decades, the threat of war in the Taiwan Strait was regarded as an unrealistic scenario propounded by policy "hawks" in China and the United States. The argument went that the Chinese leadership was unwilling to put the country's economic rise at risk by sparking hostilities against Taiwan and, potentially, the U.S. Furthermore, while hardliners in Beijing threatened war against Taiwan "separatists," the relatively weak state of the Chinese military underpinned the reality that the PLA simply did not have the capabilities, let alone the operational experience, to attempt to conquer Taiwan by force. All the more so if such a conflict prompted an intervention by the U.S. military. Thus, for decades, Beijing lacked both the *intent* and *capabilities* to act upon its threat to use force to resolve the Taiwan "question." That is no longer the case.

As China's economy grew, aided in large part by its accession to the WTO with Western assistance, so did its military capabilities. Growth in defense spending in the decade to 2015 was in the double digits annually, then averaging about 8 percent through 2024. From a declared budget of US$20 billion in 2002,[1] that amount had reached US$231.3 billion in 2024, with personnel, training and maintenance, and equipment each accounting for approximately one third of the total.[2] China is now the world's second largest spender on defense after the U.S. According to the U.S. Department of Defense, "The PRC can support continued growth in defense spending for at least the next five to 10 years, based on economic data and growth projections."[3]

As CSIS notes in a ChinaPower report on the Chinese military, the lack of transparency in China, particularly on matters pertaining to national security, means that actual defense expenditure may be substantially higher, as official budgets do not include various defense outlays such as some aspects of China's space program, research and development, and defense mobilization funds, among others.[4]

Besides the quantitative impact of growing military expenditure, China also embarked on a major military modernization program, which was reflected in the acquisition of newer platforms and training for complex, multi-service war scenarios. From a traditionally Army-centric force focusing on defense of the mainland, the PLA quickly expanded the other branches, namely the PLA Navy (PLAN), PLA Air Force (PLAAF), and the PLA Rocket Force (PLARF), gradually arming its military with the capability for force projection (the PLARF was formerly known as the Second Artillery Corps). China's indigenous defense industry also expanded by leaps and bounds (often aided by the theft of foreign military technology), with the result that the PLA increasingly featured domestically made platforms rather than arms procured from Russia or Ukraine.

By the turn of the twenty-first century, most assessments concluded that China had overturned the balance of power in the Taiwan Strait that had favored Taiwan, whose defense spending since 2000 has been mostly stagnant. Taipei's inability or unwillingness to increase its defense spending to levels that reflected the military threat posed by China was the result of a number of factors. This included resistance by opposition parties (2000–8), de-prioritization of the military during rapprochement with the PRC (2008–16), and other priorities due to public pressure despite a renewed commitment to national defense under the Tsai administration (2016–24).

Taiwan had a defense budget in 2025 of NT\$647 billion (US\$20.24 billion), or 2.45 percent of gross domestic product (GDP),[5] still below the minimum of 3 percent of GDP that many analysts argue is necessary to demonstrate real commitment to defense. Taiwan's defense budget is now approximately equal to that of the PRC's declared budget *in 2002* and at least 11.5 times smaller than China's official defense budget for 2024 (1.7 percent of GDP), the latest figures available at the time of writing.

The reluctance by Taiwanese governments to substantially increase defense spending is largely the result of democratic pressures to prioritize other areas, such as national healthcare (one of the best in the world, with an extremely high price tag). It is also attributed to the long-held belief that China's threatened use of force against Taiwan is little more than bluster and posturing. After all, many argued, for decades Beijing has made similar threats that never materialized (this is known as "continuity bias").

Another factor that has negatively affected the public's willingness to see more of their tax money allocated to national defense is the long-held belief that, come what may, the U.S. military would rush to Taiwan's rescue if China attacked. On this issue, the U.S. has cultivated for some time what is known as a policy of "strategic ambiguity." Washington has kept Taipei and Beijing guessing as to whether, and under which conditions, the U.S. military would involve itself in a war over Taiwan.

A survey commissioned by the Institute for National Defense and Security Research (INDSR), the Defense Ministry–funded think tank, showed that as of October 2024, 66.7 percent of respondents saw extreme weather as a serious threat to Taiwan, surpassing the PRC's territorial ambitions (63.9 percent) and stagnant economic development (63.3 percent).[6] The same survey revealed that 24 percent believed that a Chinese invasion of Taiwan in the next five years was a likely scenario, while approximately 62 percent believed it was unlikely. The calm and pragmatism that has characterized the Taiwanese people's threat perceptions has undoubtedly contributed to Taiwan's resilience. It has prevented panic and stock market crashes whenever China holds major military exercises to coerce Taiwan. However, this pragmatism relies on a reading of Chinese intentions and capabilities that may no longer reflect reality. And on this issue, the gap between Taiwan's government/elite and the public, which seeks "the good life," has widened under the Tsai and Lai administrations.

According to a recent poll by the Institute of European and American Studies at Academia Sinica,[7] Taiwan's premier research institution, more than 80 percent of Taiwanese believe the threat from China has increased in recent years. However, those shifting views on China have not translated into a willingness overall to substantially increase defense spending – at least not at the expense of other areas.

All this is further complicated by threat perceptions along party lines. People who traditionally vote "blue" (KMT) are less likely to believe that the China threat will translate into an invasion. Supporters of the "green" (DPP) camp, for their part, tend to regard the threat from China as a more existential issue. The same poll by Academia Sinica also shows that 62.9 percent of respondents believed signals by the U.S. (Biden administration) that Washington was resolved to defend Taiwan and that the U.S. military would intervene on Taiwan's behalf, while 60.3 percent regarded U.S. arms sales to Taiwan as a signal of likelihood that the U.S. would use force to help Taiwan. Further research, however, has demonstrated high variation in the belief that the U.S. would come to Taiwan's rescue depending on party affiliation.

Generally, DPP voters are much more likely than their KMT counterparts to have a positive outlook on U.S. willingness to defend Taiwan. In both cases, perceptions of a potential U.S. military intervention based on party affiliation may have an unexpected effect on the public's support for higher defense spending: why spend more on defense when the U.S. cavalry is certain to come charging in? Conversely, why allocate a larger share of government expenditures if the belief is that the U.S. will *not* come to Taiwan's rescue, making resistance futile?

Opinion polls on whether the Taiwanese would be willing to fight to defend their country or way of life against a Chinese invasion also differ, depending on how the questions are framed. A 2021 poll published by the state-funded Taiwan Foundation for Democracy (TFD) shows that approximately 72.5 percent of the Taiwanese population would fight to defend Taiwan if China invaded Taiwan to force unification (in other words, an "unprovoked" attack), while 62.7 percent said they would fight following a declaration by Taiwan of *de jure* independence (a "provoked" attack).[8] Another 2021 poll conducted by *Global Views Monthly* showed that 40.3 percent were "willing" to fight themselves or let their family members fight, against 51.3 percent who said they were "not willing."[9]

The extent to which opinion polls are accurate representations of public readiness to fight also depends on the circumstances at the time of hostilities. Would Taiwan face the threat alone, or does it expect to receive foreign assistance? How well trained and ready are the Reserve forces, or civilians? We should add that answering this question "in the abstract" may yield higher percentages than in reality, where the shock of actual combat will likely diminish an individual's enthusiasm for warfighting. Conversely, the public's desire to fight may also be kindled by disproportionate suffering or large collateral damage amid a foreign attack by sparking a "rally around the flag" effect. The conditions imposed by an invader for the cessation of hostilities (e.g., "war of annihilation" versus a negotiated agreement that promises the retention of certain freedoms) will also conceivably have an effect on citizens' willingness to sacrifice blood to preserve their country and way of life.

Growing fears in elite circles are mainly due to two main reasons: the emergence of Xi Jinping as a highly ideological leader with unprecedented powers, and a PLA that within a few years is expected to have sufficient capabilities and preparedness to be able to launch an attack. Although Putin's decision to do the unthinkable in 2022 by invading Ukraine is no guarantee that Xi would embark on similar adventurism, the assumption that Xi or a successor would never consider the use of force is an extraordinarily risky one. Taiwan therefore cannot afford to ignore that possibility, however small it may appear.

Although no Chinese leader has given an actual timeline for an invasion of Taiwan, Xi has nevertheless instructed the PLA to have the capabilities to do so, if ordered, by 2027, the 100th anniversary of the founding of the PLA. Former Australian prime minister Kevin Rudd observes in his book *The Avoidable War* that "Xi, intending to remain in power into the 2030s, wants to be in a position to be able to act militarily to secure Taiwan from as early as the late 2020s should he choose – or at least to have a sufficient military edge against the US by that time to cause Taipei to seek political terms."[10]

Some analysts have cautioned that this could spark major armed conflict between China and the U.S. As the historian Odd Arne Westad observed in a 2024 article in *Foreign Affairs*, "All current evidence points toward China making military plans to one day invade Taiwan, producing a war between China and the United States just as the Schlieffen Plan helped produce a war between Germany and Britain."[11]

Others, while acknowledging that China may be closer to being able to use force against Taiwan, note that developments in Ukraine may have caused some concerns in Beijing. This includes CIA Director William Burns, who told an interview with CBS's *Face the Nation* in February 2023 that "We do know, as has been made public, that President Xi has instructed the PLA, the Chinese military leadership, to be ready by 2027 to invade Taiwan, but that doesn't mean that he's decided to invade in 2027 or any other year as well." According to Burns, China may have become more hesitant due to the war in Ukraine. "I think our judgment at least is that President Xi and his military leadership have doubts today about whether they could accomplish that invasion."[12]

Additionally, revelations of high-level corruption within the PLA and CMC in 2024, resulting in the dismissal of several figures from the PLARF and CMC, suggests that PLA modernization and preparedness may not be at the level where Xi wants them to be. His crackdown on graft within the armed forces also appears to have been aimed at ensuring strict loyalty to Xi, perhaps more so than ending corrupt practices within the military.[13]

Other assessments, based on the Xi "cult of personality," PLA defense modernization, and Chinese demographics, evaluate that "Xi Jinping has a strategic window, in the 2030 timeframe."[14] Another important element is the geopolitical context in which the Chinese leadership would consider using force against Taiwan. This includes (1) Taiwan's ability (and perceived commitment) to mount a credible deterrent against a Chinese invasion, (2) the nature of U.S. support for Taiwan – including deployment of sufficient capabilities in the region to promptly and credibly respond to a contingency in the Taiwan Strait – (3) expected responses by regional countries such as Japan, the Philippines, and Australia and (4) the potential for economic sanctions imposed by the international community.

Whether China believes it has successfully deterred U.S. involvement in a war in the Taiwan Strait through its A2/AD capabilities, such as anti-ship ballistic missiles, submarines and other long-range capabilities, or its strategic nuclear forces, would also factor in Beijing's calculations. A period of reduced U.S. military commitment to the Indo-Pacific resulting from an isolationist administration in Washington could lead Beijing to conclude that it must seize the opportunity to act against Taiwan. One or more major crisis elsewhere that overstretches the U.S. military, such as major war in Europe, the Middle East, or the Korean Peninsula, could also encourage Beijing to act. The possibility that the Beijing–Moscow–led axis could "tag-team" with other bad actors to spark simultaneous crises that could then be exploited is also something that policy analysts are beginning to take seriously.

It is therefore clear that a more robust U.S. military deployment in the region, with greater burden-sharing with regional allies and partners, will help reduce the likelihood that Beijing will choose the war option. A more involved Japanese Self-Defense Forces, with fewer restrictions on its rules of engagement, and a calm geopolitical environment that does not distract Washington, would likely have a similar effect on decision makers in Beijing. Any projection on the likelihood of war in the Taiwan Strait must take uncontrollable variables (unknowns) into account. (Another hard-to-predict development that could trigger military adventurism is political instability within China, in which, for reasons of regime survival, the CCP would seek an external distraction.) Having briefly introduced the context in which decisions of war and peace will be made in the coming years, let us now turn to the military capabilities of China and Taiwan.

Military Capabilities Across the Taiwan Strait

While not the sole factor as to whether a government will decide to use force against an opponent, the size of one's military is an important element in the balance of power. Other factors, such as levels of training and jointness, how modern a military arsenal is, enemy preparedness and the likelihood that an external power will intervene on behalf of the weaker opponent, will also factor into leadership calculations.

Both quantitatively and qualitatively, China today has a clear edge over Taiwan, the result, as we saw earlier, of two decades of substantial investment in the PLA. As the following table shows, in almost every aspect of China's and Taiwan's Order of Battle (ORBAT), China has a major quantitative advantage. But that only tells half the story. Increasingly, the PLA is equipped with platforms that are modern and increasingly less reliant on the "systems of systems" – a mix of Russian and Chinese technology, or the result of tech transfer – that used to feature in many of China's military platforms.

Additionally, military reforms launched by the Chinese leadership have emphasized jointness – the ability to act together as force multipliers – in the four branches of the Chinese military. This has been reflected in the training exercises conducted by the PLA in recent years in preparation for the complex operations that would be involved in an attack against Taiwan. Recently, the PLAAF has intensified night-time training, while PLAN and CCG vessels have intensified training in winter conditions. Both are important elements in the military's ability to wage war under various conditions. The PLA has also ramped up Joint Combat Readiness Patrols, meant to assess integrated operations capabilities of various military branches, around Taiwan.

The PLAAF and PLAN have also used the daily sorties around Taiwan, near or across the median line, and into Taiwan's Air Defense Identification Zone (ADIZ) to familiarize themselves with Taiwan's environment. Starting in 2024, most PLA aircraft activity around Taiwan involved crossings into the Taiwan side of the median line; such intrusions were rarer in earlier years. According to statistics from Taiwan's Ministry of National Defense, in 2023 a total of 1,674 PLA aircraft – from the total 4,679 that operated around Taiwan – intruded into Taiwan's ADIZ,[15] about the same number (1,737) as in 2022. This was up from 972 in 2021 and 380 in 2020.[16]

The figures for 2024 present an even more daunting picture: 3,026 incursions into Taiwan's ADIZ (an increase of 80 percent from the previous year), 5,110 PLA aircraft operating near Taiwan, and 2,501 PLAN warships tracked by Taiwan. Additionally, the largest number of sorties by PLA aircraft in a single day, 153, was recorded that year. Such numbers are expected to continue to increase in the coming years.

PLAN vessels deployed to Taiwan's east in the Yonaguni Channel between Taiwan and Japan-controlled Yonaguni island have also conducted hydrographic surveying. Analysts expect that the PLA could use that area to attack Taiwan, though most believe that China could not control the Strait of Miyako between Taiwan and Japan. In 2022, PLAN vessels were deployed around Taiwan for a total of 147 days (six days with more than ten vessels and thirty-nine with five to nine vessels). In 2023, that number increased to 365, with twenty-four days during which ten or more vessels were deployed, and 168 with five to nine vessels.[17] This military presence has also allowed the Chinese military to collect important intelligence about Taiwan's responses to military contingencies. The price tag for this major escalation in military activity whas been high. According to a report to Taiwan's Legislative Yuan, China spent an estimated US$15.3 billion, or 7 percent of its overall defense budget, on military exercises in the West Pacific in 2023.[18] In other words, the PLA used the equivalent of *three quarters* of Taiwan's overall defense budget on exercises alone.

The U.S. Department of Defense's "Military and Security Developments Involving the People's Republic of China" annual report for 2021 states that for an invasion of Taiwan, the PLA has organized six combined-arms brigades capable of conducting amphibious operations, comprising four brigades in the Eastern Theater Command – with Taiwan within its range of operations – and two brigades in Southern Theater Command.[19] The PLA aviation and air assault brigades would also play a role in the event of large-scale landing operations.

Military Capabilities in the Taiwan Strait

	China (Total/Taiwan Area Deployment)	Taiwan
Total Ground Force Personnel	1,050,000/420,000	89,000
Group Armies/Army Corps	13/5	3
Combined Arms Brigades	82/31 (6 amphibious)	7
Artillery Brigades	15/5	3
Army Aviation Brigades	13/4	2
Air Assault Brigades	3/1	0
Airborne Brigades	7/7	0
Marine Brigades	8/5	2
Tanks	4,200/1,100	900
Artillery Pieces	7,600/2,300	1,300
Combat Aircraft	1,900/750	300
Bombers/Attack	500/300	0
Transport	500/40	50
Special Mission Aircraft	250/150	20
Aircraft Carriers	2/1	0
Amphibious Assault Ships	3/3	0
Cruisers	8/4	0
Destroyers	42/30	4
Frigates	47/30	22
Corvettes	50/40	0
Medium Landing Ships/Tank Landing Ships/Amphibious Transport Dock	57/50	50
Attack Submarines	47/31	4
Nuclear-Powered Attack Submarines	6/2	0
Nuclear-Powered Ballistic Missile Submarines	6/6	0
Coastal Patrol (Missile)	60/60	43
Coast Guard Ships	142/?	168

Note: This table does not include the approximately US$20 billion in arms purchased by Taiwan from the U.S. in recent years, most of which has yet to be delivered and is facing delays due to U.S. arms transfers to Ukraine after its invasion by Russia in February 2022. According to the U.S.-Taiwan Business Council, most of this backlog is expected to be delivered by mid-2026.

Source: Author's figure based on data from the U.S. Department of Defense Annual Report to Congress, 2023.

Focus on the balance of power in the Taiwan Strait – the number of combat aircraft or destroyers each side can deploy – can draw attention away from other important variables that influence how each government makes decisions on matters of war and peace. This includes the military objectives of each side and how the weaker actor in the relationship organizes its forces in response to this asymmetry. The PLA today has a clear advantage over Taiwan in terms of the number of soldiers, aircraft, vessels, and missiles it can throw into a military conflict. Therefore, Taipei long ago abandoned the belief that it can compete with the PRC on a boat-versus-boat or plane-versus-plane basis. This has forced it to re-evaluate its definition of victory and to rethink how to best use its limited resources to maximum effect.

Taiwan cannot hope to defeat its much greater opponent in a conventional armed conflict (not to mention the fact that China possesses a nuclear arsenal, which Taiwan does not). Moreover, major hostilities in the Taiwan Strait would almost certainly be disastrous for Taiwan. Taipei's doctrine has therefore shifted to one of *deterrence*. In other words, much of Taiwan's military today is geared toward maximizing the pain it could inflict on an invading force as it attempted to cross the Taiwan Strait. The goal is to make the Chinese leadership think twice about the probability of any invasion of Taiwan coming at relatively low cost.

To achieve this, Taiwan has gradually moved away from acquiring large, high-profile military platforms (often procured from the U.S.), and is instead investing heavily in the acquisition or indigenous development of smaller, radar-evasive and dispersible platforms, making them harder to target. Such weapons include ground-, sea-, and air-launched missiles, autonomous vehicles, and other equipment that is much less expensive than traditional platforms. This "asymmetric" defense posture aims to make Taiwan difficult to absorb, promising a high level of pain for any attempt to invade it.

With foreign technical assistance, Taiwan has also embarked on a multi-billion-dollar Indigenous Defense Submarine (IDS) program, with the aim of building eight submarines.[20]

The development of various cruise missiles by Taiwan's National Chung Shan Institute of Science and Technology (NCSIST) has benefited from greater permissiveness on the part of the U.S. In the past, the U.S. opposed Taiwan having armaments that were not defensive in nature. Taiwan has gradually shifted from a passive defense posture – waiting for the enemy to land on the beaches – to one that puts greater emphasis on *counterforce*, the ability to strike military sites on enemy territory. Without protests from Washington, Taiwan now deploys cruise missiles with enough range to strike targets in China. A missile with a range of 1,500 km is also reportedly under development. An enemy that bristles with small, dispersed missile systems which can sink vessels, shoot down aircraft, and hit targets inside China is bound to make the Beijing leadership pause.

Meanwhile, with U.S. encouragement and assistance, the Taiwanese military has also begun to focus on smaller, more mobile army units that can quickly be shifted from one area to another as contingencies require. This means moving away from the conventional, armor-heavy postures that had characterized Taiwan's approach to defense.

One element in Taiwan's favor is the fact that it has been preparing for a PLA invasion for decades. It therefore knows where the threat will likely come from. Unlike Russia, which only had to cross a land border to invade Ukraine, China would have to ferry tens, if not hundreds of thousands of soldiers across the Taiwan Strait to occupy Taiwan, an extraordinary challenge in terms of logistics during which transit PLA transporters would be at high risk of being sunk by Taiwanese (or American) missiles. Most military experts agree that an amphibious assault is the most challenging of all types of military operations. Taiwan's geography is also an asset, with only a limited number of locations suitable for amphibious landings, against which the Taiwanese military will have made the necessary preparations. Only fourteen small beaches are assessed to be suitable for amphibious landings, and those are bordered by mountains, cliffs, and dense urban infrastructure. Moreover, most of those beaches are assessed as too small to support the offloading of large numbers of troops and heavy military equipment needed to successfully prosecute an invasion. Consequently, the heavy offloading would have to occur at port facilities in Taiwan *after* they were captured.[21]

Currently, the PLA does not have enough transport ships (e.g., Yuzhao-class Type 071 landing platform, dock, or LPD, and Yushen-class Type 075 amphibious assault ships) to carry PLA soldiers across the Taiwan Strait. It is churning new ones, including the new Type 076, which will reportedly be the largest amphibious assault ship deployed by any navy in the world.[22] This lack of transport capability suggests that, for the foreseeable future, the PLA would need to use or convert civilian transporters, such as roll-on/roll-off ("ro-ro") ferries, to accomplish the task.[23] Those are heavy and slow vessels, meaning they would be prime targets for Taiwan's anti-ship missiles as they transit the Strait. The sinking or simply disabling of just one major ship, including an aircraft carrier, could force the PLA to allocate major resources to conduct a rescue operation, thus adding operational complexity to – and diverting capabilities from – an ongoing invasion.

To make matters even more complicated for Beijing, weather conditions in the Taiwan Strait are unsuitable for most of the year. Between late October and April, high waves, strong winds, fog, heavy rain – Taiwan has two monsoon seasons – are too treacherous for any navy to initiate major operations at sea. The PLA would therefore only have two brief "windows of attack" – between May and July; and in October – to launch large-scale naval operations against Taiwan.

China's Rocket and Nuclear Forces

Any military attack on Taiwan (and U.S. military bases in the region) would involve the PLA's formidable rocket force. According to the China Aerospace Studies Institute (CASI), "The PLA Rocket Force (PLARF) continues to have the largest and broadest missile program of any military on the planet. Unencumbered by arms control treaties, the PLARF developed an entire array of rockets and missiles from short range to intercontinental, from tactical to strategic, and from conventional to nuclear."[24] Data from the U.S. Department of Defense show the PLARF currently has an estimated 150 ground-launched cruise missile (GLCM) launchers (300 missiles); 200 short-range ballistic missile (SRBM) launchers (1,000 missiles) with a range of 300–1,000 km; 300 medium-range ballistic missiles (MRBM) launchers (1,000 missiles) with a range of 1,000–3,000 km; 250 intermediate-range ballistic missiles (IRBM) launchers (500 missiles) with a range of 3,000–5,500 km; and 500 intercontinental ballistic missile (ICBM) launchers (350 missiles) with a range greater than 5,500 km.[25] Many of the GLCM, SRBM, and MRBM launchers are intended for a Taiwan contingency. The MRBMs and IRBMs, such as the DF-26, would serve the dual purpose of deterring and/or attacking U.S. military bases in Japan, Guam, and Hawaii with conventional and, if need be, nuclear warheads. The PLARF also has four brigades of hypersonic weapons, an area where, according to CASI, the PLA is "demonstrably ahead of the U.S." Base 61, located in Huangshan, Anhui Province, would be the principal base involved in missile attacks against Taiwan.[26]

Nuclear-armed ICBMs, for their part, would serve as a deterrent, with the ability to strike targets in the Continental United States (PLAN vessels and long-range bombers also have a strike capability with land-attack cruise missiles, or LACM). Many of China's nuclear launchers and warheads are concealed in advanced underground facilities capable of surviving a nuclear first-strike by an adversary. The Pentagon states that "PLA studies discuss using warning or demonstration strikes – strikes against select military, political, and economic targets with clear awing effects – as part of deterrence."

The Pentagon's 2023 report on the PLA observes that "Over the next decade, the PRC will continue to rapidly modern-ize, diversify, and expand its nuclear forces. Compared to the PLA's nuclear modernization efforts a decade ago, current efforts dwarf previous attempts in both scale and complex-ity." China has been expanding its land-, sea-, and air-based nuclear delivery triad. As of May 2023, China is estimated to possess more than 500 operational nuclear warheads, an arse-nal that is projected to reach 700 by 2027 and 1,000 by 2030. China has a "categorical" No First Use (NFU) nuclear policy, although Chinese defense experts have opined that Beijing could consider a nuclear response to conventional strikes that compromise its nuclear deterrent.[27]

While the likelihood that a war over Taiwan would escalate to nuclear strikes by the U.S. and China is considered to be relatively low,[28] the potential for such escalation if the conflict becomes protracted or Beijing concludes it is losing the con-flict should not be entirely discounted. In a 2023 report for the Atlantic Council, Gregory Weaver observes that "China's nuclear forces potentially play both deterrence and warfight-ing roles in a Taiwan invasion scenario."[29] Moreover, "Only some of those roles are consistent with China's declared policy of 'No First Use' of nuclear weapons." (Weaver also argues that the U.S. should evaluate the possibility of using limited nuclear strikes to defeat an attempted invasion of Taiwan.)

China's nuclear arsenal would serve three purposes: (1) deter a conventional intervention by a foreign power in a Taiwan Strait scenario; (2) deter U.S. threats of nuclear strikes against the PRC; and (3) deter limited nuclear strikes by the U.S. to defeat a Chinese invasion. All three would conceivably align with China's NFU policy. However, Beijing could also use or threaten the use of nuclear weapons as part of its warfighting strategy against Taiwan. Here again, Weaver gives three options: (1) a limited nuclear strike to force Taipei to seek termination of hostilities on Beijing's terms;[30] (2) limited strikes to restore deterrence after limited nuclear strikes by the U.S. to defeat the invading force; and (3) limited nuclear strikes – first-use or retaliatory – against key U.S./allied capabilities to substantially alter the balance in the conflict.

There is also the possibility that Beijing would rule that its NFU policy does not apply in a war over Taiwan, as it would regard the conflict to be a "domestic" issue (technically the NFU policy does not apply if the target of a nuclear strike is one's own territory). First-use of nuclear weapons against Taiwan could be demonstrative (coercive), to decapitate the political leadership in Taipei, or to destroy military assets such as naval, army, and air force bases, with a somewhat smaller likelihood of large numbers of civilian casualties.

Design vs. Accident

Several factors could contribute to escalation and spark armed conflict in the Taiwan Strait. Not all of them are by design. For several years, Beijing has warned that a declaration of *de jure* independence by Taiwan would compel China to respond using "non-peaceful means." Article 8 of the Anti-Secession Law, adopted in 2005, states that

> In the event that the "Taiwan independence" secessionist forces should act under any name or by any means to cause the fact of Taiwan's secession from China, or that major incidents entailing Taiwan's secession from China should occur, or that possibilities for a peaceful reunification should be completely exhausted, the state shall employ non-peaceful means and other necessary measures to protect China's sovereignty and

territorial integrity. The State Council and the Central Military Commission shall decide on and execute the non-peaceful means and other necessary measures as provided for in the preceding paragraph and shall promptly report to the Standing Committee of the National People's Congress.[31]

We should note that a determination by Beijing that "possibilities for a peaceful reunification should be completely exhausted" would constitute *casus belli*. This, in fact, is a much likelier scenario than a declaration of independence by Taiwan (as we saw earlier, a majority of the public continues to prefer de facto independence under the "status quo"). The people of Taiwan know that a declaration of independence would run the risk of prompting military action by China. This largely accounts for the high support the "status quo" continues to have among the Taiwanese. Nobody wants to see their country destroyed in an armed conflict. (From this, we can also conclude that more people would support independence if they had the assurance that such a move would not end in devastation.)

Taiwanese politicians want to be elected (or re-elected). Therefore, as they operate in a democratic environment, they must propose policies that reflect the wishes of the public. The likelihood that a president or government would declare independence (or unification) over the heads of the public, or hold a referendum on the matter, is therefore extraordinarily slim. The two most recent DPP presidents, Tsai and Lai (the latter perhaps more begrudgingly),[32] have stated their embrace of the "status quo." While such policies have sparked discontent among the "deep-greens" (supporters of *de jure* independence), the decision was made with the knowledge that policies that tend more aggressively toward independence would cost Taiwan most, if not all, of its international support, including that of the U.S. And they would increase the likelihood of armed conflict.

The vaguer elements of the Anti-Secession Law, where Beijing concludes that all options for "peaceful reunification" have been exhausted, are therefore a more probable cause for the Chinese leadership making the *deliberate* decision to use force against Taiwan. Such a decision, moreover, would be according to Beijing's timeline and based on the Chinese leadership's assessment of PLA capabilities and readiness, the effectiveness of Taiwan's and U.S. deterrence, and the geopolitical context.

Other, nondeliberate, developments could also lead to escalation and armed conflict in the Taiwan Strait. With the PRC in recent years deciding to ramp up its military, paramilitary, and militia activity around Taiwan, with daily intrusions into Taiwan's ADIZ and across the median line, the risks of miscommunication, accidents, and collisions have increased. Other types of "grey zone" operations around Taiwan's outlying island chains of Kinmen and Matsu by the CCG and "maritime militia," such as intrusions and increasingly aggressive maneuvers into restricted zones around the islands, also increase the risks of accidents. New regulations, such as the China Coast Guard Regulation No. 3 that came into effect in June 2024, which the United States Indo-Pacific Command (INDOPACOM) describes as "a vehicle for the PRC to impose domestic jurisdiction on foreign flagged vessels and foreign persons beyond its lawful territorial sea,"[33] all substantially increase the possibility that "inadvertent" crises will lead to escalation.

Chinese military assets have also been operating closer to Taiwan's 24 nm territorial sea baseline and nearer its territorial space (12 nm). The latter is a "danger zone" that, if approached on a direct course, would conceivably force Taiwan to shoot down the intruder (aircraft in the zone between 24–12 nm would be issued a warning and be chased off by interceptors).

Besides increasing the risks of accidents and escalation, such activity by the Chinese military and paramilitary raises questions about Taipei's potential response. In June 2024, Taiwan's defense minister, Wellington Koo, stated that if a Chinese military aircraft enters Taiwan's territorial airspace or waters, Taiwan's military could "exercise the right to self-defense and launch self-defense counterattacks accordingly."[34] Koo's predecessor, Chiu Kuo-cheng, warned in March 2023 that "China has changed the status quo of the Taiwan Strait by flying drones, aircraft and balloons over our airspace. We would be forced to respond should Chinese military vessels and aircraft come near or enter the nation's airspace and territorial waters, even if they are in disputed areas."[35] Chiu nevertheless added that "We would restrain ourselves from launching the first strike to avoid giving China an excuse to attack Taiwan."

From these two statements, we can already see that, within the space of a single year, the responses by the two Taiwanese defense ministers differed over how the Taiwanese military would respond to intrusions by the PLA. Any firm response by Taipei would be regarded by Beijing as provocative and, following an expected disinformation campaign, necessitate retaliation. The CCP could not show weakness in the face of such provocation, and therefore would be compelled to escalate, especially if an incident involved the death or capture of Chinese nationals. Beijing has further blurred the lines by using paramilitary (e.g., the CCG) and maritime militia assets, as well as unmanned vehicles, creating the possibility that any action taken by the Taiwanese military would be regarded as disproportionate and therefore escalatory. This, again, would create the need for the Chinese leadership to respond forcefully.

The February 2024 incident, in which two Chinese drowned off Kinmen while being pursued by the Taiwanese coast guard, and the political storm that ensued, underscore the potential for Beijing to exploit any incident, large and small, to escalate tensions. A more serious accident, perhaps involving military assets, could result in more serious retaliation by the Chinese side. Tit-for-tat responses could quickly propel Taiwan and

China up the escalatory ladder, with a relatively minor incident potentially triggering a serious crisis. As mentioned earlier, any crisis would be accompanied by a robust cognitive warfare and disinformation campaign by Beijing to portray the Taiwanese side as the provocateur. This would also inflame nationalistic sentiment within China, which in turn would force the CCP to demonstrate strength. The incentives for de-escalation could therefore be weakened before a crisis has even begun to escalate. This would be particularly true if Beijing manufactured a crisis and sought escalation all along. Many wars throughout history were thus started, not through ostensibly deliberate decisions by the politicians involved, but rather by accident (or the impression thereof). This is arguably the most feasible source of major armed hostilities in the Taiwan Strait for the foreseeable future.

Naval Quarantine and Blockade

Besides all-out war, there are limited options at Beijing's disposal that, while having a military or paramilitary component, stop short of warfare. Beijing has two instruments in this respect: (1) a limited "quarantine" of Taiwan using "grey zone" tactics and nonmilitary means to limit access to key areas around Taiwan and select port facilities; and (2) a full, PLA-led naval blockade of Taiwan. The terms "quarantine" and "blockade" are sometimes used interchangeably. However, they are distinct instruments with substantial variation in terms of the platforms involved, the scope, and duration of the operation.

Beijing's chances of prevailing in either scenario would be contingent on the geopolitical environment at the time, as well as reactions from the countries that would inevitably be affected by measures that restrict passage in one of the world's most crucial economic corridors. In other words, regardless of how Beijing would frame such a move, a quarantine or naval blockade would not occur in a vacuum and would run the risk of prompting countervailing actions by regional powers and the international community.

In a recent report based on wargaming and exchanges with officials, the Center for Strategic and International Studies (CSIS) writes that

> The purpose of a quarantine is not to completely seal Taiwan off from the world but to assert China's control over Taiwan by setting the terms for traffic in and out of the island. A key goal is to compel countries and companies to comply with China's terms. If foreign actors largely comply with the quarantine, it strengthens China's narrative that it has control over Taiwan and undermines Taipei's sovereignty claims.[36]

In another report, RAND Corp observes that "Unlike in a blockade scenario, China's goals for the quarantine would not be to completely cut off food and supplies to Taiwan, but rather to demonstrate de facto sovereignty by controlling the air and maritime space around the island, as well as which cargo deliveries, ships, aircraft, and people have access to Taiwan."[37]

According to Rand, which sees a potentially greater role for the PLA in a blockade than the CSIS authors, Beijing's first move in a quarantine of Taiwan could be the declaration of an Exclusive Economic Zone (EEZ) around the island. Beijing would then enforce that EEZ with the deployment of CCG vessels, while PLAAF aircraft would conduct patrols around Taiwan and PLAN vessels would hold exercises to deter potential countermoves by the U.S. and Japanese military. The RAND authors also envision maritime militia ships "swarming" and ramming any vessel that attempts to break through the quarantine.

The limited and nonmilitary nature of a quarantine, while challenging in itself, would involve less complexity than a full naval blockade and would therefore be more easily implemented. The principal actors in such a contingency would be the CCG, the Maritime Safety Administration, and China's maritime militia, with support by the PLAN. Moreover, such a move would be less likely to result in an intervention by the U.S. and other countries. According to CSIS's China Power Project, "Only 13 percent of surveyed U.S. experts and 9 percent of Taiwan experts were 'completely confident' that the United States would intervene militarily to defend Taiwan from a quarantine."[38]

Furthermore, the "grey zone" nature of a quarantine would complicate Taipei's efforts to counter it. A decision to respond by military means could spark escalation, with the possibility that the PLAN, PLAAF, and PLARF would be used to counter-attack Taiwanese or U.S. forces. Such escalation would take us closer to a naval quarantine or all-out war.

China's National Defense University defines a "joint block-ade campaign" as "an offensive campaign that is implemented by Navy-, Air Force-, Second Artillery[39]- and Army campaign large formations with the assistive concerted efforts of the armed police force and militia . . . to sever enemy economic and military connections with the outside world."[40] A separate CSIS study concludes that Taiwan's geography as an island and high dependence on trade, with imports and exports in 2022 accounting for 61 percent and 69 percent of its GDP respectively, makes it particularly vulnerable to a blockade.[41] To make matters worse, Taiwan is also extremely dependent on imported energy. Despite a commitment to renewable energy, it remains approximately 97 percent dependent on energy imports. It is also highly dependent on imports for food (about 70 percent). Such dependence make Taiwan highly vulnerable to attempts to cut it off from the outside world.

Taiwan reportedly has energy reserves of no more than six months (less than two months for coal and natural gas; food reserves are also estimated at about six months). By sustain-ing a blockade over a period of several months, China could force Taipei to capitulate before it completely runs out of food or the energy network shuts down. Following the large-scale live-fire PLA exercises in August 2022 initiated in response to U.S. House Speaker Pelosi's visit to Taiwan, some analysts began suggesting that such exercises were practice runs for a potential blockade. "If an exercise over days could begin to disrupt the supply chain for the world's twenty-first largest economy, how would one playing out over weeks or months impact Taiwan?" CNN national security analyst Jim Sciutto asks in a recent book on great power conflict. "Would it push the island to relent without a single directly fired shot?"[42]

Still, there is no guarantee that a blockade would break the will of the Taiwanese, especially if it prompted a reaction by the international community. Moreover, unlike a limited quarantine effort, a naval blockade that attempts to prevent all traffic from and into Taiwan would require a much greater deployment of Chinese forces, this time including the PLAN and PLAAF. Completely sealing off Taiwan, especially if Beijing sought to ensure that no outside assistance (food and energy) were possible, would mean deployment not only around Taiwan but also into the West Pacific. Such a blockade effort would risk affecting commercial traffic in the area and therefore have a detrimental impact on the economies of regional countries such as Japan, South Korea, and the Philippines. The deployment of PLA forces in the West Pacific (Taiwan's "rear"), between Japan and Taiwan (East China Sea and the Strait of Miyako), and between the Philippines and Taiwan (the Bashi Channel) would also expose Chinese surface combatants to strikes by U.S. or Japanese submarines and make the likelihood of escalation much higher.[43]

Once they come into service, Taiwan's Indigenous Defense Submarines would also play an essential role in countering a naval blockade. The PLA has acknowledged its shortcomings in anti-submarine warfare (ASW) and has in recent years sought to address the issue.[44]

It is doubtful that the international community would stand by for the several weeks it would take the PRC to asphyxiate Taiwan through a naval/air blockade. Once such efforts threaten global economic stability, other countries would be bound to intervene. Therefore, even if it is considered a less provocative and more plausible option than an invasion of Taiwan, with some analysts referring to such a strategy as "the most strategically viable option for the PRC,"[45] a sustained blockade comports serious risks and involves high uncertainty. It would almost guarantee external intervention the longer it is imposed, given the serious effects such a gambit would have on the global economy.

Furthermore, the chances that such a strategy would deliver Beijing's ultimate objective – capitulation of Taiwan, followed by negotiations for "reunification" on Beijing's terms – are probably not high enough for the Chinese government to conclude that a blockade is the best option. In fact, a failed blockade, one whose end result is not the annexation of Taiwan, possibly with greater involvement by the international community in the Taiwan Strait, could cause serious damage to the CCP's reputation. Dmitry Alperovitch, coauthor with Garrett M. Graff of the book *World on the Brink: How America Can Beat China in the Race for the Twenty-First Century*, shares the opinion that a blockade of Taiwan would be far more difficult than most analysts seem to conclude. "[A]n economic blockade in lieu of a full-scale military invasion has a low probability of success and, therefore, Beijing is unlikely to pursue such an operation and, indeed, hasn't attempted it yet even though it has had the capability to do so for decades." Furthermore, he adds, "an attempted economic blockade would almost inevitably lead to war or a humiliating defeat by China."[46]

Short of a full economic blockade, China can use its military to wage economic warfare against Taiwan. Large-scale live-fire exercises, such as those initiated in response to the Pelosi visit in 2022, can contribute to a sense of embattlement. Although the Taiwanese public has responded pragmatically to Beijing's military muscle flexing, coverage of such developments by international media has tended to be alarmist, at times hyperbolic. This runs the risk of rattling foreign investors, board directors, business leaders, lending institutions, and insurers, who could conclude that Taiwan has become too high-risk. Following the Pelosi visit and the PLA exercises, two large foreign corporations in the energy sector approached this author and commissioned threat assessments. With these, they were hoping to assuage the fears of their company leadership and lenders by providing a more detailed and reasoned assessment of the likelihood of war in the Taiwan Strait and its potential impact on their multi-billion-dollar investments in Taiwan. There was no doubt that the headlines that had accompanied the military exercises had sowed fears among the people who had the power to decide whether to invest their money in Taiwan or elsewhere.

If Beijing's aim was to scare foreign investors and multinationals away from Taiwan through large-scale displays of military might, this strategy has not been successful – at least not yet. In its 2023 Business Climate Survey, the first since the Pelosi visit in 2022, the American Chamber of Commerce in Taiwan found that 88 percent of respondents planned to maintain or to increase their investment in Taiwan in the upcoming year. Moreover, the survey found that "At 2.8 on a scale of 1–5, the level of anxiety about increased cross-Strait tensions remains moderate ... 67% of companies reported that their operations were unaffected by the increased Chinese military activity in the second half of 2022."[47] The following year, with PLA activity around Taiwan continuing to intensify, the AmCham survey found that "Confidence in Taiwan is flying high – an impressive 92% of respondents plan to maintain or increase their investment in Taiwan in the upcoming year," adding that "A majority of companies reported that their operations have not been severely disrupted by tension across the Taiwan Strait. Those disrupted reported concerns or policy changes from offshore headquarters, staff anxiety, and reduced business from China as the main causes."[48]

According to Taiwan's Ministry of Economic Affairs, a total of 2,310 foreign direct investment (FDI) projects worth a total amount of US$11.254 billion were approved from January to December 2023, a decrease of 9.98 percent in the number of projects and a decrease of 15.40 percent in the total amount of FDI from the same period of 2022. The extent to which rising tensions and PLA saber-rattling in the Taiwan Strait contributed to this drop, as opposed to other factors, remains to be seen and will have to be assessed as tensions ramp up.[49]

Invasion, War of Annihilation

The most extreme and riskiest strategy for the Chinese leadership to annex Taiwan is an outright invasion. This is also the strategy that is the most likely to spark great power conflict between China and the U.S., with grave consequences for the international community. As we have seen, in setting the goal for China to have a "world-class military," Xi has ordered the PLA to have acquired sufficient capabilities to be able to use force against Taiwan by 2027. This date does not constitute an ultimatum to Taipei or a set a time for an invasion. But it nevertheless suggests that Beijing could conclude it has the *capabilities* to match *intent*, two of the key determinants in a state's decision to use force. Also important, as we have seen, is the global context in which the decision to use force would be made: whether Beijing concluded that external conditions – within Taiwan and geopolitically – seemed optimal for achieving its objectives militarily. This, of course, is the "rational," or calculated, decision to go to war. Another road to such a decision, as we just saw, could be a series of escalations that spin out of control.

An invasion of Taiwan would suggest that Beijing has run out of patience with Taipei and the Taiwanese people. It would also mean that deterrence has failed. By that point, the CCP would have concluded that all options for "peaceful reunification" have been exhausted and that it is therefore "compelled" to use force to resolve the dispute. And Beijing has been running out of patience. Back in 2019, some leading Chinese defense intellectuals were already expressing their frustrations. At a conference that year, retired lieutenant general Wang Hongguang warned that time was running out on "peaceful reunification," adding that "The 'independent forces' are now the majority in Taiwan and this has become an irreversible trend." Wang also observed – rightly, one might add – that "public opinion on the mainland and Taiwan is moving in opposite directions and getting further and further apart." This, Wang said, meant that "time is running out and it will be an unaffordable burden for both sides of the Taiwan Strait if we have to wait another five to 10 years for us to liberate or reunite with Taiwan." The only option to resolve this impasse, he said, was to use military force.[50]

While Beijing may show patience and hope that "sharp power" will eventually soften up or fragment Taiwan, years of such a strategy have failed to break Taiwan's democratic firewall and resilience. In fact, this strategy has tended to alienate the people of Taiwan and reinforce their desire to maintain their democratic way of life. Hong Kong's fate and the unpalatable "one country, two systems" formula have fueled greater weariness of Beijing's intentions and trustworthiness.

Contrary to some popular depictions, China could not launch a surprise invasion of Taiwan, not even if it were hiding behind military exercises, as Russia did prior to its annexation of Crimea. The period of time the PRC would need to prepare for a military annexation of Taiwan would be counted in months – from six to twelve, depending on estimates. Preparations would involve a complex series of logistical efforts, including stockpiling, mobilization, fueling, and other logistical footprints that would be detected by Taiwanese, U.S., Japanese, and other allied intelligence agencies (as well as commercial imagery intelligence). As former CIA analyst John Culver has noted, production, stockpiling, and deployment of the large amounts of precision-guided munitions, ballistic and cruise missiles, ground-to-air, air-to-air, and artillery systems would have to commence at least a year before the launch of an invasion.[51]

Moreover, having learned lessons from Russia's war in Ukraine, China would also take steps to insulate its economy, key industries, food supplies, and other sectors from punitive sanctions that, like military preparations, would not go undetected. Taiwan's vast human intelligence (HUMINT) networks in China, which includes spies and ordinary Taiwanese working there, would not fail to notice signs of massive logistical preparations across China, much as it noticed, before the entire international community did in late 2019, the first signs of the emergence of Covid-19 in Wuhan, China. Six to twelve months prior to an invasion, the PLA would also have initiated a services-wide "stop loss" by freezing demobilizations of enlisted military personnel and officers. Other telltale signs would include the construction of field hospitals near naval facilities in the Eastern and Southern Theater Commands. Full mobilization would need to be called at least four months prior to invasion. This inevitable telegraphing of intentions would give Taiwan, the U.S., and other powers a lead of several months to prepare against an invasion.

A decision to launch an amphibious assault against Taiwan would not be taken lightly. In fact, military historians and analysts argue that, of all types of military action, an amphibious assault is the most challenging, with no assurances of success and a high likelihood of high casualties. During World War II, the Allies abandoned Operation Causeway, the planned invasion of Taiwan prior to an assault on Japan's main islands. An invasion was projected to be too costly, rivaling the scale of the D-Day landings in Normandy.[52] The Nazis also abandoned plans (Operation Sea Lion) for an amphibious assault on the UK after the leadership concluded it would be too complicated, with the German navy, "even assuming air superiority was achievable," doubting "whether a large army could be transported across the Channel in the face of the overwhelming power of the Royal Navy."[53] Even the Normandy landings (Operation Neptune) by the Allies was a huge challenge despite the optimal conditions under which the operation took place – key among those the Allies having complete air superiority.[54]

Months before it initiates hostilities against Taiwan, Beijing would be expected to launch a major disinformation campaign aimed at convincing the international community that it does *not* intend to start a war. Moscow used a similar strategy before its invasion of Ukraine, telling foreign leaders and audiences that "There are no plans or intentions to attack Ukraine"[55] and "The movement of troops on our territory shouldn't be a cause for anyone's concern."[56] In a similar sleight of hand, during a meeting with European Commission President Ursula von der Leyen in April 2023, Xi reportedly claimed that it was the U.S. that was trying to "trick" or "provoke" China into attacking Taiwan, but that he would not fall into this trap.[57] In other words, alleged machinations by Taipei and Washington would be to blame for war over Taiwan, not Beijing.

As the PLA begins operations, Beijing would then likely refocus its disinformation campaign to depict its actions as a necessary and "defensive" response to provocation, possibly using an incident, such as a collision in the Taiwan Strait, as justification. Such narratives could also attempt to depict a military operation as action against an unpalatable regime, similar to Moscow's claims that its actions were motivated by a desire to "de-Nazify" Ukraine.

In the days and weeks before launching an invasion, PLA activity beyond the immediate theater of operations, such as in the Bashi Channel, the Strait of Miyako, and in the Western Pacific would intensify as part of preparations to deter intervention by the U.S., Japan, and other allied forces. Once hostilities have begun, the Chinese leadership would also seek to reinforce its nuclear deterrent through signaling, possibly by announcing it had put its nuclear arsenal on a higher state of alert.

The first salvo against Taiwan would involve a series of cyberattacks on its critical infrastructure, including government agencies, military sites, transportation, energy networks, telecommunications, and banking. China would also attempt to sever undersea telecom cables connecting Taiwan to its outlying islands and the international community, as well as its satellite communication architecture. Pro-CCP proxies, including crime syndicates and undercover agents, would also be activated and would likely conduct sabotage against physical sites across Taiwan. Proxies could also target the government leadership and other politicians who have been accused of "separatism" by Beijing.

If the Chinese leadership expected intervention by U.S. forces in a Taiwan conflict, the PLARF and PLAAF would also aim to destroy U.S. military bases in the region, most notably in Okinawa and Yokosuka,[58] as well as in the northern Philippines.[59] Further off, this would also potentially involve attacks on Guam and Hawaii. U.S. military deployments near Taiwan pose a dilemma for Beijing: under the view that an assault against Taiwan is an "internal matter," it could choose to minimize the likelihood of foreign intervention by not attacking U.S. military bases in the region and hope that its nuclear deterrent, diplomacy, and disinformation would be enough to convince foreign leaders they had better stay out of the conflict. However, failure to knock out U.S. military assets this close to Taiwan would mean that if Washington decides to intervene, it would have substantial assets to bring to bear. Those assets could determine the course of the war.

A Chinese attack on U.S. military bases on Japanese territory would also likely be regarded as a declaration of war by the Japanese government, which in turn would trigger the U.S.-Japan Defense Treaty. Moreover, as World War II made clear, predicting how the American public would react to major loss of American lives at the hands of a foreign aggressor is difficult, though as imperial Japan quickly learned, there is a good chance that the response would be muscular. The entry of both the U.S. and Japan Self-Defense Forces (JSDF) into a conflict over Taiwan, with the Japanese military conceivably playing a more supportive role, would greatly complicate Beijing's ability to achieve its objectives.

The PLARF, PLAN, and PLAAF would open hostilities with bombardment of military (navy, army and air bases, radar sites, command and control networks), government, and key infrastructure sites (including fuel depots) around Taiwan, as well as on the outlying islands of Kinmen, Matsu, and Penghu, where the Taiwanese military has assets (including missile sites). Penghu in particular, host to a Navy base, would have to be neutralized before the PLAN can transport the hundreds of thousands of soldiers, as well as heavy equipment, it would need to occupy Taiwan. Beijing could also seek to decapitate the Taiwanese leadership and destroy continuity of government sites with missile strikes. The war in Ukraine has also demonstrated the utility of armed unmanned aerial drones to launch attacks against metropolitan centers and other key targets. China would likely utilize such assets against Taiwan in the early phase of an invasion scenario. Chinese unmanned combat aerial vehicles (UCAV) such as the Tengden TB-001 have already circumnavigated Taiwan during exercises.[60]

It is highly unlikely that the Taiwan side would initiate hostilities by firing the first shot. However, as soon as the Taiwanese military determined that the PLA is about to launch a major attack against Taiwan, the Taiwanese side would use its land-attack missiles (LACM), anti-radiation drones, air-launched standoff missiles, and other weapons in a counterforce action against Chinese naval and air bases, missile and radar sites, logistics, and other sites involved in the assault. Taiwanese vessels would also lay mines at key areas in the Taiwan Strait and along lines of approach to suitable landing sites. This would be complemented along coastal areas by land-based minelayers such as the Volcano Vehicle-Launched Scatterable Mine System, which Taiwan has acquired from the U.S. (the system is due for delivery in 2026).[61]

Given Taiwan's high population density and proximity of many military bases to civilian centers, once Taiwan's air defenses have been breached, a major bombardment of Taiwan, however "precise" PLA missiles may have become, would entail substantial collateral, which could serve to rally international support to Taiwan's cause, especially if the Taiwanese leadership orchestrated an effective public diplomacy campaign as Zelenskyy did in Ukraine.

Early in the war, the PLAAF, in conjunction with the other branches of the Chinese military, would seek to achieve air superiority in the Taiwan Strait by destroying or grounding the ROC Air Force. This would include PLAN aircraft launched from aircraft carriers deployed in Taiwan's rear (West Pacific). Once it has achieved air superiority, PLA naval assets would mobilize to initiate the crossing of the Taiwan Strait, 130 km wide at its narrowest point. Using a variety of vessels, including landing ships, amphibious transport docks, and roll-on/roll-off ("ro-ro") ferries, the PLA would then face attacks by Taiwan's land- and ship-launched anti-ship cruise missiles,[62] torpedoes, and bombardment by ROCAF aircraft that survived initial bombardment as they approach the limited number of suitable beaches for an amphibious assault.

Such a crossing would be immensely more challenging if the U.S. military decided to join in the defense of Taiwan, with U.S. Navy and Air Force assets targeting PLAAF and PLAN platforms in the Taiwan Strait, north and south of Taiwan, and in the West Pacific. As PLAN ships approach Taiwan's beaches, the Taiwanese military would activate highly mobile and dispersible coastal defense systems – rocket launchers, anti-armor missiles, tanks, attack helicopters, and armed UAVs – to attack approaching transport vessels. In this phase of an operation, the potential for casualties among invading forces would be extremely high. PLA troops that successfully cross beach areas and put boots on the ground in Taiwan would then be greeted by Taiwan's mobile army units, Special Forces, and the Reserve.

Although China has the military capabilities to defeat Taiwan through a protracted conflict or war of annihilation, the PLA would suffer heavy losses (that's the deterrent part). A wargame by CSIS, whose findings were published in a January 2023 report titled "The First Battle of the Next War: Wargaming a Chinese Invasion of Taiwan," underscores this point. According to the exercise, China would suffer "catastrophic losses," with the PLAN losing "a staggering" 138 major ships, among them eighty-six amphibious ships and fifty-two major warships, leaving the navy "in shambles." The PLA would also lose as many as 161 aircraft, with tens of thousands of PLA soldiers killed, wounded, or captured.[63] Thus, even if China succeeded in capturing Taiwan militarily, it could only do so at high cost and through a campaign over several weeks or months.

According to CSIS, losses for the Taiwan side would also be severe if not crippling, with half of its air force and entire naval fleet destroyed. Tens, if not hundreds of thousands, of Taiwanese would be killed or injured in the conflict, many of them civilians, with thousands more displaced and seeking refuge in other countries. If the U.S. joined the conflict, losses on the American side would include two aircraft carriers, between seven and twenty major warships, with aircraft losses between 168 and 372. In all, U.S. and allied casualties could be in the tens of thousands.

Given Taiwan's limited food and energy stockpiles, it is difficult to predict how long it could resist aggression by a much more powerful opponent. It is also hard to predict how the Taiwanese public would react to an invasion scenario. For one thing, unlike Ukrainians, they cannot flee a war zone by simply crossing a land border into neighboring countries. While not everybody would choose to fight, with nowhere to flee, a substantial number of people in Taiwan would likely resist invasion. This would therefore require a large-scale pacification campaign by the PLA, the People's Armed Police (PAP), and Chinese law enforcement. Guerrilla-style harassment by armed resistance groups and Special Forces in difficult environments such as dense urban areas and mountain ranges could cause headaches for Chinese occupation forces while contributing to further international opprobrium and sanctions as evidence of a bloodbath makes headlines worldwide.

Despite claims by the CCP that both sides of the Taiwan Strait are "one family," the resentment caused by the long-standing refusal of the Taiwanese people to be subjugated by China would conceivably lead to abuses by occupying forces, as witnessed in Ukraine at the hands of the Russian military. As China installs a Vichy-style puppet regime – possibly comprising elements from a "shadow government" created by Beijing prior to an invasion[64] – large numbers of Taiwanese would need to be held in detention camps, while the rest of the population would be subjected to re-education, as China's ambassador to France, Lu Shaye, told French media in an interview in 2022.[65]

As this section has shown, China would likely prevail in an invasion of Taiwan. But doing so would not be a walk in the park and could come at a very high cost for the Chinese side. There are also several elements of unpredictability that could complicate Beijing's efforts, chief among them an intervention by the U.S. and a handful of other countries.

Impact of an Annexation of Taiwan

Extreme human suffering aside, the costs to the international community of a war over Taiwan would be staggering. Bloomberg Economics puts the price tag at US$10 trillion, or about 10 percent of the global GDP – a greater blow to the global economy than the Covid-19 pandemic, Global Financial Crisis, and war in Ukraine *combined*. "War over Taiwan would have a cost in blood and treasure so vast that even those unhappiest with the status quo have reason not to risk it," it observes.[66] Taiwan's economy would be devastated, with a drop in GDP as high as 40 percent and much of its industry in shambles. The invasion and occupation of Taiwan would also spark a major refugee crisis, with millions of Taiwanese refusing to be governed by a repressive regime controlled by Beijing.

China would also suffer directly from the dislocations associated with the conflict, including devastation along its coast facing Taiwan. Due to China's high reliance on high-tech components from Taiwan, any disruption to Taiwan's industrial base would affect thousands of firms on the Chinese side. International economic sanctions imposed on China following an attack on Taiwan would also undermine the Chinese economy, although the extent of the damage would depend on the level of unity within the international community, the nature of the sanctions, and how well prepared Beijing was to weather expected economic retaliation. Bloomberg estimates that the economic blow to China could be as severe as a 16.7 percent drop in GDP.

According to Jude Blanchette and Gerard DiPippo, sanctions and export controls on China by major economies would likely last years after the conflict. "In Washington, Tokyo, and some European capitals, there would be little to no political appetite to resume normal economic relations with a belligerent China."[67] As the authors point out, the G7 economies, "a reasonable proxy for the U.S. alliance network" account for "a collective GDP 65 percent larger than China's, even at purchasing power parity (PPP) exchange rates favorable to China, and directly absorb 41 percent of China's exports." They continue:

> China has little prospect of eliminating its key external economic dependences – technology, commodities, and the U.S. dollar – in the medium term. After a conflict, China would largely maintain access to commodities from emerging markets and developing countries. However, China would struggle to overcome technology export controls and sanctions based on the global dollar network, upon which its remaining trading partners would also remain reliant.

The repercussions of a war in the Taiwan Strait would be global, as inevitable disruptions in, or destruction of, Taiwan's semiconductor base would have widespread effects. Taiwan produces 60 percent of the world's semiconductors – about 20 percent more than the Organization of the Petroleum Exporting Countries's (OPEC) share of the global oil market – and 90 percent of the most advanced chips.[68] Everything from smartphones, computers, cars, electronic appliances to infrastructure systems and advanced military technology relies on the semiconductors that are developed and produced by Taiwan's unique chip ecosystem and science parks. Most are produced by Taiwan Semiconductor Manufacturing Corporation (TSMC). Even in the small likelihood that TSMC fabrication facilities (fabs) and those of other Taiwanese firms involved in semiconductor production were not obliterated in a Chinese armed campaign against Taiwan, sanctions by the U.S., Japan, and the EU on Taiwanese companies that would now technically be owned by the PRC, or stricter controls on the export of advanced machinery and materials, would negatively affect global production.[69] Foreign business groups in the PRC would also potentially face catastrophic disruptions to their operations, which in turn could undermine a Chinese economy that continues to rely heavily on foreign investment.[70]

Diplomatically, a Chinese invasion of Taiwan would have a serious impact on Beijing's relations within its region and with the rest of the world. The blow to its reputation resulting from its decision to attack Taiwan would be severe. It would also create incentives for larger defense spending and mobilization across the Indo-Pacific, thus leaving China in a much more inhospitable neighborhood. Most countries would realize that the annexation of Taiwan was only a first step in China's expansionist ambitions. Countries along China's periphery, such as South Korea, Japan, the Philippines, Vietnam, and India, would seek closer defense agreements with the U.S. or the creation of a more permanent security architecture in Asia to counterbalance the PRC. The idea that China remains committed to a "peaceful rise" would no longer be believed.

With the loss of Taiwan, which the leadership in Tokyo regards as essential to its own national security, Japan would have to adjust its defense posture in response to the now-permanent presence of the PLA on Taiwan. This would lead to major militarization, closer collaboration with the U.S., and possibly a decision in Tokyo to seek a nuclear deterrent, a move that would have serious effects on nonproliferation efforts and which would likely spark a nuclear arms race in Asia.

A Chinese invasion of Taiwan would create what Chinese scholars already predicted following Russia's invasion of Ukraine – the further division of the world into two increasingly hostile ideological camps, with the U.S.-led democratic order on one side and revisionist authoritarian states led by Russia, China, and Iran on the other. The back-to-back invasions of Ukraine and Taiwan by Russia and China, respectively, would raise pressing questions about the ability of the current international order to deter major wars. This could encourage others to resort to force to resolve political disputes, with the expectation that the international community is unable to stop them. An invasion of Taiwan would result in a less stable, less predictable, and more dangerous world with repercussions that extend well beyond the Taiwan Strait.

Finally, the annexation of Taiwan would extinguish a highly successful democracy, one that contradicts the self-serving claim that democracy cannot flourish within a "Chinese" civilization. It would deny members of the liberal-democratic camp an important and engaged partner in democracy promotion. It would shut down a safe haven to NGOs and journalists in a region where basic freedoms are often violated by governments. And it would remove an ally in the preservation of stability in the Indo-Pacific. Besides the loss of a home and freedoms for the people of Taiwan, annexation by China would constitute a net loss for the entire international community.

6

Avoiding the Nightmare

So far, despite all the threatening rhetoric, China has not invaded Taiwan. This suggests that Beijing continues to calculate that any attempt would fail or be too costly. This view, of course, assumes that the Chinese leadership is thinking rationally by weighing the costs and benefits of a policy – in this case, the decision to initiate war against Taiwan. As long as China's *capabilities* were insufficient to give certain victory at an acceptable cost, Beijing was deterred from acting on its intent. But as we have seen, the balance of power in the Taiwan Strait has shifted in Beijing's favor. As Jared M. McKinney and Peter Harris have argued, "It is only because deterrence across the Taiwan Strait was strong that past crises over the island's political status could unfold without causing an invasion. Now that deterrence has weakened, there are few if any guardrails to prevent current or future crises from escalating to become a full-blown war."[1]

China's power, including that of its military, has grown to such an extent that deterrence in the Taiwan Strait may no longer provide the assurance that war remains a distant probability. To this we must add the growing belief that the U.S. is in decline, too distracted by domestic infighting, and no longer capable of – or interested in – assuming the role of global sheriff. All this also contributes to eroding deterrence in the Taiwan Strait. The imbalance of power in the Taiwan Strait and doubts over U.S. commitments to defending Taiwan have created a "deterrence gap." Consequently, even though war is not inevitable, it may nevertheless have become a likelier prospect. Reinvigorating deterrence against a Chinese military option for Taiwan therefore becomes an indispensable element for Taiwan's survival and stability in the Indo-Pacific.

The concept of deterrence has often been associated with the military realm. This is largely due to the emergence of nuclear deterrence strategies during the Cold War. In reality, however, deterrence has many components: some military, and several in other areas. Successful deterrence stems from a country's or coalition's ability to promise a multifaceted, coherent, and sustained series of actions, in concert, that maximizes the punitive effects of a counteraction in response to an act of aggression. While there is no guarantee of success, the costlier a set of countervailing moves is expected to be, the likelier it is that decision makers, upon evaluating the costs and benefits of a certain action, will decide that the risks are too high and choose patience, or alternative policies, to achieve their political objectives.

Admittedly, the extent to which deterrence works when it is applied to messianic, nihilistic, or unstable regimes that are fighting for their survival is not fully comprehended and can differ from one case to another. Moreover, despots like Vladimir Putin or Xi Jinping may not be receiving all the information they need to make decisions about war and peace. This can be due to the fact that they have surrounded themselves with sycophants, or because advisers are unable to provide them with information that contradicts their worldview. At the end of the day, deterrence only acts on a leadership if the potential aggressor has as much information as possible before a decision is made to initiate armed hostilities.

This section proposes a series of deterrence elements for Taiwan. They include: (1) military capabilities and will to fight; (2) whole-of-society preparedness; (3) state resilience; (4) economic independence; and (5) strategic communication. Additionally, Taiwan's resilience is augmented by several external factors, including: (1) signals of military support by allies and partners; (2) threatened sanctions against the aggressor; and (3) engagement of Taiwan by the international community. The remainder of this chapter briefly discusses each of those elements, with recommendations on how to increase their aggregate effect against coercion and aggression by Beijing. To paraphrase a common aphorism in war studies, deterrence is costly, but war is far costlier.

Military Capabilities and Will to Fight

A country's military might and its people's demonstrated will to fight to defend their land are two of the most important elements of deterrence. As we saw earlier, China has overturned the military status quo in the Taiwan Strait. Still, operating in conjunction with a number of other instruments, a weaker opponent's military deterrent can continue to factor into the calculations of the stronger opponent. It can signal that the cost of military action, even if it resulted in military victory, would be too high – if not for the leadership, then for the public in whose name the decision to wage war was taken (this, of course, is less true for autocratic systems than in democratic ones).

With its smaller economy and much smaller defense budget, Taiwan must therefore maximize the deterrent value of its armed forces in ways that avoid playing to China's strengths, while exploiting its weaknesses. Much of this strategy involves adopting an asymmetrical approach, a shift that has encountered some resistance from a conservative Taiwanese military establishment. A better use of Taiwan's limited resources is one that prioritizes cheaper, small, mobile, lethal, dispersible, and hard to detect units and platforms that can spring into action to saturate an area where enemy forces are concentrated.[2] This also means developing or acquiring the ability to strike targets inside enemy territory as part of a counterforce capability, such as armed drones and land-attack cruise missiles (LACM).

In the past two decades, the Taiwanese military has allocated a substantial part of its budget to develop and mass produce anti-ship and land attack cruise missiles (the Hsiung Feng, or "Brave Wind" family of missiles). Those can be launched from a variety of fixed, road-mobile, naval, and air platforms. Moreover, Taiwanese shipbuilders have shifted away from the production of very large surface combatants and are prioritizing radar-evasive corvettes that have a higher chance of surviving initial bombardment in a war scenario.

Taiwan has also been increasing its air-defense capabilities, with the acquisition of PAC-2 and PAC-3 missile defense systems as well as the indigenous Tien Kung systems, all forming part of a layered defense system that prioritizes high-value targets (major cities, military bases, and so on). The very high number of ballistic and cruise missiles in the PLA arsenal (and high number of launchers) means that Taiwan's air defenses could not intercept every missile in a major barrage; however, its air defense architecture is sufficient to counter limited strikes.

A shift from an armor-heavy doctrine to highly mobile small army and Special Forces units equipped with anti-armor missiles and shoulder-launched missile systems has also been occurring, with support and training from the U.S. military.

Due to China's grey zone tactics, especially the constant intrusions by large numbers of PLA aircraft into Taiwan's side of the median line and ADIZ, Taiwan cannot completely abandon conventional interceptors and combat aircraft, as this would cede Taiwan's airspace to the PLA. Thus – and this has been a major focus of disagreement between military personnel and experts in Taiwan and the U.S. – despite a shift toward an asymmetrical defense posture, Taipei must nevertheless continue to allocate a substantial share of its defense budget to platforms such as the F-16V or, in future, more advanced aircraft.

Regardless of whether they involve smaller defense systems or traditional platforms such as aircraft and surface combatants, continued U.S. arms sales and foreign military financing play an important role in signaling political support for Taipei. This goes a long way in assuaging fears of abandonment in Taiwan. Beijing's expressions of anger following the announcement of arms packages to Taiwan underscores the continued importance of this type of engagement between Taipei and Washington. However, as supply chain issues and delays caused by the prioritization of arms transfers to Ukraine have made clear, Taiwan must continue to develop its indigenous defense-industrial base, which can have beneficial downstream effects on the economy and in job creation. There are also encouraging signs that the U.S., cognizant of the challenges posed by the disruptions, is increasingly open to the possibility of jointly developing and producing military equipment with partners in Taiwan – including unmanned aerial vehicles.[3] Aware of the growing importance of burden-sharing in the Indo-Pacific, the U.S. could also become more open to facilitating the transfer of advanced military technology to Taiwan and other partners in the region.

Taiwan must continue to build up redundancy in its command and control network to ensure operational continuity following an initial attack by China. As the Ukrainian experience also shows, Taipei should develop a secondary military communications system, preferably one whose existence the PRC is unaware of. The Chinese military would be expected to launch attacks – kinetic and cyber – to knock command and control offline in the initial stages of a war. The more command and control assets the Taiwanese military has, the likelier it is that some will survive an initial attack. And, consequently, the longer it will be able to put up a fight.

Taiwan must also strengthen its stockpiles of oil, as well as harden key military sites (army, naval, and air bases, radar sites, and so on).

Taiwan continues to face major challenges in areas that are essential to its deterrent. This includes recruiting a sufficiently large number of men and women to fill the professional military ranks. Taiwan is already struggling to recruit and train a sufficient number of pilots for its combat aircraft. Taiwan's low birthrate is and will continue to be an impediment in this regard. As are continued perceptions that a career in the military is less appealing than a higher-paid job in the private sector. In 2023, Taiwan's active force stood at 169,000 service members (approximately 160,000 volunteers augmented by conscripts),[4] with the ability (in theory) to recall as many as 2 million reservists.

After years of decline, the Taiwanese government under the Tsai administration has extended the military conscription period to one year, yet this remains insufficient to offset shortfalls in the recruitment of professional soldiers. Efforts to remedy the situation by providing adequate training are underway, though live-fire training remains inadequate. (In recent years, conscripts who underwent training often derisively referred to it as a "summer camp.") Assurances that a conscript or recruit will receive robust training and be provided with skills that will be useful once they return to the private sector after completing their service would go a long way in repairing the reputation of the armed forces. That, in turn, would likely have a beneficial effect on recruitment levels.

Reform of and improved training for the Reserve Forces also continues at a slower pace than the situation requires. In 2024, a total of 120,000 reservists were scheduled to receive training;

however, the actual number was revised downwards to 58,000 due to scheduling delays. The previous year, only 6,505 reservists underwent training.[5] On January 1, 2022, the Ministry of National Defense's Reserve Command was reorganized under the "All-Out Defense Mobilization" initiative and renamed as the "Armed Forces Reserve Command – All-Out Defense Mobilization." The initiative combined military and civilian agencies in defense preparation, though like many such institutions in Asia, the military establishment remains wary of empowering (and arming) civilians in preparations for war.

All in all, despite some improvements, the Taiwanese military would face major challenges in rapidly mobilizing its forces as well as ensuring continuity of operations in a protracted war scenario. There is still time to address those shortcomings, and the sooner they are dealt with, the better chances Taiwan will have of deterring and countering an attack by China. Such improvements would also encourage a will to fight among the Taiwanese, who need to know that their military is prepared and provides them with the best training and the equipment they need to defend their country.

Whole-of-Society Preparedness

The Russian invasion of Ukraine has underscored the importance of civil defense. The supportive role of nonmilitary actors can make essential contributions to resilience and a state's ability to remain in the fight. Such lessons were noticed by Taiwan, where civic groups, among them the Kuma Academy,[6] Forward Alliance[7] (the latter working in tandem with the U.S.-based Spirit of America),[8] the Citizens' League, and the Taichung Self-Training Group, among others, have endeavored to provide training to the public in disaster relief, forest survival, and other areas. Data from the Kuma Academy and Forward Alliance show that in 2023 women accounted for 60 percent and about 70 percent of their trainees and volunteers, respectively.[9] With encouragement and coordination by the Ministry of the Interior, fire agencies, police stations, and municipal units have also redoubled efforts to prepare for various types of emergencies, including war scenarios. Taiwan has substantial experience with natural catastrophes, from typhoons to devastating earthquakes, which already provides it with the tools it would need to mobilize during wartime. Such preparedness would go a long way in ensuring that society continues to function even in times of war.

Many challenges remain, however. This includes coordination with the armed forces for a whole-of-society response amid armed conflict, as well as ensuring that the public knows where air raid shelters are located and that those are sufficiently provisioned. Much greater work needs to be done to provide training to civilians, ensuring that each knows his or her role, and that the entire civilian response is well coordinated by the civil-military leadership. Local, ad hoc responses to an emergency, which may be enough to deal with a landslide or collapsed building, would come up short in wartime.

Efforts to give a fighting role to civilians as members of a trained paramilitary force in wartime have encountered even greater difficulties. Several countries in Europe have such traditions, signing up citizens with prior military service or experience with firearms, such as hunters.[10] Wartime civilian force members would be given access to firearms (stored at police stations or at other sites) in times of emergency, operating alongside municipal agencies. Taiwanese organizations and think tanks have reached out to countries where such traditions exist following the Russian invasion of Ukraine to learn from their experiences and explore areas where such practices could be emulated.

However, the Taiwanese military establishment remains fearful of the idea of entrusting civilians with a paramilitary role, or the creation of a territorial defense force, and has frustrated efforts in that respect. It is possible that such hesitancy finds its origins back in China, where organized violence outside the Nationalist military led to the emergence of powerful warlords and communist fighters. For similar reasons, military establishments across Asia tend to oppose arming their citizens. Short of doing so, the Taiwanese government should at the very least empower members of the public to play various roles in wartime, such as intelligence collection, medical services, logistics, countering disinformation, or the manufacturing of small explosive devices.

State Resilience

Taiwan's critical infrastructure is an inviting target for China, which could seek to disrupt it to cause social chaos and undermine public confidence in the Taiwanese government, or before an invasion by the Chinese military. Cyberattacks and sabotage by local proxies against infrastructure and government installations would aim to disrupt telecommunications, banking, public transportation, and energy distribution. Coordinated Russian cyberattacks against Estonia in April 2007 amid a row over the relocation of a Bronze Soldier statue from downtown Tallinn to a military facility outside the city offer a precedent for this type of action. In Estonia, government agencies, banks, and media outlets were taken offline after massive internet traffic generated by botnets and automated online requests.[11]

Besides targeting government, telecommunication, and banking, China would also exploit existing weaknesses in Taiwan's energy supply, storage, and distribution networks. These deficiencies have been highlighted in recent years by a series of blackouts. In addition to physical security at various key sites, the Taiwanese government must continue to modernize power plants and other networked elements of the country's infrastructure.[12] It must also increase redundancy, parallel systems, and auxiliary storage facilities. Grid stabilization, perhaps emulating the project at Hornsdale in South Australia, should be a priority, as well as investment in large-scale battery energy storage systems to store and distribute energy collected by solar panels, wind farms, and other alternative energy sources.

Such measures would reduce the frequency of blackouts in peacetime, while complicating efforts by China or saboteurs to knock out Taiwan's energy sector in a single blow. They would also assuage fears in various sectors of the economy – local and foreign firms alike – that necessitate large and stable energy supply for their operations, including at science parks. The Taiwanese government should also aim to increase strategic reserves of oil, coal, gas, and food stocks beyond the current two to six months and continue to diversify its sources of imports while striving to increase domestic production through renewable energy. Such efforts would build up resilience against quarantine, blockade, and invasion by China. Taiwan should also disperse and harden reserve storage facilities to ensure survivability in case of physical attack.

Scholars have also identified vulnerabilities in Taiwan's internet infrastructure and telecommunication networks, with "choke points" creating potential targets for disruption by electronic (cyber) or physical attacks (e.g., severing of undersea cables by Chinese vessels).[13] The Taiwanese government is currently at work adding bandwidth and redundancy to its space communications systems and ground-based terminals. The Ministry of Digital Affairs (MODA) expects to complete construction of 700 hot spots to be used for satellite communication during emergency situations by the end of 2024 as part of its Program for the Digital Resilience Validation of Emerging Technologies for Contingency or Wartime Applications, launched in 2023.[14]

Rather than rely on foreign firms like SpaceX, Taiwan also decided during the Tsai administration to create its own satellite network, with the first communication satellite scheduled to be sent into orbit in 2026. Taiwan has also entered into partnerships with the Luxembourg-based SES and Eutelsat OneWeb.[15] During its first press conference in September 2024, the Whole-of-Society Defense Resilience Committee under the Presidential Office announced it had identified more than 300 critical infrastructure facilities across the country that will be prioritized in measures aimed at strengthening critical buildings, equipment, and services and thereby ensure resilience in times of crisis.[16]

Taiwan must also develop and refine its plans to ensure continuity of government in response to the potential for a decapitation attack by the PLA. This includes secure infrastructure where a reconstituted or successor government can continue to operate once the primary government infrastructure, such as the Presidential Office, Executive Yuan, and other buildings, have been rendered unusable. Such efforts must also be communicated to the public to reassure citizens that their government can continue to operate in time of crisis.

Besides infrastructure, greater and more coordinated efforts should be made to educate, from a young age, Taiwanese about cognitive warfare and disinformation. The Ministry of Education, Ministry of Digital Affairs, Ministry of the Interior, and civil society organizations (CSOs) should work collaboratively to create curricula and awareness campaigns that can help immunize the population against China's relentless efforts to cause confusion, exacerbate polarization, and spread harmful disinformation across Taiwan's information ecosystem.

Economic Independence

Reducing economic dependence on China is an essential component of Taiwan's resilience, particularly in terms of reducing Beijing's ability to use economic sanctions to coerce the Taiwanese government. The Chinese regime has repeatedly used trade to punish, condition, and divide foreign governments. In recent years, Australia, Canada, the Philippines, South Korea, Taiwan, Lithuania, the Czech Republic, Sweden, and several other countries have been the targets of economic retaliation by the PRC over various political disputes. Beijing has resorted to direct and secondary sanctions where high economic reliance on the Chinese market promised leverage on recalcitrant governments. As we saw earlier, the EU's high reliance on Russian oil and gas had a detrimental impact on European unity in its preparations for, and response to, the Russian invasion of Ukraine. High economic dependence on authoritarian countries such as China and Russia is a recipe for trouble. States should therefore aim to build up their resilience against economic retribution, as well as freedom to adopt policies without the risk of external economic coercion.

For many years, Taiwan relied heavily on China for the export of its products and components, reaching a historical high of 43.9 percent of total trade in 2020. Until recently, Taiwan's dependence on China (and Hong Kong) for its exports rose steadily. Interestingly, this occurred regardless of the state of bilateral relations in the Taiwan Strait. From 2000 to 2008 under the DPP's Chen Shui-bian, exports to the PRC rose from 24.4 percent to 39.0 percent. Under the KMT's Ma Ying-jeou (2008–16), who strove to improve relations with the PRC, China's share of Taiwan's overall exports continued to increase, reaching 40.1 percent toward the end of his second term. Under the Tsai Ing-wen administration (2016–24), exports to China rose slightly during her first administration despite rising tensions.[17] However, from her second term, the numbers began to drop, down to 35.2 percent in 2023 – the lowest figure in twenty-one years.

The reduction in trade with the PRC can be attributed to several factors, including a slowing Chinese economy. However, a far more important factor was the decision by the Tsai and Lai administrations to diversify Taiwan's export destinations. This was partly the result of deliberate decisions by Taipei, and also the inevitable outcome of punitive economic practices by Beijing, which used sectoral sanctions – including the removal of tariff concessions negotiated under the Economic Cooperation Framework Agreement (ECFA) under the Ma administration – to punish Taiwan for its refusal to give in to China's political demands.[18]

To mitigate the impact of China's retaliatory measures on sectors such as agriculture (and in so doing reduce the potentially political effects), the Taiwanese government rapidly explored the viability of alternative export destinations, while launching public diplomacy campaigns which led to fellow democracies – Japan chief among them – opening their markets for the targeted products. Given Beijing's continued hostility toward the Lai administration, Taipei continues to seek diversification to further reduce Taiwan's economic dependence on the PRC. Incentive programs aiming to encourage China-based Taiwanese firms to "return home,"[19] compounded by an increasingly hostile environment in China, have also led to a reduction in the number of Taiwanese enterprises in the PRC, many of which have either returned to Taiwan or established their manufactures in other countries in Southeast Asia, often encouraged by incentives provided under President Tsai's New Southbound Policy.[20]

Thus, by resorting to economic coercion in hopes of achieving favorable political results, the Chinese leadership has instead compelled Taiwan to decouple from the Chinese economy and to diversify its list of export markets to reduce the impact of economic blackmail.

Besides opening their markets to Taiwanese products, like-minded democracies could further bolster Taiwan's resilience from economic warfare by signing trade liberalization agreements with Taiwan or helping it join multilateral trade groups such as the Comprehensive and Progressive Agreement for Trans-Pacific Partnership (CPTPP).

Strategic Communication

As noted earlier, any move by China against Taiwan will be preceded and accompanied by a cognitive warfare and disinformation campaign aimed at confusing the Taiwanese and the international community. In the lead-up to its invasion of Ukraine, Putin's Russia launched a similar strategy, this time aimed at transatlantic unity and the Zelenskyy regime in Kyiv, which it accused of being filled with Nazi sympathizers. In a Taiwan scenario, Beijing would first seek to convince the world that it does not intend to launch an invasion, and once hostilities begin, it would resort to disinformation to blame Taipei or Washington for the hostilities. It would also depict its military operation as a necessary "defensive" response.

In wartime, the government agencies responsible for strategic communication would need to ensure resilience to potential disruptions through kinetic or cyber means. This can be achieved by having redundancy in means of production and dissemination, as well as having a pool of spokespersons to draw from. The head of state should also be ready and willing to communicate Taiwan's will to resist to the international community, much as Zelenskyy did after the Russian invasion of his country, or Winston Churchill during World War II. Such a voice would be essential not only to reassure and rally the Taiwanese public in their country's darkest hour, but also to occupy the moral high ground and engender international support for Taiwan's cause. This would also serve as an important tool to combat disinformation. For example, during the Tsai administration, a disinformation campaign orchestrated by Chinese media alleged that the Presidential Office had plans in place to secure the president's exit from Taiwan in wartime.[21] No such plan existed.

Besides military contingencies, China continually wages cognitive warfare against Taiwan and its allies, reinforcing narratives such as China's sovereignty claims over Taiwan, the evils of "Taiwan separatism," or American imperialistic machinations. Measures to counter such narratives are as necessary in peacetime as they are in wartime, and every effort should be made to strike a proper balance between alarmism and pragmatism. On the matter of China's "sharp power" activities against Taiwan, such as Beijing's efforts to interfere with Taiwan's elections or the activities of suspected Chinese proxies, the Taiwanese government should strive to communicate the necessary information to the public. Under some circumstances, it would be useful to "sanitize" classified material for public consumption. Such initiatives can also be launched in coordination with civic groups involved in countering authoritarian influence. Merely asking the public to "trust us" when accusations of complicity with the CCP are made against individuals or institutions is insufficient.

Strategic communication, based on a counter-narrative that dispels lies while highlighting the virtues of democratic Taiwan, is an important element in Taiwan's resistance, one that can underscore the importance of Taiwan and thereby rally fellow democracies to its cause. It can also set the record straight on which side is responsible for increased tensions in the Taiwan Strait and, if coordinated with other countries, in other contested parts of the Indo-Pacific. One example of this would be for the Philippines and Taiwan to jointly present a consistent narrative about the destabilizing behavior of the China Coast Guard and maritime militia in the South China Sea and the Taiwan Strait, and how such activities are in violation of international law. Another area where strategic communication benefits Taiwan is on the matter of the PRC's historical claim over Taiwan and its misrepresentation of documents such as a country's "one China" policy (which Beijing seeks to present as coterminous with its "one China" *principle*), or U.N. General Assembly Resolution 2758, whose language Beijing has insidiously sought to reinvent as evidence of the U.N.'s recognition that Taiwan is part of China.

In recent years, Taiwan's Ministry of National Defense (MND) has issued daily reports on X and other social media platforms about PLA activity around Taiwan and into its ADIZ.[22] The maps and data provided have served to alert the international community to the growing threat posed by the Chinese military. The ministry has also made major improvements in its uses of social media, with clips and photography presenting a much more appealing image of the armed forces. Such efforts can have a beneficial impact on enrollment numbers. During his time as foreign minister, Joseph Wu also effectively used X and interviews with foreign media to share Taiwan's side of the story in the dispute in the Taiwan Strait. Several Taiwanese representatives abroad have also authored op-eds and given interviews, often in the local language, to counter claims made by Beijing.

During the Covid-19 pandemic, the "Taiwan Can Help" campaign played an important role in helping position Taiwan as a global health partner,[23] as have efforts to underscore Taiwan's centrality as the world's top manufacturer of semiconductors. The publicly funded Radio Taiwan International (RTI)[24] and Taiwan+[25] are also tools that Taiwan has been using to present Taiwan-centric content in various languages. Meanwhile, Taiwan continues to lag behind countries like South Korea in using the creative industry to bolster its brand recognition and image internationally. More funding in the sector, added to a strategic vision for how the creative industry can play a role in public diplomacy, would go a long way in helping Taiwan gain wider recognition globally.

Finally, Taiwan and its allies should do much more collaboratively to exploit weaknesses within the PRC, including factionalism within the CCP, and encourage a more thorough discussion among the Chinese people of the direction China has taken under Xi. Among other things, this can touch on tightened controls over society, economic mismanagement, a foreign policy that in recent years has had a disastrous impact on China's image and reputation internationally, and the threat of a war with Taiwan – and potentially the U.S. – that would be catastrophic for everybody involved, including the Chinese people. Given the linguistic similarities between Taiwan and China, Taiwan is in an ideal position to foment such discussions within China in ways that can weaken regime legitimacy. As Hongbin Han notes in *Contesting Cyberspace in China: Online Expression and Resilience*, despite censorship measures, the CCP cannot comprehensively control the exchange of information and criticism, especially online. "It is clear that the struggle [for information] is not simply one between the authoritarian state and digitally empowered social forces. The boundaries and landscape of online expression are shaped by internal fragmentation within the Party-state, the diverse capacities and agency of intermediary actors, and the heterogeneity of netizen groups."[26]

Signals of Military Support by Allies and Partners

A potential intervention by the U.S. military in a Taiwan Strait armed conflict has been one of the key ingredients of deterrence against a Chinese attack for decades. Despite the rapid modernization of the PLA in the past decade, the U.S. military continues to have an edge over its Chinese opponent, though it is one that is being gradually eroded. As Robert Blackwill and Richard Fontaine note in *Lost Decade*, their study of the U.S. "pivot" to Asia, "the defense pivot [is] challenged not only by numbers but by geography . . . and while Beijing can focus its own forces in the immediate vicinity,

American aircraft and naval vessels have multiple roles across several regions."[27]

For the foreseeable future, Beijing's calculations on matters of war and peace over Taiwan will therefore continue to factor in possible U.S. military assistance in the defense of Taiwan. Whether Washington should abandon its longstanding posture of "strategic ambiguity" and replace it with one of "strategic clarity" has been the object of debates in defense circles for years.[28] Of greatest importance is that U.S. rhetoric on a commitment to defending Taiwan – including instances where a U.S. president, as Joe Biden did, affirmed that the U.S. would help defend Taiwan if it were attacked by China[29] – must be reflected by the actions the U.S. government and military are taking to signal that commitment.[30] This includes continued arms sales to Taiwan,[31] joint development and production of weapons systems, and adequate levels of military capabilities in the region with bases within a range that is close enough to permit a relatively swift intervention in the Taiwan Strait.

Taiwan has been invited to join the Partnership for Indo-Pacific Industrial Resilience (PIPIR), an initiative launched by the U.S. which will involve at least twelve allies in the Indo-Pacific and Europe to address supply chain constraints on weapon production. The PIPIR seeks to address defense industrial base (DIB) vulnerabilities by fast-tracking weapon production among allies.[32]

Besides providing Taiwan with weapons that contribute to its military deterrent, arms sales send a strong signal of continued *political* support. A U.S. military role in replenishing ammunition for the Taiwanese military during hostilities would be an important contribution to Taipei's ability to keep fighting in a protracted conflict, or to bring supplies during a quarantine/blockade action by China.

The PLAN already has the largest navy in the region, and trends in U.S. naval deployments are not encouraging. The Center for Naval Analysis forecasts that the PLAN will grow from 131 ships to "270 large modern warships with a larger proportion of nuclear submarines, not counting another 160 near-seas vessels. The overall number grows to 600 Chinese maritime vessels of concern when CCG and maritime militia are factored in."[33] The current U.S. Pacific Fleet consists of about 200 navy ships, with 1,500 aircraft and 150,000 military and civilian personnel.[34]

Such numbers make it clear that, on a quantitative basis, the U.S. Navy can no longer hope to compete against the PLAN, especially as its lines of communication are much, much longer than the PLAN's would be in a Taiwan Strait war scenario. As such, the U.S. has called for, and needs to continue to insist on, more burden-sharing in the region, with countries like Japan, the Philippines, and Australia assuming more prominent roles in ensuring peace and stability in the Taiwan Strait and the region. Freedom of navigation operation (FONOP) transits through the Taiwan Strait by navy vessels from a number of countries continue to reaffirm international law and the international waters nature of the Strait. More such transits by a greater number of countries would further underscore the international community's commitment to upholding international law, while a more continuous multinational military presence in proximity to Taiwan could contribute to deterrence against an attack on Taiwan.

Although exactly what form a Japanese entry into war in the Taiwan Strait would take is unclear, Tokyo in recent years has issued various statements indicating the essentiality of Taiwan and stability in the Taiwan Strait to Japan's own national security. In its National Security Strategy issued in December 2022, the Japanese government stated that "Taiwan is an extremely important partner and a precious friend of Japan," adding that "Japan will continue to make various efforts based on its position that the cross-strait issues are expected to be resolved peacefully."[35] Yoji Koda notes that in a Taiwan contingency, the Japan Self-Defense Forces (JSDF) can play various roles, including "securing airspace, strengthening ballistic missile systems, protecting sea lines of communication (SLOC), and providing airborne and maritime intelligence, surveillance, and reconnaissance (ISR) beyond the Japanese homeland to encompass the Ryukyu islands, the Sea of Japan, and the East China Sea."[36] Importantly, he also points out the role that Japan, in conjunction with South Korea, could play to deter other adversaries, such as North Korea and Russia, from opening new fronts during hostilities in the Taiwan Strait.

As noted earlier, the U.S. military has large military deployments in Japan. If the PLA, in the initial phase of an attack on Taiwan, sought to disable U.S. naval, air, and marines bases across Japan through missile strikes, there is a high likelihood that Tokyo would regard an attack on its territory as a declaration of war. Japan, furthermore, has a defense treaty with the U.S., which would presumably obligate it to play a certain role in a U.S. defense of Taiwan, if only a supporting one limited to denying the PLA access to the Strait of Miyako north of Taiwan or into the West Pacific. The Japanese military could bring to bear substantial firepower and would thus be a potent force multiplier to the U.S. and Taiwan in a Chinese invasion of Taiwan. Recent initiatives, presumably with encouragement by Washington, have loosened some of the restrictions imposed by Japan's pacifist constitution after World War II. This includes the development and eventual deployment of long-range missile systems with the ability to strike targets in China,[37] the procurement of long-range Tomahawk cruise missiles from the U.S. (scheduled to be deployed in 2025),[38] and plans by the Japan Ground Self-Defense Force (JGSDF) to deploy short-range anti-ship missiles on islands near Taiwan.[39] Those are bound to weigh into Beijing's calculations.

New basing agreements between the U.S. and the Philippines are also creating opportunities for the deployment of anti-ship missile systems in northern parts of the Philippines facing Taiwan that could deny the PLA the ability to operate safely in the Bashi Channel. While the permanence of such agreements is vulnerable to developments in Philippine politics, the deployment of short- to medium-range missile systems in the northern Philippines would complicate PLA operations and severely curtail the ability of the PLAN and PLAAF to use waters between Taiwan and the Philippines to reach Taiwan's "rear" on the West Pacific. Moreover, as with Japan, an attack on the Philippines would trigger the latter's defense treaty with the U.S. With the Bashi Channel and the Strait of Miyako serving as "tripwires" and "choke points" against a PLA attack on Taiwan, China's ability to successfully invade Taiwan would be greatly complicated.

More distant, the Australian military and that of other allies could also deploy in the South China Sea and close to the Bashi Channel south of Taiwan during hostilities. Australia can also serve as a hub for the U.S. military from which to conduct operations in the South China Sea.

Continued statements by regional security organizations, such as NATO, 2+2 summits between the U.S. and allied countries, as well as by multilateral organizations like the EU and G7, all of which underscore the importance of peace and stability in the Taiwan Strait, are also important narrative elements that can contribute to a deterrent against Chinese military action aimed at Taiwan. However, such statements must be accompanied by concrete actions and material contributions, including FONOPs, basing in the Indo-Pacific, joint exercises, and other measures that compound the U.S.-led military presence in the region.

Threatened Sanctions Against the Aggressor

Besides the military elements of deterrence discussed above, the international community can materially increase deterrence against a Chinese attack on Taiwan by signaling the intent to use, and coordinate preparations for, a suite of economic sanctions and trade restrictions that would be unleashed against China following an unprovoked attack on Taiwan. In September 2024, the U.S. House of Representatives passed the Taiwan Conflict Deterrence Act, which in the event of war would "restrict financial services for certain immediate family of [CCP] officials" and publicize information about "illicit" financial assets of CCP officials and their families.[40] Former Representative Mike Gallagher, regarded as a China hawk, said such legislation "makes clear that should [Chinese leader Xi Jinping] choose to invade, the U.S. will not hesitate to respond with crippling and comprehensive economic sanctions on any person or company supporting a [Chinese Communist Party (CCP)] invasion of Taiwan."[41]

The top targets for potential sanctions would be China's Big Four commercial banks, China's overseas reserves, state-owned enterprises (SOE), and smaller banks with links to the PLA or China's high-tech sector.[42]

However, the extent to which threatened economic sanctions against the Chinese regime can successfully deter a Chinese attack would likely be limited by a number of factors. For one thing, Beijing would expect the imposition of punitive sanctions, especially in light of the international response to Russia's invasion of Ukraine, and would therefore make preparations to reduce their impact. Furthermore, questions remain on the willingness of the international community to act in concert in using this instrument, or to implement those instruments early enough to successfully deter an attack. Disagreements over Chinese intentions, or the scale of an expected military action against Taiwan, could also cause divisions among members of the international community and thereby undermine their effectiveness.

Putin's decision to invade Ukraine in 2022 also highlights the limits of economic deterrence. This is due to a number of factors, including the nature of the regime, calculations about the duration of conflict, and perceptions of the threatened sanctions. As noted earlier, authoritarian leaders tend to be more immune to sanctions than leaders in democracies, as they are more insulated from the potential public backlash and can use repressive measures to quiet dissent. An autocratic leader's overconfidence or incomplete advice from his advisers can also fuel expectations that an armed intervention will be of short duration and therefore that the resulting sanctions will be survivable. Finally, a regime can also doubt the international community's willingness to enact sanctions due to the importance of their own economy – in this case the Chinese economy – to the global economy, including international banking.

Despite Taiwan's high importance to supply chains and the semiconductor industry, Beijing could conclude that the depth of its economic engagement with the entire world, and the resulting dependencies, would dissuade a sufficiently large number of countries against joining a sanctions regime. There are also doubts on whether multinational corporations would be willing to suspend their operations in the PRC, as they did in Russia, due to their heavy exposure in the Chinese market and pressure from investors.

The key, therefore, is to ensure unity within major economies, such as the G7 and the EU, with the stated intent to deliver on the threat of economic sanctions should China go to war against Taiwan. Much of this requires leadership as well as efforts to reduce Beijing's ability to use economic blackmail to divide alliances. There is no guarantee of success, and there are many examples of major economies, such as Germany, breaking rank with the EU and the U.S. on decoupling from China.

Given the uncertainty over the effectiveness of threatened economic sanctions against China as a deterrent against an attack on Taiwan, other measures need to be considered – and some of them could be more threatening to Chinese decision makers. Chief among them would be the imposition of severe trade restrictions on the high technologies the PRC relies upon to modernize and fuel its economy. Through this, G7 countries, all leaders in the high-tech sector, could embargo China and deny it access to advanced technologies such as advanced semiconductors, precision machinery, advanced optical lenses, and several other areas. Such measures, added to restrictions on scientific exchanges and enrollment by Chinese students in Western universities, could threaten to cripple China's modernization efforts and retard its ability to become a world leader in R&D and the manufacturing of advanced technology.

Engagement of Taiwan by the International Community

Much of China's narrative concerning Taiwan is predicated on the claim that the Taiwan issue is an "internal matter" for the Chinese on both sides of the Taiwan Strait to resolve among themselves. Consequently, Beijing apprehends any development that makes Taiwan an issue of international concern. This goes well beyond the number of official diplomatic allies Taiwan has. Although Beijing has successfully poached a number of Taiwan's official diplomatic allies (now down to twelve) and continues to block Taipei's ability to have representation or meaningful participation at U.N. specialized agencies, Taiwan continues to expand its international presence through creative engagement, even if much of it occurs at the unofficial level. The logic behind Taipei's strategy is simple: the more Taiwan engages with the international community, the greater the impact of Chinese annexation would be on global partners.

It was with this strategy in mind that the Tsai administration revamped old laws to make it easier for international NGOs to register and set up regional offices in Taiwan. Taipei's efforts were also inadvertently assisted by the Chinese leadership, whose crackdown on civil society, censorship of the press, and growing paranoia over foreign organizations resulted in an exodus of NGOs and journalists from China and, after the crackdown there, Hong Kong. Many of them resettled in Taiwan, where they received assistance from the Ministry of Foreign Affairs and other agencies. Plans were for temporary escape to Taiwan, but as the situation continued to deteriorate in China and Hong Kong, in many instances the temporary measures became more permanent.

Taiwan's strategy bore fruit: in recent years, a constellation of international NGOs, including Reporters Without Borders (RSF), Freedom House, the International Republican Institute (IRI), National Democratic Institute (NDI), Friedrich Neumann Foundation, European Values, among several others, have opened regional offices in Taiwan. During the same period, several dozens of foreign correspondents, formerly based in China, made Taiwan their base. As a result, Taiwan as a frontline state began to receive much more extensive and positive coverage in international media, with reporting on China increasingly coming from the outside – a complete reversal of the situation just a few years ago.

Taiwan's enhanced visibility abroad created a positive feedback loop, with more tourists, curious to learn more about this hitherto neglected nation, making Taiwan their destination. And as more NGOs, news bureaus, organizations, and firms set up or expanded their footprint in Taiwan, it followed that more employees and their families made Taiwan – modern, safe, highly convenient – their home. Major international firms have also expanded their presence in Taiwan, setting up research centers and bringing thousands of workers (and their families) from abroad. The result of this rediscovery of Taiwan, made possible by the policies of the Tsai administration and the CCP's self-defeating alienation of the international community, is that more people today have a stake – personal, financial, or professional – in Taiwan than, arguably, ever before.

With incentives and public diplomacy that continues to reassure international partners that Taiwan is a safe place to live and invest, such momentum can be maintained. Foreign representative offices and embassies have also reflected that trend. With a greater presence by foreign nationals and foreign interests in Taiwan, diplomatic missions have had to expand their staff. The more international Taiwan becomes, the more difficult it will be for Beijing to argue that Taiwan is an internal matter, and the greater the costs to the international community would be if China decided to attack. Thus, the internationalization of Taiwan makes a substantial contribution to deterrence by nonmilitary means. Foreign governments would therefore be advised to regard investment in Taiwan, including trade agreements, as a form of investment in deterrence.

Facing a low birthrate and an aging society, Taiwan must also continue to liberalize its immigration policies so that more people can obtain permanent residency or citizenship. Through the addition of tens, or hundreds of thousands of new citizens who, though born elsewhere have chosen to make Taiwan their home, Taipei can not only address its demographic challenge but also counter the narrative that Taiwan is a purely *Chinese* matter. A multinational, multicultural society can help debunk Beijing's claim that it represents "Chinese compatriots," as hundreds of thousands of Taiwan's residents and citizens would not be of Han (ethnic Chinese) stock. Also, Chinese military action against Taiwan would inevitably cause casualties among non-Han residents and citizens, thus drawing in families and, perforce, governments abroad. According to the Ministry of Education, in 2016 approximately 140,000 children in Taiwanese schools had at least one parent who was from Southeast Asia, representing about 5 percent of the total. In 2020, eight out of every 100 children born in Taiwan were of mixed heritage.[43]

The CCP's fixation on blood is its own weakness, as this narrative cannot be reconciled with multiethnic societies. Taipei

and its partners within the international community should
therefore exploit that foible in China's narrative by urgently
making the necessary adjustment to facilitate immigration to,
and permanent resettlement in, Taiwan.

7

Taiwan and the Battle for Democracy's Future

In fall of 2021, NATO held a closed-door meeting with a committee of experts on the sidelines of the Halifax International Security Forum in Halifax, Canada. The meeting was part of a series of engagements as the organization was crafting its latest Strategic Concept, which would be adopted by heads of state and government at the NATO Summit in Madrid, Spain, on June 29, 2022. As one of the academics invited to give remarks at the meeting, it soon became evident that NATO was in the process of redefining its remit, and that the chief reason for this strategic rethink was China. In fact, at some point during the meeting, a German representative cut in and lamented that, until that point, the entire discussion had focused on China. Could we, she implored, start talking about Russia, which back then was already showing signs of preparation for its invasion of Ukraine the following February.

The intervention was telling: an organization that, since the end of World War II, had focused entirely on the threat from the Soviet Union and then Russia, then the Balkans in the 1990s and an out-of-area contingency in Afghanistan, was now trying to conceptualize what role it should play in Western efforts to counter China. As the final document shows, NATO has not completely abandoned its role as the principal guarantor of security in Europe. However, the reality of malign PRC influence is now recognized as a major security issue for NATO and Europe. And while it is unlikely that NATO would involve itself militarily in a Taiwan Strait or Indo-Pacific contingency, there is nevertheless a willingness on the part of its members to identify and counter the corrosive effects of Chinese interference within the transatlantic alliance. The Strategic Concept states that: China's "stated ambitions and coercive policies challenge our interests, security and values. The PRC employs a broad range of political, economic and military tools to increase its global footprint and project power, while remaining opaque about its strategy, intentions and military build-up." China's "malicious hybrid and cyber operations," it continues, added to "confrontational rhetoric and disinformation target Allies and harm Alliance security."

China, it adds,

> seeks to control key technological and industrial sectors, critical infrastructure, and strategic materials and supply chains. It uses its economic leverage to create strategic dependencies and enhance its influence. It strives to subvert the rules-based international order, including in the space, cyber and maritime domains. The deepening strategic partnership between the People's Republic of China and the Russian Federation and their mutually reinforcing attempts to undercut the rules-based international order run counter to our values and interests.[1]

The final sentence in this paragraph, which notes the growing strategic partnership between Russia and China, is key. The repercussions of the "no limits" partnership that has developed between the two countries in recent years, underscored by Beijing's economic, political, and military support of Russia's invasion of Ukraine, are only starting to be fully comprehended.

From an alliance of convenience in the past, the two countries have become the two main pillars of a nexus of authoritarian countries that are dedicated to overturning the Western-led liberal-democratic order.

As Eugene Rumer of the Carnegie Endowment for International Peace argues, the relationship between Russia and China rests on four pillars: "A common adversary – the United States; Complementary geopolitical priorities – Europe for Russia, Asia-Pacific for China – that reinforce each other in competition with the United States; Authoritarian domestic politics; and Complementary economic strengths – Russia's natural resources and China's manufacturing power."[2]

Moscow and Beijing have made historical grievances a major component of their narratives and justification for their expansionist policies. Under this narrative, the current global order is unjust, hewing to Western ideologies and principles that, they argue, are no longer suitable to address the challenges of the twenty-first century. Much of this narrative resonates with the "Global South," where a long history of exploitation by Western powers serves to reinforce the supposed legitimacy of the ideology that seeks to displace them.

In a report on authoritarian narratives, the National Endowment for Democracy writes that "Over the past decade and a half, autocracies like Russia and China have led the effort to disseminate authoritarian narratives globally, becoming more explicit in their efforts to normalize authoritarianism as an equally viable and legitimate form of government." It continues:

> While employing different tactics, the regimes in both Beijing and Moscow promote authoritarian narratives as a vital tool to amplify their influence, project the inevitability of their desired outcomes, and reshape the international landscape in ways that disadvantage democracy ... Rather than selling authoritarianism as such, authoritarian narratives focus on themes that

have popular appeal – while attributing a wide range of visceral grievances to the shortcomings of democracy.[3]

At the center of this narrative is a belief that the U.S., their ideological nemesis, is a fading power, inclined toward retrenchment, distracted, overstretched, and that therefore the time has arrived for a reconfiguration of the world order that reflects a new, multipolar order (Moscow might nevertheless resent its secondary role in what Beijing regards as a bipolar order shared between itself and the U.S.). Both countries seek to expel the U.S. and, in Russia's case, NATO, from what they consider to be their rightful spheres of influence. Russia seeks to resurrect the territorial expanse of the Soviet Union, while the PRC wants to secure its control over the Taiwan Strait and the East and South China Seas. And both countries have shown their willingness to resort to military coercion and force to change the status quo.

Amid this resurgence, other authoritarian states whose leadership has been clashing with the current world order have perceived a strategic opportunity in a seeming moment of weakness within the democratic camp. They have therefore decided to bandwagon with Russia and China, if only to secure their own, more local, interests. As a result, the world is increasingly consolidating into ideological camps, pitting the democratic order against authoritarian revisionists. The author Anne Applebaum notes that the world today is not a replay of the binary Cold War – it is not Cold War 2.0. Rather, "Among autocrats are people who call themselves communists, monarchists, nationalists, and theocrats. Their regimes have different historical roots, different goals, different aesthetics."[4] David Sanger refers to "the contours of the new cold wars" – note the plural form: "a combustible mix of simultaneous, high-stakes conflicts nestled inside each other."[5]

Through arms sales, economic assistance, political coordination, and votes at the U.N., this axis of authoritarianism finds strength in numbers and is redoubling its efforts. It does so through demonstrations of power and political warfare against institutions in the democratic camp to accelerate what they regard as an inevitable decline.[6] Divisions within the democratic camp caused by the two Trump administrations' seeming disregard for traditional alliances, added to the financial crisis and the lingering effects of the Covid-19 pandemic, have compounded the perception that the U.S.-led order has lost its footing, no longer has strategic vision, and that with a single push the entire edifice would collapse.

In this context, the importance of Taiwan cannot be overstated. Much more than a simple "internal" dispute between people on both sides of the Taiwan Strait, China's ambition to annex Taiwan is one of the major parts of this authoritarian resurgence and territorial expansionism. For reasons geographical and ideological, Taiwan is a frontline state in the PRC's outward push to expand its physical and political influence in the Indo-Pacific and beyond, just as Ukraine stands in the way of similar ambitions in Putin's Moscow. The conflicts in Europe and Asia are therefore connected, with Moscow and Beijing "tag-teaming" to weaken resistance in those two theaters.

A successful annexation of Ukraine by Russia would deeply expose Europe and open the door for the further erosion of freedom within parts of the former Soviet Union. Authoritarians would be emboldened and be on the march, concluding that force is once again a means by which to achieve political objectives. The defeat of Ukraine would increase the risk that Beijing would reach similar conclusions and conclude that it, too, could get away with resorting to force to accomplish its interests. Other countries, such as Iran, Syria, Serbia, North Korea, Venezuela, and Belarus, among others, could arrive at similar conclusions and, with backing from Moscow and Beijing, also decide to adopt more drastic measures within their own, though more limited, spheres of influence.

The extinction of Ukraine and Taiwan as free, democratic nations and their absorption by their autocratic neighbors would also strike a severe blow to the democratic camp, depriving it of two partners with substantial experience in defending democratic systems against the depredations of giant authoritarian neighbors. Morally and psychologically, such outcomes would exacerbate the impotence of the democratic world order against concerted efforts to rewrite the map and rules of the game. Ultimately, it would signal that the authoritarian camp is willing to sacrifice blood and capital to achieve its objectives, while the democratic camp lacks the willpower and unity to act upon its stated ideals. Such an outcome would have catastrophic repercussions for international security. China, Russia, and the authoritarian camp would sense weakness; the assault would not end with Taiwan and Ukraine. In fact, those would only be the first shots in a concerted assault on the world as we know it.

At this point, the exact level of coordination within the autocratic camp remains unknown. Although Russia and China have professed a "no limits" strategic partnership, the degree of coordination that is occurring between the two principal members of this axis and other autocratic powers is not fully understood. Political and material support by Moscow and Beijing to smaller partners in this alliance is uneven, and in some instances ad hoc and opportunistic. For decades Beijing has provided economic, political, and military cover to the Kim regimes in Pyongyang, and more recently there have been signs that China has been deepening its relationship with Iran as well as countries in Central Asia, where it has slowly been displacing Russia as regional hegemon. Similarly, Russian collaboration with Belarus has increased, as became clear during the months preceding its invasion of Ukraine, and Moscow has maintained a good relationship with Serbia and Cuba, with evidence of more solid engagement with Venezuela.

Signs that closer strategic coordination is occurring between China, Russia, and other members of the revisionist camp would be worrying, especially if a more consolidated authoritarian camp resulted in a deepening of military support by Beijing and Moscow for those countries. Such a development would suggest that members of the authoritarian axis may be envisioning a "tag-teaming" strategy whereby a handful of states could simultaneously spark major contingencies in their respective theaters and in so doing overstretch the U.S. military. During the Obama administration, the U.S. Department of Defense already concluded that it no longer had the capabilities to involve itself in two major simultaneous military contingencies. Recent wars in Ukraine and the Middle East (Israel–Hamas, Israel–Hezbollah) have already forced the U.S. military to redeploy forces from the Indo-Pacific theater to the Middle East, meaning that as long as conflict in other theaters continues, the U.S. military will be in a weakened position vis-à-vis its adversaries in that theater.

Imagine, then, a scenario where Russia, locked in a protracted war of attrition in Europe, coordinates with Belarus and Serbia to open new fronts in the Baltics and Balkans; at the same time, Iran and Syria (along with their militant proxies) open a new front against Israel or other U.S. allies in the Middle East; Venezuela moves to invade Guyana; the Taliban regime, courted by Beijing since the U.S. withdrawal, resumes its hosting of international terrorist organizations like al Qaeda; rebels in Somalia and Yemen intensify their destabilizing activities in their respective regions; and nuclear North Korea ramps up its missile tests and intensifies its threatening behavior against the South and Japan.

Iran, in particular, has the greatest potential to spark a major conflagration in the Middle East and thereby open a third front to challenge U.S. military primacy.[7] In his book *Wars of Ambition*, Afshon Ostovar notes that "Moscow and Beijing treat Iran not as an ally, but as a point of leverage in regional relations and a tool directed against the West."[8] Although, as he argues, Iran "is as used as it is useful" in this triangular relationship, Tehran probably could not be ordered by Beijing or Moscow to launch a war against Israel. However, if the Iranian regime engaged in a war of its own choosing, both Beijing and Moscow would likely provide political and military support, if only to ensure that the conflict remains protracted and compels the U.S. to shift substantial parts of its military assets to the region – and away from the Indo-Pacific. (For political and religious reasons, it is highly unlikely that Washington will ever abandon Israel to its fate in a war against Iran and its proxies in the region, even when doing so undermines American interests elsewhere.)[9]

At current (and projected) force levels, the U.S. military would not have the necessary resources to deal successfully with all of the above contingencies should they occur simultaneously. The U.S. would therefore be forced to make extremely difficult choices: it could either attempt to involve itself in all those contingencies, which would threaten overstretch and offer only limited chances of successfully handling the conflicts. Or it would be compelled to prioritize – in other words, to abandon some allies to their fate while concentrating its forces on one or two priority contingencies. In either scenario, the U.S.'s reputation would be dealt a severe blow, as it would be regarded as no longer capable of fulfilling its security commitments.

Whether the U.S. tries to resolve all conflicts or stays out of some of them, the outcome would be the same: in some theaters, the authoritarian axis would succeed and further dismember the democratic camp. A weakened U.S., or one that is perceived to be weaker, would create a dangerous situation in which the leadership in Beijing may conclude that an unprecedented window of opportunity has opened for it to resolve the Taiwan issue once and for all. In other words, perceptions of U.S. weakness resulting from overstretch or a series of defeats would markedly reduce the deterrent effect the U.S. military has had in the Taiwan Strait.

This nightmarish scenario tells us that we should not underestimate the will among members of the autocratic camp to join forces in ways that would distract, overstretch, and weaken the ability of the U.S. to uphold security and stability in its various theaters of operation. It also serves as a reminder that, with finite capabilities, budgetary challenges, isolationist tendencies, and in a world that is increasingly bi- or multipolar, the U.S. can no longer go it alone.

It is therefore essential that security partners of the U.S., such as NATO or countries like Japan, South Korea, and Australia, among others, do more burden-sharing. For this to become possible, those countries will need to invest more in their militaries, adopt new defense postures that are more forward-looking, less risk-averse, and based on a commitment to create more permanent and coherent regional security alliances.

For its part, NATO would be well advised to concentrate its military commitments in Europe – what Rynning refers to as "NATO classic" – rather than expand into other theaters, including the Indo-Pacific, however tempting such a move may be to some. Instead, the alliance should aim to create a force that is capable of defending Europe against aggression so that the U.S. military can concentrate on the Indo-Pacific. This would by no means signify that the U.S. has abandoned Europe, as the U.S. would continue to be *primus inter pares* within the organization. However, it would constitute a realistic assessment of the geopolitical environment and the kind of burden-sharing that is essential for the democratic camp's ability to counter the threats that will soon emanate from different directions. If China and Russia can "tag-team," so can the West. This does not mean that NATO has no role to play in the Indo-Pacific. Rather, it would force the alliance to do what it does best in the context of the wider world – in other words, in the ideological battle between the two camps. As Rynning writes, "Taiwan's independence – which China has threatened to end – is thus not a freak issue that allies can choose to ignore."[10]

Burden-sharing would risk sparking new arms races in different regions, and in Japan's case this could force a reassessment of its pacifist constitution. None of this is ideal, and the resulting tensions would make our world a potentially more dangerous place. Be that as it may, the aim of strengthened security alliances and key partners like Japan assuming a more prominent role in ensuring stability and security in their respective regions should always be one of deterrence, under the logic that capabilities and coordination within the democratic camp would reduce the likelihood that the authoritarian side will resort to force to change the status quo. There is no guarantee of success, as deterrence works best when the object of deterrence acts rationally, has access to all the information it needs to make decisions of war and peace, and is vulnerable to electoral retribution following bad decisions. All those factors are largely lacking in autocracies.

Such a reorganization and task allocations would therefore be a gamble, with the aim of avoiding conflict but having sufficient capabilities to respond should deterrence fail. The other option – ceding ground to the authoritarians – would be a disastrous one. It would ensure that revisionist powers would be free to act as they see fit against their weaker opponents. This would be an anarchic world order, one where might is right.

Conclusion

As this book has sought to demonstrate, the conflict over Taiwan's status and how it will be resolved should be a matter of concern for the entire international community. The fate of the island-nation's 23.5 million people will have direct repercussions for the future of democracy, the global economy, the future of technology,[11] and the ambitions of authoritarian regimes to create a world that is more hospitable to their anti-democratic outlook. Thus, contrary to what former Australian Prime Minister Paul Keating said during an interview with ABC News in August 2024,[12] Taiwan is not just "Chinese real estate," nor should Australia, as he counseled, avoid involvement in a conflict between China and Taiwan due to the fact that Taiwan is not a vital interest of Australia.

And yet, Keating is right, just not in the way he intended to be. For all their talk about "Taiwanese compatriots" being part of one big Chinese family, the well-being of the people of Taiwan is not a top priority for Xi and the CCP. For them, Taiwan is a piece of real estate that stands in the way of their greater geopolitical ambitions. And above all, Xi hungers for his historical legacy, the kind of project that usually does not bode well for the people who entertain such illusions of grandeur. Thus, regardless of what form it takes – "peaceful reunification" or annexation by force – we can be certain that this would entail the extinction of one of the most vibrant and essential democracies in Asia.

Such an outcome would strike a powerful blow against other democracies and civil societies in nations across the region that are striving for democracy in their countries (many such groups have benefited from Taiwan's example and support by Taiwanese institutions). It would also puncture the democratic camp's reputation by demonstrating that it does not have the moral fiber, will, and capacity to defend its own values. Like wolves, the authoritarians would smell weakness and thirst for more. *Pace* Keating and the many others who have argued that Taiwan is not their fight, a world in which Taiwan has fallen would be a world that has become more dangerous for all. It is far wiser, therefore, to hold the line. And to be successful, Taiwan needs to pull its weight and it needs all the help it can get from the international community.

Part of the solution lies in renewed attempts to revitalize democracy, its institutions, and the narratives that underpin belief in and support for democracy as the two incompatible systems battle each other to define the twenty-first century. Long, unsuccessful campaigns in Afghanistan and Iraq, slowing Western economies, political polarization, poor leadership, Brexit, Trump, rampant disinformation and the appeal of "soft-authoritarianism" and a pushback against liberalism have all contributed to perceptions that democracy has run out of steam and may no longer be suitable to address today's challenges. This moral deflation has in turn opened the door for regimes such as the CCP to argue that their mercantilist-authoritarian model is the solution, that it is more effective and delivers results more quickly.

The appeal of such a narrative should not come entirely as a surprise. After all, we have allowed our democracies to atrophy through a series of poor decisions, apathy, and the very feeling of inevitable decline that Beijing has amplified through its narrative. We must awaken from our stupor and find a new commitment to reviving and perfecting our democracies and institutions of governance. And this must be done in concert, as part of a countervailing strategy against the coalition of authoritarians. "This is not a short-term battle for access or influence," the National Endowment for Democracy's Joseph Siegle writes. "Rather, it is about sustaining a global coalition of governments and societies committed to popular participation, freedom of expression, freedom of thought and belief, and the rule of law."[13]

This is a battle in which Taiwan can play a central role. Not only in the reductive, utilitarian form that has been proposed over the years – as an example of a "Chinese democracy" that could encourage change in the PRC. Although there is value to this argument, Taiwan deserves better than to be treated as a means to an end. It has inherent value as a distinct society, a prime example of democratization without bloodshed, and as its handling of the Covid-19 pandemic demonstrated, it disproves the lie that only autocratic regimes can properly handle major emergencies like pandemics and continue to prosper economically in the process. Taiwan is the living proof that democracies can be trusted with surveillance technology, can ensure the safety of their people, and can achieve economic growth even in times of global pandemic. Furthermore, it did that under the constant threat of Chinese aggression.

Taiwan provides the kind of counter-narrative that is needed to push back against authoritarian revisionism. And we should return the favor to the authoritarians by using narratives that expose the deficiencies and shortcomings of autocracy. Technology can play an important role in this. However, before we can do any of this, we need to shed the defeatism and sense of inevitability that has gripped our minds for far too long. China is not a 1,000-pound gorilla; it is not all-powerful, all-seeing, and unstoppable. This is another lesson that Taiwan, through its defiant survival, can teach the international community, as other revisionist regimes accumulate power and challenge the existing order.

Rather than an unstoppable adversary, the party-state in China is beset with high controls and rigidity that undermine the free-thinking that sparks technological and ideational innovation; the regime is paranoid: it does not trust and in fact fears its people, which weakens the bonds between citizens and their government. The CCP, particularly under Xi, has become rigidly ideological, with "Xi Jinping Thought" on everything personalizing governance in almost caricatural ways. This, in turn, has alarmed critics within the Party who already resented Xi's decision to dispense with tradition by making himself emperor for life. Under such conditions, the leadership is feared, it is not loved, meaning that at the first sign of weakness, Xi's opponents could decide to get rid of him. All this fosters instability, which never ceases to exist under the patina of party-state self-confidence.

The rigidity of autocratic regimes is a strength as long as those regimes have the ability to control the environment, but the lack of elasticity and creativity that characterizes authoritarianism can also be a regime's greatest weakness. Autocratic regimes operating under leaders like Xi believe themselves to be the epitome of governance and are therefore far less adaptive than iterations of the CCP that existed before Xi. In this, democracies have a net advantage: though messy and eternally subject to electoral cycles, democracy is animated by a striving for perfection – one that can never be achieved, but that nevertheless fuels imagination and constant improvement.

It would be difficult to imagine a country where such aspirations run stronger in a people's bloodstream than in Taiwan. It is far from perfect: it is divided, at times unsure of itself, and never in complete agreement on its identity. Yet, Taiwan is a precious example of a world that can be, that can thrive under the shadow of military coercion and threatened war. In a time when revisionist authoritarian regimes are becoming increasingly self-assured and assertive, where despots have no compunction in massacring tens of thousands of people to fulfill their megalomaniac aspirations, the world needs the example of the people of Taiwan. Its history through the years – from colonial times through decades of Martial Law rule followed by democratization – is a prime example of resilience, persistence, creativity, and a refusal to give up even when the rest of the world regarded it as an inconvenience, as many did until recently and some still do to this day.

Notes

Preface

1 The PLA launched major military drills around Taiwan on both the week that I began drafting this manuscript, in late May 2024, and again in October 2024 as I was putting the finishing touches to the draft.

Introduction

1 This section is intended as a very brief primer on the intermingled histories of Taiwan and China, while the remainder of this book focuses primarily on the recent phase of the conflict. Readers who are already familiar with Taiwan's contemporary history can skip over this section. Those who seek a thorough history of Taiwan in English language, however, are encouraged to read recent publications such as Sulmaan Wasif Khan's *The Struggle for Taiwan: A History of America, China, and the Island Caught Between*, Jonathan Clements' *Rebel Island: The Incredible History of Taiwan*, Jonathan Manthorpe's *Forbidden Nation: A History of Taiwan*, and Nancy Bernkopf Tucker's *Dangerous Strait: The U.S.-Taiwan-China Crisis* as good places to start. All four books have helped inform this section.

2 Paine, S.C.M. *The Sino-Japanese War of 1894–1895* (New York: Cambridge University Press, 2003), pp. 271–277.

3 Cohen, Warren I. *America's Response to China: A History of Sino-American Relations* (New York: Columbia University Press, 2010), pp. 186–187.

4 My father-in-law did his military service as a physician on Dongyin, one of the islets that comprise the Matsu chain. He was not deployed there during the crisis in 1958, however.

5 Glaser, Bonnie S. and Jessica Drun. "The Distortion of UN Resolution 2758 and Limits on Taiwan's Access to the United Nations," German Marshall Fund, March 24, 2022.

6 Upon establishing official diplomatic relations with the PRC, countries usually adopted language in which they "took note of" or "acknowledged" Beijing's claims over Taiwan. Later, Beijing would strive to negate this rhetorical subtlety by maintaining that countries adhere to the "one China" principle, which states that Taiwan is part of China and that there is only one China – the PRC. In Beijing's view, the defeat of Chiang's Nationalist forces in 1949 meant that the PRC was a successor state to the ROC.

7 Located on what is now Freedom Lane, the office has been turned into a human rights museum. In a twist of irony, the lead police officer at the site when Cheng set his office ablaze was Hou You-yih, who would be the KMT's presidential candidate in the 2024 elections. Asked in 2023 for his views on the incident, Hou said he would do it all over again, remarks that understandably were not well received by civil society and DPP supporters.

8 Jacobs, J. Bruce. *Democratizing Taiwan* (Leiden: Brill, 2012), pp. 74–83.

9 Tucker, Nancy Bernkopf. *Strait Talk: United States–Taiwan Relations and the Crisis with China* (Cambridge: Harvard University Press, 2009), pp. 213–224.

10 Phillips, Steven. "Building a Taiwanese Republic: The Independence Movement, 1945–Present." *Dangerous Strait: The U.S.-Taiwan-China Crisis*, Nancy Berknopf Tucker, ed. (New York: Columbia University Press, 2005), pp. 65–66. In Lee's view,

the ROC (Taiwan) did not need to declare independence, as the ROC had been an independent state since 1912. Lee came to be regarded as the spiritual leader of the Taiwan independence movement.

11 Bush, Richard C. *Untying the Knot: Making Peace in the Taiwan Strait* (Washington, D.C.: Brookings Institution Press, 2005), pp. 214–16.

12 Bush, 155–198.

13 Author interview with former U.S. Deputy Secretary of Defense Paul Wolfowitz, October 2011.

14 Tsao, Nadia. "US official denies Bush called Chen a 'troublemaker,'" *Taipei Times*, October 24, 2003. However, Bush did single out Chen, saying, "comments and actions made by the leader of Taiwan indicate that he may be willing to make decisions unilaterally, to change the status quo, which we oppose." See Brian Knowlton, *International Herald Tribune*, December 10, 2003.

15 I use "people of Taiwan" and "Taiwanese" interchangeably throughout this book. No disrespect is intended toward the people in Taiwan who identify themselves as "Chinese" or "ethnically Chinese" and citizens of the Republic of China.

Chapter 1: The Unbridgeable Divide

1 Khan, Sulmaan Wasif. *The Struggle for Taiwan: A History of America, China, and the Island Caught Between* (London: Allen Lane, 2024), p. 179.

2 Ko, Shu-ling. "ARATS chief Chen arrives to protests," *Taipei Times*, December 22, 2009.

3 *Taiwan's Social Movements Under Ma Ying-jeou: From the Wild Strawberries to the Sunflowers*, Dafydd Fell, ed. (London: Routledge, 2017).

4 Hornby, Lucy. "Taiwan and China sign trade pact," Reuters, June 29, 2010.

5 For a useful discussion on this subject, see Scott L. Kastner, *Political Conflict and Economic Interdependence Across the*

Taiwan Strait and Beyond (Stanford: Stanford University Press, 2009).

6 President Ma meets participants attending International Conference on Asia-Pacific in Transition, Mainland Affairs Office. https://www.mac.gov.tw/en/News_Content.aspx?n=FE0 7F9DA122E29D4&sms=3A4E63FA5107487D&s=CF95F21DEA FEE794.

7 Presidents since 1947: Ma Ying-jeou (12th–13th terms), Presidential Office. https://english.president.gov.tw/Page/88.

8 Stand, James. "Taiwan's Media Uproar: A New Generation Comes of Age," Council on Foreign Relations, December 18, 2012.

9 See Fell, *Taiwan's Social Movements Under Ma Ying-jeou: From the Wild Strawberries to the Sunflowers*, and J. Michael Cole, *Convergence or Conflict in the Taiwan Strait: The Illusion of Peace?* (London: Routledge, 2017), pp. 104–125.

10 Schumpeter, Joseph. *Capitalism, Socialism, and Democracy* (New York: Harper, 1947).

11 Schell, Jonathan. *The Unconquerable World: Power, Nonviolence, and the Will of the People* (New York: Henry Holt, 2003).

12 Wang, Chris. "Protesters occupy government building," *Taipei Times*, August 20, 2013.

13 Ho, Ming-sho. *Challenging Beijing's Mandate of Heaven: Taiwan's Sunflower Movement and Hong Kong's Umbrella Movement* (Philadelphia: Temple University Press, 2019).

14 Cole, J. Michael. "On the role of organized crime and other substate actors in Chinese political warfare against Taiwan." Ministry of Justice Investigation Bureau: *Prospect & Exploration*, vol. 18, No. 6, pp. 55–88.

15 Garnaut, John. "China's rulers team up with notorious 'White Wolf' of Taiwan," *Sydney Morning Herald*, July 11, 2014.

16 "Taiwan students storm education ministry in textbook protest," BBC, July 31, 2015.

17 "Taiwan's KMT party ditches Hung Hsiu-chu as candidate," BBC, October 17, 2015.

18 "Opening remarks by President Ma Ying-jeou at his meeting with mainland Chinese leader Xi Jinping in Singapore." Mainland Affairs Council. https://www.mac.gov.tw/en/News_Content.as px?n=FE07F9DA122E29D4&sms=3A4E63FA5107487D&s=63B 15546262C861C.

19 Recommended readings on the demise of Hong Kong include Michael Sheridan, *The Gate to China: A New History of the People's Republic & Hong Kong* (London: William Collins, 2021), Richard W. Bush, *Hong Kong in the Shadow of China: Living With the Leviathan* (Washington, D.C.: Brookings Institution Press, 2016), and Shibani Mahtani and Timothy McLaughlin, *Among the Braves: Hope, Struggle, and Exile in the Battle for Hong Kong and the Future of Global Democracy* (New York: Hachette, 2023).

20 "How Taiwan became a linchpin in the fight against Covid-19," BBC, https://www.bbc.com/storyworks/future/taiwan-the-worlds-tech-partner/how-taiwan-became-a-linchpin-in-the-fight-against-covid-19.

Chapter 2: Xi's Unbridled Ambitions

1 Fukuyama, Francis. *Identity: The Demand for Dignity and the Politics of Resentment* (New York: Farrar, Straus and Giroux), p. xiv.

2 Khan, Sulmaan Wasif. *Haunted by Chaos: China's Grand Strategy from Mao Zedong to Xi Jinping* (Cambridge: Harvard University Press, 2018), p. 208.

3 Minzner, Carl. *End of an Era: How China's Revival is Undermining Its Rise* (New York: Oxford University Press, 2018), p. 59.

4 Cai, Xia. "The Weakness of Xi Jinping," *Foreign Affairs*, September/October 2022, p. 86.

5 Chan, Alfred L. *Xi Jinping: Political Career, Governance, and Leadership, 1953–2018* (New York: Oxford University Press, 2022), pp. 58–99.

6 Lam, Willy Wo-lap. *Chinese Politics in the Era of Xi Jinping: Renaissance, Reform, or Retrogression?* (New York: Routledge, 2015), p. 44.

7 Wong, Chun Han. *Party of One: The Rise of Xi Jinping and China's Superpower Future* (New York: Avid Reader Press, 2023), p. 162.

8 "Highlights of Xi's speech at gathering marking 40th anniversary of Message to Compatriots in Taiwan," Xinhua News Agency, January 2, 2019.

9 The main factors in the local elections for municipal heads, borough chiefs and others typically focused on that which affects the daily lives of ordinary citizens, and had little to do with the more elevated affairs of foreign policy and cross-Strait relations. Nevertheless, there is reason to believe that KMT voters used the local elections to punish the Tsai administration for pushing the highly necessary albeit controversial pension reform for retired civil servants, teachers, and the military.

10 Bush, Richard C. "What Xi Jinping said about Taiwan at the 19th Party Congress," Brookings Institution, October 19, 2017.

11 "Highlights of Xi's speech at gathering marking 40th anniversary of Message to Compatriots in Taiwan," Xinhua News Agency, January 2, 2019.

12 Hille, Kathrin. "China's Communist party toughens Taiwan rhetoric with call to 'fight' independence," *Financial Times*, February 23, 2024.

13 "China toughens language, warns Taiwan that independence 'means war,'" *Economic Times*, January 28, 2021.

14 Cole, J. Michael. "China Ends 'Median Line' in the Taiwan Strait: The Start of a Crisis?" *National Interest*, September 22, 2020.

15 Not to be confused with Taiwan's airspace, a frequent mistake by media covering rising tensions in the Taiwan Strait.

16 "Opinions on Punishing Crimes of Separatism and Inciting Separatism by 'Taiwan independence' Die-hards in Accordance with Law," China Law Translate. https://www.chinalawtranslate.com/en/taiwan-independence/.

17 Chen, Jody. "Chinese Government Expands Criminalization of Taiwanese Identity," Human Rights Watch, July 4, 2024.
18 Wong, p. 16.
19 Doshi, Rush. *The Long Game: China's Grand Strategy to Displace American Order* (New York: Oxford University Press, 2021), p. 35.
20 Shirk, Susan L. *Overreach: How China Derailed Its Peaceful Rise* (New York: Oxford University Press, 2023), p. 31.
21 Shirk defines China's "core interests" as "an interest so crucial to the fate of the nation that it would use military force to defend it." *Overreach*, p. 131.
22 China had a score of 9/100, with −2/40 on political rights and 11/60 on civil liberties, according to Freedom House's 2024 ranking, while Taiwan had an overall score of 94/100, with 38/40 on political rights and 56/60 on civil liberties.
23 Heath, Allister. "Xi Jinping is rapidly running out of time – and he knows it," *Telegraph*, May 10, 2023.
24 Yiu, Pak, Grace Li, and Mitsuru Obe. "China's aging population threatens a Japan-style lost decade," *Nikkei Asia*, March 22, 2023.
25 Bicker, Laura. "China's ageing population: A demographic crisis is unfolding for Xi," BBC, April 3, 2024.
26 Yiu, Pak. "China to see biggest millionaire exodus in 2024 as many head to U.S.," *Nikkei Asia*, June 18, 2024.
27 Steele, Evie. "IMF Predicts China Economy Slowing Over Next Four Years," Voice of America, February 2, 2024.

Chapter 3: Attacking Taiwan's Democracy

1 Cole, J. Michael. "Chinese PLA Simulates 'Attack' on Taiwan's Presidential Office," *The Diplomat*, July 22, 2015.
2 "Mainland says Tsai's speech on cross-Straits ties 'an incomplete test answer,'" *People's Daily*, May 21, 2016.
3 Hsiao, Russell. "PRC Ramps Up United Front with 31 New Measures Targeting People and Businesses," *Global Taiwan Brief*, March 21, 2018.

4 Jennings, Ralph. "Why China's Financial Incentives for Taiwanese Flatlined," *Voice of America*, March 20, 2019.

5 "TAO: Mainland Suspends Official Cross-Strait Interactions for Lack of 1992 Consensus," Official KMT website, May 23, 2016.

6 Leading Small Groups and Leading Groups bring together senior CCP officials with the aim of advising the Party Politburo on a broad range of issues (e.g., united front work, Taiwan work, foreign affairs work) and to coordinate implementation of policy decisions made by the Politburo. See Alice Miller, "The CCP Central Committee's Leading Small Groups," Hoover Institution China Leadership Monitor No. 26. https://www.hoover.org/sites/default/files/uploads/documents/CLM26AM.pdf.

7 Groot, Jerry. "The Expansion of the United Front Under Xi Jinping," Australian Centre on China in the World, 2015. https://www.thechinastory.org/yearbooks/yearbook-2015/forum-ascent/the-expansion-of-the-united-front-under-xi-jinping/.

8 Joske, Alex. "The Central United Front Work Leading Small Group Institutionalising united front work," *Sinopsis*, July 23, 2019.

9 "Select Committee Unveils CCP Influence Memo, 'United Front 101,'" Select Committee on the CCP, November 27, 2023.

10 Nakazawa, Katsuji. "Analysis: Xi puts top brain in charge of Taiwan unification strategy," *Nikkei Asia*, January 26, 2023.

11 Dang, Yuanyue and William Zheng. "China's third plenum highlights the quiet rise of political theorist Wang Huning," *South China Morning Post*, August 10, 2024.

12 Cole, J. Michael. "Veteran Chinese Official Song Tao Assumes the Taiwan Portfolio," *Global Taiwan Brief*, January 11, 2023.

13 "What Is Soft Power?" Council on Foreign Relations, May 16, 2023.

14 "Sharp Power: Rising Authoritarian Influence," National Endowment for Democracy, December 5, 2017.

15 Cole, J. Michael. "Candidate Claims 'Nobody Loves Taiwan More Than Xi Jinping,'" *Taiwan Sentinel*, October 21, 2019.

16 "Former legislative candidate indicted over ties to China," *Taipei Times*, March 3, 2024.

17 The CUPP "broke up" with the CPA in 2018 after it was discovered that the latter was accepting financial donations from the PRC.

18 Cole, "On the role," p. 74.

19 "Cognitive Warfare: Strengthening and Defending the Mind," NATO, April 5, 2023.

20 Walsh, Don. "Taiwan Strait: The Ocean's Most Contested Place," U.S. Naval Institute *Proceedings*, Vol. 149/11/1,449, November 2023.

21 See Stephen Dziedzic, "Australia backs Taiwan in Senate motion likely to infuriate China," ABC News, August 22, 2024; and Theodoros Benakis, "Netherlands House of Representatives resolution calls for Taiwan's representation in the UN," *European Interest*, September 13, 2024.

22 "Former High-Ranking New York State Government Employee Charged with Acting as an Undisclosed Agent of the People's Republic of China and the Chinese Communist Party," Department of Justice, September 3, 2024.

23 Wong, Scott and Ken Dilanian. "FBI warns some lawmakers that China aims to create fake stories about them to erode support for Taiwan," NBC News, December 17, 2024.

24 "Cuba turns away Taiwanese tourists." Radio Taiwan International, March 26, 2024.

25 "China's Hunt for Taiwanese Overseas." Safeguard Defenders, November 30, 2021.

26 Goh, Brenda and John Ruwitch. "China cracks down on foreign companies calling Taiwan, other regions countries," Reuters, January 12, 2018.

27 Other examples of Chinese disinformation targeting the U.S.'s reputation among the Taiwanese include claims that the U.S. had demanded that Taiwan build a biosafety level 4 lab to develop

biological warfare agents, and allegations that in case of war, the U.S. military would destroy Taiwan's TSMC, the world's largest manufacturer of advanced semiconductors.

28 Wen, Kuei-hsiang and Sean Lin. "Faced with China flight path moves, Taiwan to stay the course: Source," *Focus Taiwan*, April 20, 2024.

29 Hsieh, Yi-hsuan and Sunny Lai. "Chinese vessels patrol Taiwan Strait to close jurisdictional gap: Experts," *Focus Taiwan*, August 19, 2024.

30 Davidson, Helen. "Beijing condemns Taiwan after two Chinese fishers die in speedboat crash," *Guardian*, February 15, 2024.

31 "Decision of the Standing Committee of the National People's Congress on the Exercising of the Marine Right Safeguarding and Law Enforcement Functions and Powers by the China Coast Guard," PKU Law. http://www.pkulaw.cn/fulltext_form.aspx ?Db=chl&Gid=316153. Amendments to the Law of the People's Republic of China on People's Armed Police in June 2020 further consolidated the authority of the PAP and the CMC over the CCG. Article 9, Chapter 2 ("Organization and Command") of the Armed Police Law stipulates that the PAP includes the CCG. Additionally, Article 22, Paragraph 1 of the National Defense Law of the People's Republic of China and Article 9 of the Armed Police Law state that the Ministry of National Defense, the PAP, and the CCG are unified as one organization.

32 Luo, Shuxian and Jonathan G. Panter. "China's Maritime Militia and Fishing Fleets: A Primer for Operational Staffs and Tactical Leaders," *Military Review*, January–February 2021.

33 Johnstone, Christopher B. and Bonnie Lin. "Responding to a More Coercive Chinese Coast Guard and a Potential PRC Quarantine of Taiwan," Center for Strategic and International Studies, June 7, 2024.

34 Gan, Nectar and Ben Westcott. "US senators took a military aircraft to Taiwan to announce vaccine donation. To Beijing, that is a major provocation," CNN, June 7, 2021.

35 Kuo, Lily. "China's military extends drills near Taiwan after Pelosi trip," *Washington Post*, August 8, 2022.

36 Snyder, Timothy. *The Road to Unfreedom: Russia, Europe, America* (New York: Tim Duggan, 2018) p. 255.

37 Thompson, James, Liu Chien-pang, and Lin Chang-shun. "TPP leader Ko Wen-je detained incommunicado in anti-corruption case," *Focus Taiwan*, September 5, 2024.

38 Chen, Yeh and Evelyn Kao. "Court orders detention of ex-vice premier over corruption allegations," *Focus Taiwan*, July 11, 2024.

39 Chau, Thompson. "China accuses Taiwan president of 'hunting down' rivals like Ko Wen-je," *Nikkei Asia*, September 11, 2024. See also http://www.gwytb.gov.cn/m/speech/202409/t20240911_12649284.htm.

40 "CDC says doubts over Medigen vaccine's safety 'seriously wrong,'" *Focus Taiwan*, January 3, 2024.

41 Chung, Jake. "KMT files lawsuit on domestic vaccine EUA," *Taipei Times*, July 21, 2021.

42 Cook, Christine. "Vaccine Hesitancy and Misinformation/Disinformation in Taiwan," Center for Asia-Pacific Resilience and Innovation, May 2024.

43 "2024 Taiwan Election: The Increasing Polarization of Taiwanese Politics – Reinforcement of Conspiracy Narratives and Cognitive Biases," DoubleThink Lab, April 8, 2024.

44 "KMT, TPP pass controversial measures," *Taipei Times*, May 29, 2024.

45 Fan Cheng-hsiang, Lin Ching-yin, Lai Yu-chen, and Frances Huang. "Opposition cuts 2025 central government budget by NT$93.98 billion," *Focus Taiwan*, January 18, 2025.

46 "DPP criticizes Ma's proposal to amend Anti-Infiltration Act," TVBS, April 22, 2024.

Chapter 4: The Impact of Ukraine

1 "China condemns opening of Taiwan office in Lithuania as 'egregious act'," *Guardian*, November 19, 2021.

2 "Article by Vladimir Putin 'On the Historical Unity of Russians and Ukrainians,'" President of Russia official website, July 12, 2021. http://en.kremlin.ru/events/president/news/66181.

3 "U.S. intel accurately predicted Russia's invasion plans. Did it matter?" CNBC, February 25, 2022.

4 Emmott, Robin, Sabine Siebold, and Andrius Sytas. "Lithuania, EU say Belarus using refugees as 'political weapon,'" Reuters, July 13, 2021.

5 Tanaka, Miya. "Ex-U.S. Indo-Pacific commander sticks to 2027 window on Taiwan attack," Kyodo News, January 23, 2023.

6 Twenty seven countries joined the PfP, namely: Albania, Armenia, Austria, Azerbaijan, Belarus, Bulgaria, Czech Republic, Estonia, Finland, The Former Yugoslav Republic of Macedonia, Georgia, Hungary, Kazakstan, Kyrgyzstan, Latvia, Lithuania, Moldova, Poland, Romania, Russia, Slovakia, Slovenia, Sweden, Switzerland, Turkmenistan, Ukraine, and Uzbekistan. See "NATO Partnership for Peace," U.S. Department of State Archive. https://1997-2001.state.gov/regions/eur/nato_fs-pfp.html.

7 Sarotte, M. E. *Not One Inch: America, Russia, and the Making of Post-Cold War Stalemate* (New Haven: Yale University Press, 2021), p. 187.

8 "NATO-Russia relations," North Atlantic Treaty Organization Factsheet, February 2022. https://www.nato.int/nato_static_fl2014/assets/pdf/2022/2/pdf/220214-factsheet_NATO-Russia_Relations_e.pdf. The NRC met eleven times between 2016, when it reconvened following Russia's annexation of part of Ukraine, and January 12, 2022, the last meeting before Russia invaded Ukraine the following month.

9 Rynning, Sten. *NATO: From Cold War to Ukraine, a History of the World's Most Powerful Alliance* (London: Yale University Press, 2024), p. 204.

10 Zubok, Vladislav M. *Collapse: The Fall of the Soviet Union* (London: Yale University Press, 2021), p. 436.

11 Rynning, p. 174.

12 Rynning, p. 196.

13 NATO member countries. https://www.nato.int/cps/en/natohq /topics_52044.htm#coldwar2.

14 Sarotte, p. 348.

15 Rynning, p. 106.

16 Kimmage, Michael. *Collisions: The Origins of the War in Ukraine and the New Global Instability* (New York: Oxford University Press, 2024), pp. 200–201.

17 The best introduction to how the CCP has used historical grievances to fuel nationalism remains Zheng Wang's *Never Forget National Humiliation: Historical Memory in Chinese Politics and Foreign Relations* (New York: Columbia University Press, 2012).

18 See "Why is Ukraine the West's Fault?" https://www.youtube .com/watch?v=JrMiSQAGOS4.

19 "Chomsky Says US' Eastward Expansion to Blame For Putin's 'Monstrous' War in Ukraine," *Statecraft*, April 8, 2022.

20 For a useful discussion on how Russia's invasion of Ukraine has shaken strategic assumptions in Washington, Moscow, and Beijing, see John K. Culver and Sarah Kirchberger. "US-China lessons from Ukraine: Fueling more dangerous Taiwan tensions," Atlantic Council, June 15, 2023.

21 Bonenberger, Adrian. "Ukraine's Military Pulled Itself Out of the Ruins of 2014," *Foreign Policy*, May 9, 2022. See also "U.S. Security Assistance to Ukraine," Congressional Research Service, May 22, 2024.

22 In their book *Conflict: The Evolution of Warfare from 1945 to Ukraine* (New York: HarperCollins, 2023), p. 148, General David Petraeus and historian Andrew Roberts write that "Ideally, attacking forces ought to outnumber defenders by three to one and concentrate on vulnerable points."

23 Wintour, Patrick. "Russia has amassed up to 190,000 troops on Ukraine borders, US warns," *Guardian*, February 18, 2022.

24 Wuthnow, Joel. "Rightsizing Chinese Military Lessons from Ukraine," *Strategic Forum*, Institute for National Strategic Studies, September 2022.

25 Medeiros, Evan, Brian Hart, Elizabeth Wishnick, and Joseph Webster. "Chinese Assessments of the War in Ukraine, 2 Years on," Center for Strategic and International Studies *Interpret: China*, June 11, 2024.

26 Situation in Ukraine: ICC judges issue arrest warrants against Vladimir Vladimirovich Putin and Maria Alekseyevna Lvova-Belova, International Criminal Court, March 17, 2023.

27 Orr, Bernard, Guy Faulconbridge, and Andrew Osborn. "Putin and Xi pledge a new era and condemn the United States," Reuters, May 17, 2024.

28 Kardas, Szymon. "Conscious uncoupling: Europeans' Russian gas challenge in 2023," European Council on Foreign Relations, February 13, 2023. According to another study, EU imports of fossil fuels from Russia dropped from a high of US$16 billion per month in early 2022 to about US$1 billion per month by the end of 2023. See Ben McWilliams, Giovanni Sgaravatti, Simone Tagliapietra, and Georg Zachmann. "The European Union-Russia energy divorce: state of play," Bruegel, February 22, 2024.

29 Emiliozzi, Simone, Fabrizio Ferriani, and Andrea Gazzani. "The European energy crisis and the consequences for the global natural gas market," Centre for Economic Policy Research, January 11, 2024.

30 Gross, Samantha and Constanze Stelzenmüller. "Europe's messy Russian gas divorce," Brookings Institution, June 18, 2024.

31 Green, Mark A. "China Is the Top Trading Partner to More Than 120 Countries," Wilson Center, January 17, 2023.

32 "What are the sanctions on Russia and have they affected its economy?" BBC, February 23, 2024.

33 Rynning, 229.

34 Galeotti, Mark. *Putin's Wars: From Chechnya to Ukraine* (Oxford: Osprey, 2022), p. 178.

35 Freedman, Lawrence. *Ukraine and the Art of Strategy* (New York: Oxford University Press, 2019), pp. 86–87. See also Laurence Freedman, *Command: The Politics of Military Operations from*

Korea to Ukraine (New York: Oxford University Press, 2022), p. 370.

36 "Taiwan suspects Chinese ships cut islands' internet cables," Associated Press, April 18, 2023.

37 Chang, Wayne and Simone McCarthy. "A cut undersea internet cable is making Taiwan worried about 'gray zone' tactics from Beijing," CNN, January 10, 2025.

38 See James Andrew Lewis. "Cyberattack on Civilian Critical Infrastructures in a Taiwan Scenario," Center for Strategic and International Studies, August 11, 2023.

39 Liu, Kwangyin. "Blackout exposes Taiwan electrical grid's major vulnerabilities," *CommonWealth*, March 10, 2022.

40 "Taiwan arrests Chinese man who took speedboat into Taipei harbour," Reuters, June 10, 2024.

Chapter 5: The Catastrophe: War in the Taiwan Strait

1 Annual Report on the Military Power of the People's Republic of China, 2002, U.S. Department of Defense.

2 "What Does China Really Spend on its Military?" CSIS ChinaPower. https://chinapower.csis.org/military-spending/.

3 "Military and Security Developments Involving the People's Republic of China," U.S. Department of Defense Annual Report to Congress, 2023.

4 For example, the International Institute for Strategic Studies (IISS) estimates China's defense budget in 2023 was US$319 billion.

5 Teng, Pei-ju. "Taiwan's defense spending to reach NT$647 billion, 2.45% of GDP in 2025," *Focus Taiwan*, August 22, 2024.

6 Lin, Sean. "Most Taiwanese see PRC's territorial aims as 'serious threat': Survey," *Focus Taiwan*, October 9, 2024.

7 "2024 Survey Results of the 'American Portrait'. Institute of European and American Studies, Academia Sinica, July 18, 2024.

8 "2021 TFD Survey on Taiwanese View of Democratic Values and Governance." Taiwan Foundation for Democracy, December 29, 2021.

9 *Global Views Monthly.* https://www.gvm.com.tw/article/115557.

10 Rudd, Kevin. *The Avoidable War: The Dangers of a Catastrophic Conflict Between the US and Xi Jinping's China* (New York: PublicAffairs, 2022).

11 Westad, Odd Arne. "Sleepwalking Toward War," *Foreign Affairs,* July/August 2024, pp. 78–89.

12 Yen, Hope. "CIA chief: China has some doubt on ability to invade Taiwan," Associated Press, February 27, 2023.

13 Char, James. "Xi's anti-graft purge of the PLA is limited and has dubious motives," *Nikkei Asia,* August 13, 2024.

14 Amonson, Kyle and Dane Egli. "The Ambitious Dragon: Beijing's Calculus for Invading Taiwan by 2030," *Journal of Indo-Pacific Affairs,* March–April 2023.

15 Waldron, Greg. "Fighters, ASW aircraft dominate China's 2023 aerial incursions against Taiwan," *Flight Global,* January 3, 2024.

16 Lewis, Ben. "2022 in ADIZ Violations: China Dials Up the Pressure on Taiwan," Center for Strategic and International Studies, March 23, 2023.

17 Research Project on China's Defense Affairs. "The Number of PLA Navy Vessels around Taiwan." https://rcdatw.org/.

18 Lee, Yimou. "Exclusive: China spent \$15.3 billion on Pacific exercises in 2023, internal Taiwan estimates show," Reuters, August 27, 2024.

19 "Military and Security Developments Involving the People's Republic of China." https://media.defense.gov/2021/Nov/03/2002885874/-1/-1/0/2021-CMPR-FINAL.PDF.

20 Garcia, Carlos, Walid Berrazeg, and Sarah Wu. "Taiwan reveals first domestically made submarine in defence milestone," Reuters, September 28, 2023.

21 Easton, Ian. *The Chinese Invasion Threat: Taiwan's Defense and American Strategy in Asia* (Manchester: Eastbridge Books, 2019).

22 Funaiole, Matthew P., Brian Hart, Aidan Powers-Riggs, and Joseph S. Bermudez Jr. "China's Massive Next-Generation Amphibious Assault Ship Takes Shape," Center for Strategic and International Studies, August 1, 2024.

23 Hunter, Gregor Stuart. "China preparing armada of ferries to invade Taiwan," *Telegraph*, May 26, 2024.

24 "PLA Aerospace Power: A Primer on Trends in China's Military Air, Space, and Missile Forces 4th Edition," China Aerospace Studies Institute, July 22, 2024.

25 U.S. Department of Defense Annual Report to Congress, 2023.

26 Ma, Xiu. "PLA Rocket Force Organization," China Aerospace Studies Institute, October 24, 2022.

27 Gallagher, Nancy W. "China on Arms Control, Nonproliferation, and Strategic Stability." *China's Strategic Arsenal: Worldview, Doctrine, and Systems*. James M. Smith and Paul J. Bolt, eds (Washington, D.C.: Georgetown University Press, 2021), p. 224.

28 Torode, Greg, Gerry Doyle, and Laurie Chen. "U.S. and China hold first informal nuclear talks in five years," Reuters, June 22, 2024.

29 Weaver, Gregory. "The role of nuclear weapons in a Taiwan crisis," Atlantic Council, November 22, 2023.

30 Short of a nuclear strike against Taiwan, Beijing could also engage in signaling with a nuclear demonstration "by actually detonating a nuclear device without having direct military effects." See Matthew Keoenig. "Deliberate Nuclear Use in a War Over Taiwan: Scenarios and Considerations for the United States," Atlantic Council, 2023.

31 "Anti-Secession Law." European Parliament. https://www.euro parl.europa.eu/meetdocs/2004_2009/documents/fd/d-cn20050 42601/d-cn2005042601en.pdf.

32 Hsia, Hsiao-hwa and Huang Chun-mei. "'No need' to declare independence, Taiwan presidential hopeful says," Radio Free Asia, January 9, 2024. See also Lily Kuo. "Tsai Ing-wen says China must 'face reality' of Taiwan's independence," *Guardian*, January 15, 2020.

33 "China Coast Guard Regulation No. 3." https://www.pacom.mil /Portals/55/Documents/Legal/J06 TACAID – CCG Regulation 3 (FINAL) – VER 2.pdf?ver=DbFQtB0oqN0l2NcJ_55HNA==.

34 Wu, Shu-wei, Matt Yu, and Evelyn Kao. "Taiwan can exercise self-defense if territorial airspace violated: Minister," *Focus Taiwan*, June 6, 2024.

35 Shan, Shelley. "China may test Taiwan's 24-nautical-mile limit: Chiu," *Taipei Times*, March 7, 2023.

36 Lin, Bonny, Brian Hart, Matthew P. Funaiole, Samantha Lu, and Truly Tinsley. "How China Could Quarantine Taiwan," Center for Strategic and International Studies, June 5, 2024.

37 Martin, Bradley, Kristen Gunness, Paula DeLuca and Melissa Shostak. "Implications of a Coercive Quarantine of Taiwan by the People's Republic of China," Rand Corporation, 2022.

38 Lin, Bonny, Brian Hart, Chen Ming-Chi, Shen Ming-Shih, Samantha Lu, Truly Tinsley, and Yu-Jie (Grace) Liao. "Surveying the Experts: U.S. and Taiwan Views on China's Approach to Taiwan in 2024 and Beyond," *China Power*, January 22, 2024.

39 Known as the PLA Rocket Force (PLARF) since January 1, 2016.

40 "In Their Own Words: Foreign Military Thought – Science of Campaigns," China Aerospace Studies Institute, 2006.

41 Lin, Bonny, Brian Hart, Matthew P. Funaiole, Samantha Lu, and Truly Tinsley. "How China Could Blockade Taiwan," Center for Strategic and International Studies, August 22, 2024.

42 Sciutto, Jim. *The Return of Great Powers: Russia, China, and the Next World War* (New York: Dutton, 2024), p. 167. See also Silva Shih, Steven Yeo, Sylvia Lee, Yingyu Chen, Meg Wu, "Maps: China's 72-hour 'Taiwan blockade,'" *CommonWealth*, August 15, 2022.

43 In a 2023 testimony to U.S. Congress, Ely Ratner, assistant secretary of defense for Indo-Pacific security affairs, stated that "These risks underscore the extent to which peace and stability across the Taiwan Strait matter for modern life across the Indo-Pacific region, global prosperity around the world, and the economic and national security interests of the American people . . . Military aggression across the strait – whether in the form of an outright invasion, a blockade or other means – would risk human life and global prosperity unimaginable in this century."

See Jim Garamone. "U.S. Strengthening Deterrence in Taiwan Strait," U.S. Department of Defense, September 19, 2023.

44 Tirk, Eli and Daniel Salisbury. "PLAN Anti-Submarine Warfare Aircraft – Sensors, Weapons, & Operational Concepts," China Maritime Studies Institute, May 7, 2024.

45 Jestrab, Marek. "A maritime blockade of Taiwan by the People's Republic of China: A strategy to defeat fear and coercion," Atlantic Council, December 12, 2023. Jestrab writes, "a non-kinetic blockade is appealing to the PRC, as it is the lowest level of coercive action that could remain below the threshold of open hostilities and still achieve its national objectives."

46 Alperovitch, Dmitry. "A Chinese Economic Blockade of Taiwan Would Fail or Launch a War," *War on the Rocks*, June 5, 2024.

47 "Business Climate Survey, 2023 Report." American Chamber of Commerce in Taiwan. https://amcham.com.tw/wp-content/uploads/2023/02/AmCham-Taiwan-2023-Business-Climate-Survey.pdf. The survey was conducted between November 15 and December 16, 2022.

48 "Business Climate Survey, 2024 Report," American Chamber of Commerce in Taiwan. https://amcham.com.tw/wp-content/uploads/2024/01/AmCham-2024-Business-Climate-Survey.pdf.

49 "Taiwan FDI Statistics Summary Analysis (December 2023)." Ministry of Economic Affairs, January 15, 2024. https://www.moea.gov.tw/MNS/english/news/News.aspx?kind=6&menu_id=176&news_id=113606.

50 Liu, Zhen. "Taiwan running out of time to discuss peaceful reunification, says former Chinese general," *South China Morning Post*, December 22, 2019.

51 Culver, John. "How We Would Know When China Is Preparing to Invade Taiwan," Carnegie Endowment for Democracy, October 3, 2022.

52 Toll, Ian W. *Twilight of the Gods: War in the Western Pacific: 1944–1945* (New York: W.W. & Norton, 2020), p. 56. See also Benjamin Jensen. "Not So Fast: Insights from a 1944 War Plan Help Explain Why Invading Taiwan Is a Costly Gamble," *War on*

the *Rocks*, September 8, 2022, and Ian Easton, "China Maritime Report No. 42: Invasion Plans: Operation Causeway and Taiwan's Defense in World War II," China Maritime Studies Institute, U.S. Naval War College, October 2024.

53 McDonough, Frank. *The Hitler Years: Disaster: 1940–1945* (London: Head of Zeus, 2020), pp. 70–71.

54 Allied casualties on D-Day are estimated at 10,250, of which 4,440 were killed. Commonwealth War Graves. https://www.cwgc.org/our-work/blog/d-day-casualties-in-numbers/.

55 Martínez, A., Greg Myre, and Jenna McLaughlin. "In high-stakes meeting, Russia tells U.S. it isn't planning to invade Ukraine," NPR, January 10, 2022.

56 "Kremlin denies plans to invade Ukraine, alleges NATO threats," Associated Press, November 12, 2021.

57 Sevastopulo, Demetri and Joe Leahy. "Xi Jinping claimed US wants China to attack Taiwan," *Financial Times*, June 15, 2024.

58 See "Deployment of U.S. Forces in Japan." https://www.mofa.go.jp/region/n-america/us/security/pdfs/arrange_ref7.pdf.

59 In April 2023, the U.S. and the Philippines announced that four more military bases would be made accessible to the U.S. military, of which two, Isabela and Cagayan, face north toward Taiwan, under expansion of the Enhanced Defense Cooperation Agreement (EDCA). See Karen Lema. "Philippines reveals locations of 4 new strategic sites for U.S. military pact," Reuters, April 3, 2023.

60 Dotson, John. "China Commences Military Drone Flights Circumnavigating Taiwan," Global Taiwan Institute, May 17, 2023.

61 "US to sell Taiwan anti-tank mine-laying Volcano system," *Defense News*, December 29, 2022.

62 Taiwan has implemented a project to build Coast Guard offshore patrol corvettes that, in wartime, can quickly be converted to missile corvettes to augment the Republic of China Navy's (ROCN) surface combatant fleet. At this writing, eight Anping-

class 600-tonne CGA missile corvettes have been delivered as part of the project. In May 2022, the CGA test-fired a Hsiung Feng 2 anti-ship cruise missile from Anping-class vessel CG-601.

63 Cancian, Mark F., Matthew Cancian, and Eric Heginbotham. "The First Battle of the Next War: Wargaming a Chinese Invasion of Taiwan," Center for Strategic and International Studies, January 2023.

64 In August 2024, researchers at Xiamen University's Cross-Strait Institute of Urban Planning published a short paper with recommendations following the "reunification" of Taiwan. Among them was the creation of a "shadow government" in Taiwan. The paper was quickly deleted. See "Start Taiwan Takeover Preparations as Soon as Possible," CSIS Interpret: China, August 5, 2024.

65 Carbonaro, Giulia. "China Would Re-Educate Taiwan in Event of Reunification, Ambassador Says," *Newsweek*, August 5, 2022.

66 Welch, Jennifer, Jenny Leonard, Maeva Cousin, Gerard DiPippo, and Tom Orlik. "Xi, Biden and the $10 Trillion Cost of War Over Taiwan," Bloomberg, January 9, 2024.

67 Blanchette, Jude and Gerard DiPippo. "'Reunification' with Taiwan through Force Would Be a Pyrrhic Victory for China," Center for Strategic and International Studies, November 22, 2022.

68 "Taiwan's dominance of the chip industry makes it more important," *Economist*, March 6, 2023.

69 Miller, Chris. "The Chips That Make Taiwan the Center of the World," *Time*, October 5, 2022.

70 Wonacott, Peter. "Costly Conflict: Here's How China's Military Options for Taiwan Backfire," United States Institute of Peace, October 9, 2024.

Chapter 6: Avoiding the Nightmare

1 McKinney, Jared M. and Peter Harris. "Understanding the Deterrence Gap in the Taiwan Strait," *War on the Rocks*, February 12, 2024.

2 Kanapathy, Ivan. "Countering China's Use of Force." *The Boiling Moat: Urgent Steps to Defend Taiwan*, Matt Pottinger, ed. (Stanford: Hoover Institution, 2024), pp. 83–103.

3 Hille, Kathrin. "US and Taiwan seek to strengthen drone supply chain to keep out China," *Financial Times*, September 20, 2024. During a press conference in early September 2024, AIT Director Raymond Greene said he "would not rule out Taiwan being one of th[e] partners in the future" for the joint production of military material and supplies. Yeh, Joseph. "New U.S. envoy vows to help enhance Taiwan's resilience, security," *Focus Taiwan*, September 4, 2024.

4 Hunzeker, Michael A., Enoch Wu, and Kobi Marom. "A New Military Culture for Taiwan." *The Boiling Moat*, pp. 61–62. While providing many useful recommendations on how to improve Taiwan's defense preparedness, the chapter arguably suffers from its references to some authors who have an unwarranted defeatist perspective on Taiwan's armed forces – a few of them due to ulterior motives.

5 Huang, Ching-hsuan, Chen Yu-fu, and William Hetherington. "58,000 to be called for alternate service," *Taipei Times*, July 1, 2024.

6 Former United Microelectronics Corp chairman Robert Tsao donated US$33 million to the Kuma Academy to help it set up a training program in civilian defense to complement regular and reserve forces. Tsao hopes that as many as 3.3 million "civilian warriors" can be trained to help defend Taiwan against a potential invasion. See Calderwood, Kathleen, Xin-yun Wu, and West Matteeussen. "As China flexes its military muscles, everyday citizens in Taiwan are preparing for war," ABC News, January 2, 2024.

7 "In Brief with Enoch Wu, Founder of Forward Alliance." 9DASHLINE, April 5, 2023.

8 "Help Taiwan and its people protect their democracy." Spirit of America. https://spiritofamerica.org/project/help-prepare-taiwan-for-an-emergency.

9 Hsu, Shih-kai. "'We have to be ready ourselves before we can help anyone else,'" Radio Free Asia, January 30, 2024.

10 See for example, "Lithuania sets up wartime civilian force – explainer," *LRT*, May 5, 2024.

11 McGuinness, Damien. "How a cyber attack transformed Estonia," BBC, April 27, 2017.

12 See "The Construction Plan for Enhancing Power Grid Resilience." Taipower, July 28, 2023. https://service.taipower.com.tw/csr/en/news/GK/detail; Jordan McGillis. "Taiwan's Electrical Grid and the Need for Greater System Resilience," *Global Taiwan Brief*, June 14, 2023; and J. Michael Cole. "Critical Infrastructure Remains a Blind Spot in Taiwan's Defense Preparedness," *Global Taiwan Brief*, June 2, 2021.

13 Sokolski, Henry. "War game reveals Chinese attacks on communications could paralyze Taiwan," *SpaceNews*, September 16, 2024.

14 Lai, Sunny. "MODA targets completion of 700 satellite hot spots by end of 2024," *Focus Taiwan*, March 27, 2024.

15 Tobin, Meaghan and John Liu. "Why Taiwan Is Building a Satellite Network Without Elon Musk," *New York Times*, March 14, 2024; and Eric Cheung. "Developing Taiwan's own 'starlink' crucial for island-wide emergency, space agency says," CNN, May 4, 2024.

16 Wen, Kuei-hsiang, Wu Shu-wie, and Teng Pei-ju. "Government plans enhanced protection for critical infrastructure," *Focus Taiwan*, September 27, 2024.

17 Shen, Howard. "Taiwan's Surprising Drop in Trade Dependence on Mainland China," *The Diplomat*, March 8, 2024.

18 "China suspends tariff concessions on 134 items under Taiwan trade deal," Reuters, May 31, 2024.

19 "Government Welcomes Mainland-based Taiwanese Companies to Return and Invest in Taiwan; MAC is Actively Involved for Assistance." Mainland Affairs Council, January 26, 2020. https://www.mac.gov.tw/en/News_Content.aspx?n=2BA0753CBE348412&s=B4C4630713948064.

20 Chau, Thompson and Cheng Ting-Fang. "Taiwanese companies in China flocking to Southeast Asia: survey," *Nikkei Asia*, October 8, 2022.

21 Lee, Yimou. "China aims to sap Taiwan morale with 'escape plan' misinformation, sources say," Reuters, July 7, 2023.

22 Official MND R.O.C. Twitter [X] account. https://x.com/MoND efense.

23 Taiwan Ministry of Health and Welfare. https://covid19.mohw .gov.tw/ch/cp-4843-53644-205.html.

24 Radio Taiwan International. https://en.rti.org.tw/.

25 Taiwan+. https://www.taiwanplus.com/.

26 Han, Hongbin. *Contesting Cyberspace in China: Online Expression and Resilience* (New York: Columbia University Press, 2018), p. 175.

27 Blackwill, Robert D. and Richard Fontaine. *Lost Decade: The US Pivot to Asia and the Rise of Chinese Power* (New York: Oxford University Press, 2024), p. 229. Oriana Skylar Mastro notes that the PRC has thirty-nine air bases within 800 km of Taiwan, while the USAF has two within 1,000 km of the Taiwan Strait (cited in Blackwill and Fontaine).

28 Bosco, Joe. "Strategic ambiguity on Taiwan no longer works – it's time for strategic clarity," *The Hill*, September 1, 2020.

29 Ruwitch, John. "Biden, again, says U.S. would help Taiwan if China attacks," NPR, September 19, 2022.

30 See Jonathan Masters and Will Merrow. "U.S. Military Support for Taiwan in Five Charts," Council on Foreign Relations, September 25, 2024.

31 Total value of U.S. arms sales to Taiwan over the years: Bill Clinton (1993–2001): US$8.702 billion; George W. Bush (2001–2009): US$15.614 billion; Barack Obama (2009–2017): US$13.962 billion; Donald Trump (2017–2021): US$18.278 billion; Joe Biden (2021–present): US$5.709 billion. Source: U.S.-Taiwan Business Council. "USTBC President Offers Follow-up Comments Examining Data on Taiwan Arms Sales," September 20, 2024. https://www.us-taiwan.org/resources/ustbc-president

-follow-up-comments-examining-data-on-taiwan-arms-sales/.

32 Clark, Joseph. "DOD Official Details U.S. Collaboration With Indo-Pacific Partners on Defense Industrial Base," U.S. Department of Defense, June 27, 2024. See also Shih, Hsiu-chuan and Sean Lin. "Taiwan to join U.S.-led initiative to tackle weapons supply constraints," *Focus Taiwan*, September 24, 2024.

33 Sadler, Brent Droste. *U.S. Naval Power in the 21st Century: A New Strategy for Facing the Chinese and Russian Threat* (Annapolis: Naval Institute Press, 2023), p. 210.

34 "U.S. Pacific Fleet advances Indo-Pacific regional maritime security and enhances stability." https://www.cpf.navy.mil/About-Us/.

35 Tokuchi, Hideshi. "Japan's New National Security Strategy – An Awakened Japan and Its Implications for Taiwan," Prospect Foundation, January 17, 2023.

36 Koda, Yoji. "The Sun Also Rises." *The Boiling Moat*, p. 202.

37 Yamaguchi, Mari. "Japan signs $2.8 billion deals for long-range missile development," *Defense News*, April 12, 2023.

38 Yamaguchi, Mari. "Japan signs agreement to purchase 400 Tomahawk missiles as US envoy lauds its defense buildup," Associated Press, January 18, 2024.

39 Takahashi, Kosuke. "JGSDF Plans to Build a Missile Firing Range on Japan's Easternmost Island," *The Diplomat*, July 26, 2024.

40 H.R.554 – 118th Congress (2023–2024). https://www.congress.gov/bill/118th-congress/house-bill/554/text.

41 Quoted in Gerard DiPippo and Jude Blanchette. "Sunk Costs: The Difficulty of Using Sanctions to Deter China in a Taiwan Crisis," Center for Strategic and International Studies, June 12, 2023.

42 Vest, Charlie and Agatha Kratz. "Sanctioning China in a Taiwan crisis: Scenarios and risks," Atlantic Council, June 21, 2023.

43 Yang, Aili. "New immigrant inflow – is Taiwan ready?" *CommonWealth*, March 17, 2021.

Chapter 7: Taiwan and the Battle for Democracy's Future

1 "NATO 2022 Strategic Concept. Adopted by Heads of State and Government at the NATO Summit in Madrid, 29 June 2022." https://www.nato.int/nato_static_fl2014/assets/pdf/2022/6/pdf /290622-strategic-concept.pdf.

2 Rumer, Eugene. "Taiwan and the Limits of the Russia-China Friendship," Carnegie Endowment for International Peace, September 3, 2024.

3 Siegle, Joseph. "Winning the Battle of Ideas: Exposing Global Authoritarian Narratives and Revitalizing Democratic Principles," National Endowment for Democracy, February 2024.

4 Applebaum, Anne. *Autocracy, Inc: The Dictators Who Want to Run the World* (New York: Doubleday, 2024), p. 2.

5 Sanger, David E. *The New Cold Wars: China's Rise, Russia's Invasion, and America's Struggle to Defend the West* (New York: Crown, 2024), p. 436.

6 Kendall-Taylor, Andrea and Richard Fontaine. "The Axis of Upheaval," *Foreign Affairs*, May–June 2024, pp. 50–63.

7 As this book is being written, Israel is locked in a months-long war with Hamas in Gaza and has launched a new invasion of Southern Lebanon after assassinating Lebanese Hezbollah leader Hassan Nasrallah in an airstrike, part of a series of strikes against the Hezbollah and Islamic Revolutionary Guard Corps leadership in recent months. Iran has retaliated with a missile barrage against military sites in Israel, which in turn has vowed to retaliate. U.S. Navy vessels deployed to the region played a role in intercepting Iranian ballistic missiles headed for Israel.

8 Ostovar, Afshon. *Wars of Ambition: The United States, Iran, and the Struggle for the Middle East* (New York: Oxford University Press, 2024), p. 269.

9 For an excellent analysis of the U.S.–Israel relationship, see Walter Russell Mead. *The Arc of a Covenant: The United States, Israel, and the Fate of the Jewish People* (New York: Alfred A. Knopf, 2022).

10 Rynning, *NATO*, p. 275.

11 For a useful discussion of the battle for financial and technological power between China and the West, see Andrew Small, *No Limits: The Inside Story of China's War With the West* (New York: Melville House, 2022).

12 Johnson, Paul. "Former Australian prime minister Paul Keating attacks senior members of Albanese government over AUKUS agreement and foreign policy," ABC News, August 8, 2024.

13 Sicgle, Joseph. "Winhing the Battle of Ideas."

Index